PRACTICAL PEDOLOGY
Studying Soils in the Field

ELLIS HORWOOD SERIES IN GEOLOGY

Editors: D. T. DONOVAN, Professor of Geology, University College London, and J. W. MURRAY, Professor of Geology, University of Exeter

A GUIDE TO CLASSIFICATION IN GEOLOGY
J. W. MURRAY, Professor of Geology, University of Exeter
THE CENOZOIC ERA: Tertiary and Quaternary
C. POMEROL, Professor, University of Paris VI
Translated by D. W. HUMPHRIES, Department of Geology, University of Sheffield, and E. E. HUMPHRIES
Edited by Professor D. CURRY and D. T. DONOVAN, University College London
INTRODUCTION TO PALAEOBIOLOGY: GENERAL PALAEONTOLOGY
B. ZIEGLER, Professor of Geology and Palaeontology, University of Stuttgart, and Director of the State Museum for Natural Science, Stuttgart
FAULT AND FOLD TECTONICS
W. JAROSZEWSKI, Faculty of Geology, University of Warsaw
RADIOACTIVITY IN GEOLOGY: Principles and Applications
E. M. DURRANCE, Department of Geology, University of Exeter

ELLIS HORWOOD SERIES IN APPLIED GEOLOGY

A GUIDE TO PUMPING TESTS
F. C. BRASSINGTON, Principal Hydrogeologist, North West Water Authority
QUATERNARY GEOLOGY: Processes and Products
JOHN A. CATT, Rothamsted Experimental Station, Harpenden, UK
TUNNELLING GEOLOGY AND GEOTECHNICS
Editors: M. C. KNIGHTS and T. W. MELLORS, Consulting Engineers, W. S. Atkins & Partners
MODERN STANDARDS FOR AGGREGATES
D. C. PIKE, Consultant in Aggregates, Reading
LASER HOLOGRAPHY IN GEOPHYSICS
S. TAKEMOTO, Disaster Prevention Research Unit, Kyoto University, Japan

BRITISH MICROPALAEONTOLOGICAL SOCIETY SERIES

NANNOFOSSILS AND THEIR APPLICATIONS
Editor: J. A. CRUX, British Petroleum Research Centre, Sunbury-on-Thames
A STRATIGRAPHICAL INDEX OF THE PALAEOZOIC ACRITARCHES AND OTHER MARINE MICROFLORA
Editors: K. J. DORINING, Pallab Research, Sheffield, and S. G. MOLYNEUX, British Geological Survey, Nottingham
STRATIGRAPHICAL ATLAS OF FOSSIL FORAMINIFERA, 2nd Edition
Editors: D. G. JENKINS, The Open University, and J. W. MURRAY, Professor of Geology, University of Exeter
MICROFOSSILS FROM RECENT AND FOSSIL SHELF SEAS
Editors: J. W. NEALE, Professor of Micropalaeontology, University of Hull, and M. D. BRASIER, Lecturer in Geology, University of Hull
FOSSIL AND RECENT OSTRACODS
Editors: R. H. BATE, Stratigraphic Services International, Guildford, E. ROBINSON, Department of Geology, University College London, and L. SHEPPARD, Stratigraphic Services International, Guildford
A STRATIGRAPHICAL INDEX OF CALCAREOUS NANNOFOSSILS
Editor: A. R. LORD, Department of Geology, University College London
A STRATIGRAPHICAL INDEX OF CONODONTS
Editors: A. C. HIGGINS, Geological Survey of Canada, Calgary, and R. L. AUSTIN, Department of Geology, University of Southampton
CONODONTS: Investigative Techniques and Applications
Editor: R. L. AUSTIN, Department of Geology, University of Southampton
PALAEOBIOLOGY OF CONODONTS
Editor: R. J. ALDRIDGE, Department of Geology, University of Nottingham
MICROPALAEONTOLOGY OF CARBONATE ENVIRONMENTS
Editor: M. B. HART, Professor of Micropalaeontology and Head of Department of Geological Studies, Plymouth Polytechnic
OSTRACODA
Editors: R. C. WHATLEY and C. MAYBURY, University College of Wales

PRACTICAL PEDOLOGY
Studying Soils in the Field

S.G. (STUART G. McRAE, BSc, PhD
Lecturer in Land Resources Science
Wye College, University of London

ELLIS HORWOOD LIMITED
Publishers · Chichester

Halsted Press: a division of
JOHN WILEY & SONS
New York · Chichester · Brisbane · Toronto

First published in 1988 by
ELLIS HORWOOD LIMITED
Market Cross House, Cooper Street,
Chichester, West Sussex, PO19 1EB, England
The publisher's colophon is reproduced from James Gillison's drawing of the ancient Market Cross, Chichester.

Distributors:

Australia and New Zealand:
JACARANDA WILEY LIMITED
GPO Box 859, Brisbane, Queensland 4001, Australia

Canada:
JOHN WILEY & SONS CANADA LIMITED
22 Worcester Road, Rexdale, Ontario, Canada

Europe and Africa:
JOHN WILEY & SONS LIMITED
Baffins Lane, Chichester, West Sussex, England

North and South America and the rest of the world:
Halsted Press: a division of
JOHN WILEY & SONS
605 Third Avenue, New York, NY 10158, USA

South-East Asia
JOHN WILEY & SONS (SEA) PTE LIMITED
37 Jalan Pemimpin # 05–04
Block B, Union Industrial Building, Singapore 2057

Indian Subcontinent
WILEY EASTERN LIMITED
4835/24 Ansari Road
Daryaganj, New Delhi 110002, India

© 1988 S.G. McRae/Ellis Horwood Limited

British Library Cataloguing in Publication Data
McRae, S.G. (Stuart Gordon), *1942–*
Practical pedology
1. Soil science. Methodology
I. Title
631.4′01′8

Library of Congress Card No. 87–37930

ISBN 0–85312–918–5 (Ellis Horwood Limited)
ISBN 0–470–21062–1 (Halsted Press)

Phototypeset in Times by Ellis Horwood Limited
Printed in Great Britain by Butler & Tanner, Frome, Somerset

Table of contents

Preface 9

1 Understanding soils
   1.1 Introduction 11
   1.2 The main soil components 11
   1.3 Soil mineralogy 13
   1.4 The soil architecture 15
   1.5 Soil water 16
   1.6 Water movement, waterlogging and drainage 20
   1.7 The soil atmosphere 23
   1.8 Soil biology 24
   1.9 Soil chemistry 25
   1.10 Soil fertility 29
   1.11 Soil forming processes 32

2 Describing a soil sample
   2.1 Introduction 37
   2.2 Soil colour 38
   2.3 Soil texture 41
   2.4 Stoniness 48
   2.5 Soil structure 50
   2.6 Carbonates 56
   2.7 Additional properties 57
   2.8 Porosity 57
   2.9 Soil water state 59
   2.10 Handling properties (consistency) 60
   2.11 Roots and other soil flora 62
   2.12 Plant remains and organic matter 63
   2.13 Soil fauna 63
   2.14 Features of pedogenic origin 64
   2.15 The final description 64

3   Soil profile description
3.1   Equipment 66
3.2   Choosing a soil profile for study 66
3.3   Soil profile preparation. 68
3.4   Recognising, describing and sampling horizons 69
3.5   Site characteristics. 75
3.6   Examples 75

4   Naming and classifying a soil profile
4.1   Introduction 80
4.2   The soil classification system for England and Wales. 81
4.3   Legend of the FAO/UNESCO Soil Map of the World. 106
4.4   The Soil Taxonomy 119
4.5   The USDA zonal soil classification system 124

5   Making a soil map
5.1   Introduction 127
5.2   A basic soil map 127
5.3   Scales and map units 134
5.4   Preparing to make a soil map — scale and type of survey 137
5.5   Preparing to make a soil map — base map and background information 138
5.6   Equipment needed for field work 140
5.7   The field work 143
5.8   The accompanying report 147
5.9   Very detailed maps (about 1:2500) 151
5.10 Reconnaissance maps (1:100 000 and smaller scales). 151

6   Climate, soil and plant relationships
6.1   Introduction 154
6.2   Climatic properties 155
6.3   Soil properties 162
6.4   Soil temperature regimes in the Soil Taxonomy 176
6.5   FAO agro-ecological zones 177

7   Interpreting a soil map for practical purposes
7.1   Introduction 180
7.2   Kinds of soil map interpretation 181
7.3   Simple correlations 181
7.4   Derived single-factor maps 182
7.5   Suitability of land for specific agricultural purposes. 182
7.6   Crop suitabilities. 186
7.7   Land suitability for non-agricultural purposes 197
7.8   Land capability classifications 204

8   Simple soil physical and chemical analyses
8.1   Introduction 215
8.2   Soil moisture 217
8.3   Bulk density and porosity 218

8.4   Stone content. 219
8.5   Particle size analysis (pipette method) 220
8.6   Carbonates 224
8.7   Soil organic matter by wet oxidation 225
8.8   Loss on ignition 227
8.9   Total soil nitrogen. 228
8.10 Soil reaction (pH) 229
8.11 Soil salinity 230
8.12 Cation exchange capacity, exchangeable bases and exchange acidity. .232
8.13 Available nutrients, e.g. available phosphate 236
8.14 Extractable iron 238

9   Bibliography
9.1   General 241
9.2   Soil formation and distribution. 241
9.3   Soil and profile descriptions. 242
9.4   Soil classification. 242
9.5   Soil mapping and interpretations 242
9.6   Methods 244
9.7   Other references cited in the text 245

Acknowledgements 247

Index 248

Preface

For many years I have been involved in teaching soil science to beginners in the subject. In particular I have concentrated on soils as natural bodies worthy of study in their own right. This is the branch of soil science called Pedology. There are several excellent textbooks to back up the theory, but really nothing I could recommend to beginners to cover the practical work. Textbooks would indicate that the fundamental property of, say, soil texture could be described in such and such a way and could be determined by a procedure called finger assessment, but then did not go on to explain to the reader how to do it. At the other extreme the manuals of various soil survey organisations were very detailed, but in trying to cover every eventuality were far too complex for a beginner. Also they did not differentiate sufficiently clearly between important features which are likely to be encountered frequently and those of very esoteric interest.

The solution, of course, was the ubiquitous 'handout' for each of the practical sessions which tried to convey the salient points in a way the beginner could understand. I was taught this way myself, and have seen a similar approach used in many other universities and colleges both in Britain and abroad. This may be fine while there is a lecturer or demonstrator at hand to explain the difficult points, to provide demonstrations of techniques, examples of the phenomena being studied and post mortems as to why the student didn't get the right answer. What, however, of the beginner who has no tame expert standing at his or her shoulder? Could there be a book which would explain things in simple terms, and which could be used by a beginner working entirely on his or her own? Thus was born the idea for *Practical Pedology*. I have deliberately written it as if I were personally explaining things to you and I hope you find this encourages you to tackle some of the practical techniques and not be frightened off by this rather awkward but vitally important material called soil.

Much of the book is based, at least as a starting point, on some of the teaching materials used at Wye College. These have been developed over the years in collaboration with my colleagues, Jeanne Ingram and Paul Burnham. In the mists of time it is difficult to be sure exactly who was the originator of some of the material, and if I have inadvertently stolen some of their pet ideas I hope they forgive me! It has been a pleasure and a stimulation to work with both of them over the years.

Generations of Wye students have acted as guinea pigs as the material was developed. My thanks are due to all those who suffered some of the early 'handouts' and who pointed out where things were badly explained, or I had assumed something they did not know about. I owe a large 'thank you' to all those who made constructive criticisms, but of course take full responsibility myself for any residual discrepancies, ambiguities or other shortcomings in the book.

I am also grateful to Rural Planning Services plc and their clients who have provided me over the years with ample opportunities to study soils and related agricultural and planning matters.

One of the main problems for a beginner is to discover if what he or she has done is to an acceptable standard — hence the dreaded practical exam! There is no practical exam at the end of *Practical Pedology* (though there are one or two little tests in the soil classification chapter). Instead I have included, where appropriate, examples of what a professional pedologist would have been likely to produce, so you can see the sort of thing to aspire to. My thanks are due to the various fellow pedologists, FAO, the United States Department of Agriculture (USDA), and to the soil survey organisations of Manitoba, New Zealand, Ireland and Scotland for permission to use their work as 'type examples' as well as using teaching material from their manuals, maps and classification systems.

In particular I am grateful to the Soil Survey of England and Wales who have very generously allowed me to use much of their material. I greatly admire their work and wish it were more widely known and appreciated. Perhaps this book will help. In particular the recent 1:250 000 national soil map and the accompanying regional bulletins has provided not only a fascinating inventory of the soils of England and Wales but a range of interpretations whereby the information can be directly used by farmers, growers, planners and anyone interested in soil resources.

Finally I need to say 'thank you' to my long-suffering wife. It is not easy being married to a pedologist but she has borne with fortitude and good humour many years of dealing with muddy clothing (and footprints across the hall carpet) and a family car which often bears more than a passing resembalance to a tractor, with respect, at least, to the amount of soil in and on it.

Wye College (University of London)
December 1987

Stuart McRae

1

Understanding soils

1.1   INTRODUCTION

Soil is material found at the surface of the earth which sustains the vegetative cover on which animals including Man depend. It has formed over **time** by the action of the **climate** and **living organisms** on the underlying geological **parent material.** Soils differ across the landscape according to variations in these four **soil forming factors**, and to position in the landscape, i.e. the fifth soil forming factor of **topography.**

When a pit is dug to show a **soil profile** it is seen that soil is characteristically differentiated into **horizons,** layers or bands of different appearances and properties which have arisen by the action of various **soil forming processes** (see below). Pedology is the branch of soil science which is mainly concerned with these processes and the soil profiles they produce, together with the classification and mapping of soils.

Other branches of soil science are concerned mainly with the chemical, physical and biological aspects of soils particularly as they affect soil fertility and Man's ability to grow crops. The pedologist can also contribute to these studies by providing the basic information about soil resources and by interpreting the results of his studies in a form intelligible to the practical user.

Pedology is also an important intellectual study in its own right, an integral part of environmental science. The practising pedologist will quickly find he has to cope with subjects including geology, geomorphology, climatology, ecology, agriculture, forestry and civil engineering as well as the more basic disciplines of chemistry, physics and biology if he or she is fully to understand the soils being studied.

1.2   THE MAIN SOIL COMPONENTS

A closer look at a sample of soil shows that it consists of both **organic** and **mineral** fractions. The organic fraction is derived from decaying plant and animal debris and so is most abundant nearest the surface, producing the black or dark brown colours of the **topsoil** which normally has between 3 and 8% **organic matter** (by weight). The underlying **subsoil** has less, around 1–2% and so is usually lighter in colour. Fresh plant or animal debris is progressively decomposed by **soil micro-organisms,** tending to a more or less stable end product called **humus,** a black amorphous substance which has lost all its original structure. This humus has a chemical composition which amongst other characteristic features has a ratio of carbon to nitrogen of close to 12, compared with perhaps around 30 in fresh organic debris or about 100 in straw residues.

During the breakdown of organic matter by micro-organisms, plant nutrients are liberated in a form which can be absorbed by plants. Thus many plant nutrients, particularly nitrogen, phosphorus and sulphur are involved in cycles from decaying plant and animal debris, through the soil organic matter and back to the plant. In natural soils this is the main source of plant nutrients and farming systems such as shifting cultivation and the use of organic manures are in sympathy with this natural cycle. Removal of plant and animal products from the cycle upsets the balance which has to be redressed by application of chemical fertilisers.

In certain circumstances such as waterlogged and/or very acid soils the decomposition process is drastically slowed, and a surface accumulation of only partially decomposed material (**peat**) builds up sometimes to depths of several metres. The properties of these **organic soils** are often substantially different from the more normal mineral soils.

In most soils the mineral fraction predominates, derived from the weathering of the underlying geological parent material, sometimes with surface additions, e.g. alluvium deposited during a flood. Conversely losses of soil (both mineral and organic) by erosion is a worrying problem in many parts of the world.

The mineral or inorganic fraction of the soil can be subdivided in terms of particle size into **stones, sand, silt** and **clay**. There are no universally accepted size definitions (see Chapter 2) but in general terms stones are particles larger than 2 mm, and sand consists of visible particles from 2 mm down to about 0.06–0.02 mm (20 to 60 μm). Silt is the finer dust-like material down to 0.002 mm (2 μm) and clay consists of the chemically active particles smaller than 0.002 mm (2 μm). Material less than 2 mm is called the **fine earth,** on which soil analyses are conventionally carried out after stones have been sieved out.

The **soil texture** refers to the relative proportions of the sand, silt and clay. This most fundamental of soil properties will be described more fully in Chapter 2. It can be determined in the laboratory by discovering the percentages of sand, silt and clay by time-consuming techniques of sieving and settlement in water. The results are then plotted on a textural triangle (Fig. 1.1), which defines the **textural classes** according to the proportions of the three components. Textural classes include the **loams** which do not have specific particle sizes like sand, silt and clay do but represent more or less equal proportions of each of these.

In practice the textural class can be determined with acceptable accuracy by **finger assessment** (see Chapter 2) in which the relative proportions are subjectively assessed from the feel of a moist soil sample. Sand imparts grittiness, silt a smoothness and clay a stickiness.

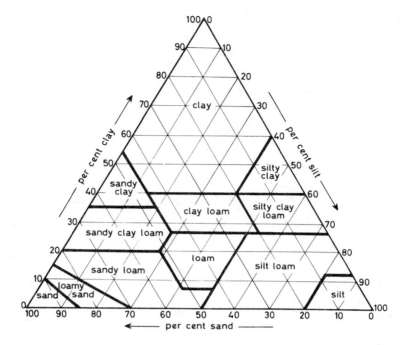

Fig. 1.1 — The soil textural triangle, relating particle size distribution to texture classes (see also Fig. 2.3).

1.3 SOIL MINERALOGY

Stones are generally rock fragments, and in most soils the sand and silt consist largely of grains of resistant minerals, chiefly quartz. In relatively young or unweathered soils the sand and silt can include substantial amounts of other minerals, depending on the nature of the geological parent material. As these weather they can make a small but significant contribution to the store of nutrients in the soil, and given time the fertility of the soil is replenished. All soil nutrients except nitrogen and to a limited extent sulphur are derived originally from weathering of the parent material unless there have been extraneous additions such as from percolating ground-water or additions of manures and fertilisers. It is for this reason that the fertility of soils is closely linked to their parent material, though the intensity of weathering and leaching is also important.

The clay fraction is made up of a specific group of minerals known, not surprisingly as the **clay minerals.** All the commonest ones have silicate structures like mica, i.e. sheet silicates or phyllosilicates, but are more hydrated. Common mineral species include illite, vermiculite and montmorillonite (or smectite) commonest in temperate region soils and kaolinite and halloysite which tend to predominate in tropical soils.

Because of their small particle size the clay minerals have a huge surface area ranging from about 5 to over $800\,m^2$ per $100\,g$. Their surfaces and edges are covered with electric charges so that they carry a net negative charge, balanced by a surrounding cloud of positively charged cations. These cations are not fixed but can be replaced by or exchanged for other cations. This is the phenomenon of **cation exchange** which is also exhibited, for slightly different reasons, by the humus and by the amorphous oxides (see below). Some typical values of **cation exchange capacity** (CEC) for pure clay minerals and for soils, where other components effectively 'dilute' the CEC, are given in Table 1.1. The cation exchange properties of a soil are extremely important and, in general terms, the higher the CEC, the more fertile the soil is likely to be.

Table 1.1 — Typical values of cation exchange capacity (me/100 g) for a range of soils, clay minerals and organic matter (see also Tables 1.5 and 1.6)

Soils[a]	Topsoil	Subsoil
Podzol (Scotland)	39.1 (humose sl)	6.0 (s)
Luvisol (England)	28.0 (scl)	19.6 (cl)
Acrisol (USA)	2.1 (ls)	10.2 (sc)
Chernozem (USSR)	33.0 (l)	25.2 (l)
Ferralsol (Thailand)	9.6 (sl)	4.0 (scl)
Planosol (Argentina)	22.8 (l)	32.8 (zc)
Arenosol (Senegal)	9.2 (ls)	6.3 (ls)
Andosol (Philippines)	61.4 (humose l)	33.9 (zl)
Histosol (England)	131.0 (peat)	—
Thionic fluvisol (Guinea)	17.5 (sl)	27.1 (sc)

[a]Named according to the FAO/UNESCO system (see Chapter 4).
Textures (given in brackets) are abbreviated: cl, clay loan; l, loam; ls, loamy sand; s, sand; sl, sandy loam; sc, sandy clay; scl, sandy clay loam; zc, silty clay; zl, silt loam.

Clay minerals and organic matter:

Kaolinite	3–15
Illite	10–40
Montmorillonite	80–150
Vermiculite	100–150
Organic matter	c. 200

Clay minerals tend to be one of the stable end products of weathering, either in the soil by decomposition of the primary minerals or present in the parent material because of earlier geological weathering, erosional and depositional processes. Some clay minerals, notably the illites, undergo further transformations in soils and it is believed, for example, that the natural potassium status of temperate and perhaps some tropical soils is closely related to their content and weathering of illitic clay minerals.

Various amorphous **iron** and **aluminium oxides** and **hydroxides** are present in virtually all soils, the former particularly conspicuous by being largely responsible for the brown and red colours of well-drained soils and greyish colours in badly drained ones. Aluminium oxides are colourless. In temperate regions these oxides, sometimes collectively called the **sesquioxides,** tend to occur as coatings to other soil particles or in small concretions or other segregations. **Manganese oxides** occur in similar, but black, concretions and segregations most commonly in badly drained soils and associated with iron oxides.

Temperate regions can typically have up to about 5% by weight of various forms of sesquioxides, some horizons having substantially more and others much less, notably the characteristic white bleached horizon of the soil type known as a podzol. Some tropical soils have much more as testified by their bright red colours. Contents of iron and aluminium oxides as high as 12% are not uncommon, and even more if the soils are derived from limestone residues or basic igneous rocks. This is because iron and aluminium oxides are the end product of tropical weathering, and commercial deposits of some iron ores and bauxite are, in effect, simply highly and deeply weathered tropical soils. Many of the chemical and physical properties of tropical soils as opposed to temperate region soils, including their low fertility, are considerably influenced by their high contents of iron and aluminium oxides and the intense weathering which has produced them.

Some soils, described as **calcareous soils**, contain free calcium carbonate (and in some cases magnesium carbonate). This is usually because they have developed over limestones or other calcareous parent materials. Shallow examples (called rendzinas) often consist essentially of a mixture of organic matter and calcium carbonate only.

Calcium carbonate can be redistributed within the soil profile by soil forming processes, particularly in arid and semi-arid areas, sometimes producing naturally cemented layers. In very arid areas gypsum (calcium sulphate) can accumulate.

Also in arid and semi-arid areas surface accumulations of **soluble salts** can be produced by saline ground-water being drawn to the surface where it evaporates leaving impregnations and crusts of sodium chloride and other salts (the so-called solonchak soils). **Salinity** may be found in regions of higher rainfall in soils recently reclaimed from or flooded by the sea, and where high amounts of fertilisers have been applied with insufficient water to leach them through the soil, producing surface efflorescences of salts in some greenhouses or the pots of household plants.

1.4 THE SOIL ARCHITECTURE

Soil particles can combine or stick together into **aggregates** or **peds**. These are what a layman examining a handful of soil would probably call 'crumbs' or 'clods' of soil. He would then be describing the **soil structure** which is not the same as the soil texture described above. If the components of the soil texture, i.e. the sand, silt and clay, are thought of as analogous to building components such as bricks, girders or joists, then the soil structure is analogous to the finished buildings. To continue the analogy, just as there are voids (i.e. rooms) and linear spaces within buildings (i.e. corridors) and larger ones between them (passages and roads) so too there are voids and channels both within and between the structural units.

An examination of soil structure is really looking at the effect of the channels between the units since it is these which define the size and shape of the units and how they fit together. The durability of the peds (analogous to the soundness of buildings) is also used in describing soil structure, e.g. 'weakly developed blocky structure'. The full range of descriptive terms for this important soil property is given in Chapter 2.

The factors which determine soil structure are soil texture, organic matter content, content of calcium carbonate, the content of iron oxides, the action of the weather, particularly wetting and drying or freezing and thawing, the activities of roots, earthworms and micro-organisms and the manipulation of the soil by cultivations and other agricultural practices. In general terms the situations in which a soil is likely to have a stable structure of a kind which will promote plant growth are those where the soils have a moderately high clay content (or low silt and fine sand), high organic matter with an active soil biology and high content of iron oxides or free calcium carbonate.

The development of soil structure is promoted by alternate wetting and drying or freezing and thawing and by an active soil fauna and flora enhanced by recent additions of easily decomposable organic matter. Carefully timed cultivations can assist by loosening the soil and breaking open incipient cracks between embryonic peds but conversely much harm can be done to soil structure if the wet soil is cultivated, run over or trampled by the hooves of stock (poaching). Man's influence on soil structure is somewhat of a mixed blessing, and some of his activities such as causing organic matter levels to drop, acidity to develop, and especially exposing the soil surface to the direct impact of rain leading to soil erosion are positively harmful.

1.5   SOIL WATER

Between and within the structural units or peds is a network of **pores** of various sizes, which are filled mainly with water when the soil is wet and air when the soil is dry (Fig. 1.2). These pores conduct water and air through the soil and provide an ideal growth environment for plant roots and the soil micro-organisms.

About half the volume of a soil is pore space (Fig. 1.3). The volume of pores, i.e. the **soil porosity** or **air capacity,** can be calculated from the **bulk density** of a soil as porosity=100−(bulk density/particle density×100). Bulk density is the weight of soil per unit volume and characteristically ranges from about 1.0 to 2.0 g/cm^3. This means a total porosity of between about 60 and 25% respectively (assuming a particle density of 2.65 g/cm^3).

When soil is wetted, e.g. by rainfall, so that all the pores fill up with water it would be described as **saturated** (Figs 1.2(a) and 1.3(a)). Under the action of gravity, however, water starts to drain out of the larger pores, the **macropores** larger than about 0.06 mm in diameter (unless there is some drainage impediment lower in the soil profile) and is replaced by air. This water is called **gravitational water** and when all of it has drained away the soil is said to be at **field capacity** (Figs 1.2(b) and 1.3(b)) with a moisture content sometimes called its **retained water capacity** (see Chapter 6).

Gravitational water eventually ends up in the ground-water (the zone of permanent saturation whose upper surface is called the **water table**) and is also the water seen issuing from the outfalls of any piped underdrainage system. The gravitational water continues to drain from the soil profile long after the source of water from the rainfall has ceased. The time taken for the system to arrive at field capacity depends on both the size and the interconnection of the actual pores involved and determines the **hydraulic permeability** of the soil mentioned again later in the Chapter. In

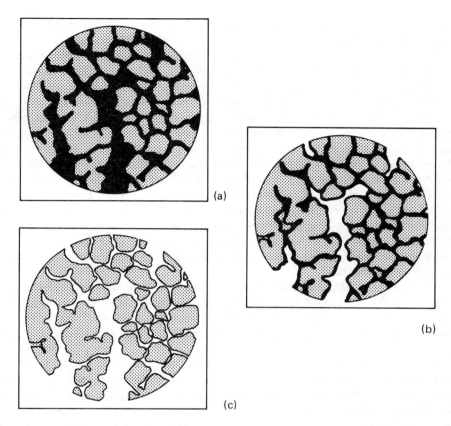

Fig. 1.2 — Soil water states: (a) at saturation; (b) at field capacity; (c) at permanent wilting point.

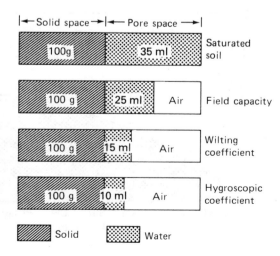

Fig. 1.3 — Typical proportions of solids, air and water in a well-structured loamy topsoil at various water states.

general, however, the sandier the soil the more quickly it is likely to arrive at field capacity, perhaps within hours, while heavier soils may take many days.

The smaller pores retain water against gravitational removal mainly because of capillary forces and so, not surprisingly, this is called the **capillary water**, held increasingly tightly the smaller the pores. The final physical category of soil water is the **hygroscopic water** held as a tight film near the particle surfaces. The amount of hygroscopic water held by a soil is called its **hygroscopic coefficient**, and at this stage the soil looks completely dry though some water still remains (Fig 1.3(d)). The moisture content of an apparently dry soil, e.g. an **air-dry** soil which has been allowed to dry out in a laboratory, is variable and determined by the temperature and humidity of its surroundings. Accordingly most soil analyses are reported on the basis of **oven-dry** soil (dried at 105–110°C in an oven for several hours).

The soil water which plants draw on when current rainfall alone does not provide sufficient for their needs is called the **available water**. It corresponds to most but not all of the capillary water, since the gravitational water is considered to be too transitory, and the hygroscopic water (and some of the capillary water in the smallest pores) is too tightly held.

It is generally advantageous for a soil to have a high **available water capacity** (AWC) and soils with low AWCs will be more droughty than those with high AWCs. The main factors determining the AWC of a soil sample (see Chapter 6) are its texture (see Fig. 1.4), stoniness, organic matter content and packing density, and on a soil profile basis the rooting depth.

Work has to be done by plant roots to extract the water, the driving force being the transpiration from the leaves. Similarly work in the form of heat has to be expended to withdraw water from a soil by natural evaporation or by oven drying. The drier the soil the harder the plant has to work to obtain the remaining moisture reserves held in progressively smaller pores. Eventually there comes a point as the

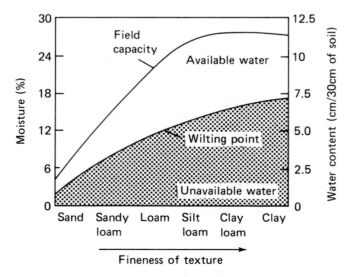

Fig. 1.4 — The relationship between soil water availability and soil texture.

soil dries out, called the **permanent wilting point** (Figs 1.2(c) and 1.3(c)), when plants can no longer exert sufficient suction to withdraw the tightly held moisture and so they wilt permanently.

The tightness with which soil can hold water is conveniently measured by the suction required to remove a certain portion of the soil water. In soil work suctions are measured in bars or millibars, like atmospheric pressure (standard atmospheric pressure is 1 bar or 1000 mbar). Most soil physicists agree that permanent wilting point corresponds to a suction of 15 bar and that the distinction between capillary and hygroscopic water is at a greater suction of 31 bar (Table 1.2). Oven drying corresponds to about 10 000 bar. They are, however, much less agreed on what suction corresponds to field capacity. Suctions of 0.33, 0.1 and 0.05 bar have all been proposed, and so the convention in use should always be checked.

Table 1.2— Relationships between different measures of soil moisture

Approximate soil work suction (atm)	Pore diameter (μm)	Soil moisture constants	Type of soil water	Appearance of soil
10 000		Oven dry		
1 000			Hygroscopic water; unavailable soil moisture	Dry
100		Hygroscopic		
30.6	0.1	coefficient		
15		Permanent	Capillary	Moist;
10	0.3	wilting	water;	best
	1.0	point	available soil moisture	moisture range for tillage
1	3.0	Old		
0.33	10	field		
0.10	30	capacity		
0.05	60	New field capacity	Gravitational water; subject to drainage	Wet
	100			
0.01	300			
0.001		Maximum moisture-holding capacity		Saturation

   In Britain it seems that a suction of 0.05 bar is the best approximation to field capacity, and so the usual definition of available water is that held at suctions between 0.05 (field capacity) and 15 bars (permanent wilting point). It corresponds to the water held in pores between about 0.06 mm (60 μm) and 0.002 mm (2 μm) in diameter. It can also be useful to know how much of the available water is held in the relatively larger pores and thus constitutes the readily available soil water, e.g. that held at suctions between 0.05 and 2 bar, corresponding to pores in the size range from 0.06 to about 0.002 mm (see Chapter 6).

1.6   WATER MOVEMENT, WATERLOGGING AND DRAINAGE

The network of larger pores, mainly those between the structural aggregates, is vital to allow the excess (gravitational) water to drain away and to allow air into the soil. The ease with which water passes through a soil is called the **permeability** of the soil. It is closely linked to soil texture and should not be confused with porosity which is a measure of the actual amount of pore space. Darcy's law for the transmission of a fluid through a porous medium allows permeability to be quantified in terms of the **hydraulic conductivity**, a proportionality constant, usually labelled K with units m/day. Some typical values of hydraulic conductivity K are given in Table 1.3.

Table 1.3 — Approximate relationships between texture, structure and hydraulic conductivity

Texture	Structure	Indicative hydraulic conductivity K	
		(cm/h)	(m/day)
Coarse sand, gravel	Single grain	⩾50	⩾12
Medium sand	Single grain	25–50	6–12
Loamy sand, fine sand	Medium crumb, single grain	12–25	3–6
Fine sandy loam, sandy loam	Coarse, subangular blocky and granular, fine crumb	6–12	1.5–3
Light clay loam, silt, silt loam, very fine sandy loam, loam	Medium prismatic and subangular blocky	2–6	0.5–1.5
Clay, silty clay, sandy clay, silty clay loam, clay loam, silt loam, silt, sandy clay loam	Fine and medium prismatic, angular blocky, platy	0.5–2	0.1–0.5
Clay, clay loam, silty clay, sandy clay loam	Very fine or fine prismatic, angular blocky, platy	0.25–0.5	0.05–0.1
Clay, heavy clay	Massive, very fine or columnar	<0.25	<0.05

Source: Landon (1984); adapted from Dent and Young (1981).

If the soil profile has a horizon or horizons of low hydraulic conductivity then the likelihood is that waterlogging will occur in or above such horizons. Gravitational water cannot drain away, and air is therefore excluded, a situation harmful to most plant roots and the beneficial soil micro-organisms. Waterlogging can also occur in low-lying positions in the landscape where the water table is close to the surface. Both these situations give rise to characteristic soil types, called gley soils, which are characterised by greyish colours and mottling, called gleying (see below), due to the chemical reduction, movement and redeposition of iron compounds in response to the anaerobic conditions.

Artificial drainage of a soil provides the means to remove water from the site, e.g. by open drains or ditches helping to lower the water table or a network of tile or plastic drainpipes installed in the subsoil, together with some treatment to encourage water to soak from the soil to the drains. This may involve permeable backfill above the drains, and secondary treatments such as mole drains or loosening the soil, i.e. improving its hydraulic conductivity, by subsoiling.

Wet soils have a low mechanical resistance and so are easily damaged if a load is imposed on them especially if it involves a shearing stress, such as by the wheels of vehicles, a heavy plough or the hooves of animals. Soil becomes smeared and the continuity of pores is broken, structure is lost and in extreme cases the soil turns into a slurry. Bulk density increases, the soil becomes compact and the hydraulic conductivity decreases further.

Plant roots, except for some adapted species such as rice, respond adversely to waterlogged soil and become stunted or are even killed off. Aerobic micro-organisms, notably those involved in organic matter decomposition are inhibited in badly drained anaerobic soils (hence the build-up of peat). However, anaerobic bacteria become active and may, for example, cause a loss of soil nitrogen by conversion to gaseous forms and convert sulphates to sulphides (hence the smell of some very badly drained soils). Beneficial macro-organisms such as earthworms (in temperate soils) and termites (in tropical soils) are also inhibited by bad soil drainage.

The concepts of permeability and hydraulic conductivity described above tend to be used for the soil in bulk. For the particular situation at the soil surface the terms infiltration and **infiltration rate** are used instead. In dry soils infiltration rates are initially high, especially in coarse textured or fissured soils, but then fall as the soil becomes wet. This is because pores become blocked by entrapped air, and pores become smaller and fewer as the soil swells or especially if the structure begins to collapse. Infiltration rates can be as high as 35 cm of water per hour in very coarse permeable soils to as low as 0.03 cm of water per hour or less in low-permeability clays.

If rainfall arrives at the soil surface at a faster rate than it can infiltrate, then it will form surface ponding in the minor undulations of level ground or will run off on slopes with consequent risk of soil erosion.

In humid areas the net movement of water is downwards. In the short term this washes out plant nutrients and bases and the soil tends to become acid (see below). In the longer term, downward percolation of water through a soil profile is one of the main agents of soil formation (see for example Fig. 1.5 and the soil forming processes of leaching, clay migration, podzolisation and ferallitisation described below). In

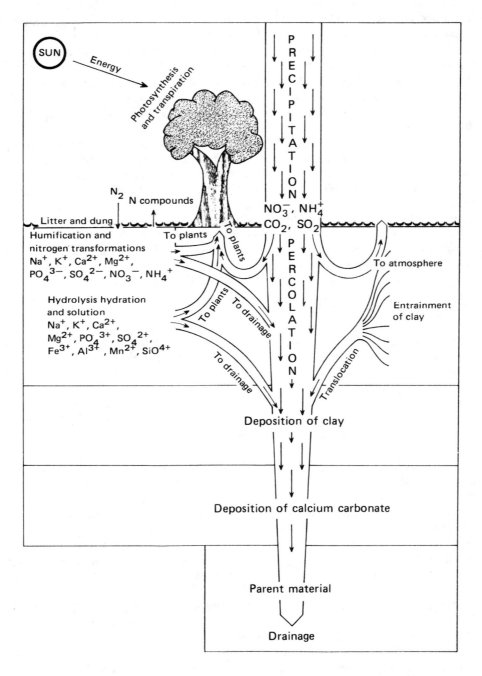

Fig. 1.5 — Water as a soil forming process. (Source: FitzPatrick 1986)

arid regions, however, water tends to move upwards rather than downwards in the profile. The upward movement is mainly by capillary rise from ground-water encouraged by evaporation from the surface and if the water is saline this can cause deposition of salts at or near the surface (the process of salinisation discussed below).

1.7 THE SOIL ATMOSPHERE

The soil atmosphere is the gaseous mixture occupying the pores which are not water filled. Its composition (Table 1.4) differs from the normal atmosphere by having less oxygen than the 20.9% of a normal atmosphere, but much more carbon dioxide, typically 0.5–5% compared with 0.03%. The carbon dioxide comes from the respiration of roots and soil organisms which use up oxygen in the process, and hence the need for a well-aerated soil to replenish the essential oxygen.

Table 1.4 — Composition of the soil air compared with that of the atmosphere

Location	Content (vol.%)		
	O_2	CO_2	N_2
Soil air			
England	20.65	0.25	79.20
Iowa	20.40	0.20	79.40
New York	15.10	4.50	81.40
Atmospheric air			
England	20.97	0.03	79.0

(Source: Brady 1974)

If there was a completely free interchange between the soil atmosphere and the open atmosphere the composition of both would equilibrate and so be very similar. The exchange of gases, i.e. soil respiration is, however, controlled mainly by the rate of gaseous diffusion which depends on the pore size distribution, pore continuity, including the presence of water which can block off pores to gaseous diffusion, and even to the tortuosity of the pores themselves. Soil temperature and any wind blowing across the soil surface also influence soil respiration. Carbon dioxide levels are therefore high and oxygen levels low in dense, poorly structured soils and/or badly drained soils. Such conditions would be called **anaerobic** and the soil **poorly aerated**. Even in well-drained, loose and open soils there can still be pockets of localised anaerobism, e.g. in the centres of large structural units.

Plant roots need oxygen to flourish and so anaerobism is harmful to them. Thus they are encouraged by well-drained, generally aerobic soils and tend to grow preferentially down cracks and fissures which are likely to be well aerated, though the reduced mechanical resistance of such paths may also be responsible.

The composition of the soil atmosphere is constantly changing with marked diurnal and seasonal fluctuations. Carbon dioxide levels can rise dramatically as soil organisms are encouraged by a rise in temperature and/or an addition of fresh organic debris. In badly drained soils there can be the production and build-up of small but phytotoxic amounts of gases such as ethylene, along with methane, once appropriately known as marsh gas.

1.8   SOIL BIOLOGY

Most of the organisms which live in soils are involved in the complex process of decomposition of fresh organic matter to humus, such as the earthworms and the saprophytic micro-organisms. The major exceptions are those which simply burrow into soils to provide their living accommodation, such as rabbits, badgers and prairie dogs, or which are predators on soil organisms, such as moles.

Earthworms are commonest in temperate region soils though there are some tropical species. They generally prefer fertile well-drained organic-rich soils which are not too acid and serve as the main agents of soil mixing and physical incorporation of fresh organic matter landing on the soil surface. In suitable undisturbed soils the topsoil will have passed through the gut of earthworms many times to produce what is, in effect, a mass of earthworm casts. Such an intimate mixture of organic and mineral matter produced by earthworms is called **mull**. In tropical soils earthworms are overshadowed by the termites which are the great soil mixers and incorporators in these regions.

When earthworms (or termites) are inhibited one of the first signs is that organic matter builds up as a discrete layer or layers on the surface and is not mixed in, e.g. the so-called **mor** or **raw humus** which builds up on very acid heathland and coniferous forests in the absence of earthworms. In such material the decomposition is a slow *in situ* process carried out by the soil microflora with gradual degradation by tiny animals such as woodlice, millipedes or springtails but little incorporation of the debris into the rest of the soil.

The decomposition of organic matter is a complex web of processes involving mainly bacteria, fungi and actinomycetes. Bacteria tend to be the commonest in most soils and the population can adapt in both numbers and composition with changes in the environment. For example there is a flush of opportunist growth as fresh organic material is added, especially if there is a mix of substrates to support a wide range of species. The population declines with time as the more easily decomposable material is used up, and near the end of the process as the material approaches the composition of true humus the fungi tend to become relatively more important.

The bacterial population is inhibited not only by lack of suitable organic matter to attack but also by temperature (the optimum range is about 20–40°C), moisture content (activity is slowed in very dry soils), aeration (activity patterns change and the general population declines with anaerobism, e.g. by waterlogging), soil reaction (optimum range is pH 6–8) and by the availability of mineral nutrients. In this last respect it is often thought that the activities of micro-organisms are wholly beneficial in returning nutrients locked up in the organic matter to forms available to higher plants and this is true in the long-term. In the short-term, micro-organisms (especially bacteria) compete vigorously with plant roots and can even cause deficiencies, notably in nitrogen when the bacteria are attacking fresh organic matter which has a low nitrogen content.

While most bacteria are involved in organic matter breakdown (the saprophytes), others are involved in transformations of plant nutrients in soils, especially transformations in the forms of nitrogen, including fixation of atmospheric nitrogen. Nitrogen fixation is carried out notably by *Rhizobium* species living symbiotically with the roots of legumes, but many free living species have also been shown to fix small amounts of atmospheric nitrogen. This microbial fixation of nitrogen is of great importance since it is virtually the only primary source of soil nitrogen other than applied by chemical fertilisers and recycled in the organic matter.

Fungi are restricted to well-aerated soils but they can tolerate more acid conditions than bacteria can and so become more dominant in acid soils. They are also more able than bacteria to decompose more resistant organic compounds such as lignins which predominate in the later stages of organic matter decomposition or where there is a lot of woody debris.

An important group of fungi are the mycorrhizae whose association with the roots of higher plants is mutually beneficial. Less beneficial, indeed positively harmful, are the many plant-disease (and some animal-disease) organisms which live in soils, mostly fungi, though bacteria and actinomycetes also cause their share of diseases.

The actinomycetes are not particularly common, but the characteristic 'earthy' smell, particularly of warm moist topsoil is thought to be produced by them. Other soil organisms include the algae, notably the blue–green algae which fix atmospheric nitrogen in rice paddy soils and a huge range of mesofauna and microfauna. Some of these feed directly on plant debris, others such as springtails, mites, protozoa, nematodes and termites feed on the microflora and others favour a carnivorous diet of other mesofauna and microfauna, e.g. centipedes, mites, ants and beetles.

1.9 SOIL CHEMISTRY

Much of the chemical activity in soils is concerned with the clay and humus, sometimes collectively referred to as the **colloidal fraction** of the soil. As explained above, these carry electrostatic charges on their surfaces giving an overall net negative charge, the **cation exchange capacity** (CEC), balanced by positive cations in the surrounding **soil solution.** The charges on the clays are due either to what is called isomorphous replacement within their atomic structures or to an edge effect of dissociation of hydroxyl and similar groups. This amount of this latter charge is pH dependent and increases as the pH rises, and hence the need to measure the CEC at a standard pH. Conversely positive charges can develop at low pH values, and hence the frequent reference to net negative charge (rather than only negative charges). These positive charges seem to be mainly associated with coatings of sesquioxides, and in some tropical soils high in sesquioxides it is possible to demonstrate a net positive charge at low pH levels. The negative charges carried by humus are due entirely to edge dissociation effects, mainly of carboxyl and phenolic groups, and so their contribution to the CEC is also pH dependent.

The cations which balance all these negative charges are interchangeable with each other in chemically equivalent amounts and so are called exchangeable. They tend to cluster near the surfaces of the clays and humus, becoming less tightly held the further away they are from the surfaces. In general the order of replacement of cations is that higher-valency ones, e.g. calcium, will tend to replace lower-valency ones, and cations which are small in their hydrated form tend to replace those which are large in their hydrated form so that, for example, potassium will replace sodium.

In practice, however, the main driving force for exchange is the concentration of particular cations in the external solution, and high concentrations will tend to force that cation onto the exchange complex, replacing the cations already held. This can be demonstrated by passing a solution of, say, sodium chloride through a column of soil. The solution which emerges will contain all the cations which were originally on the exchange sites, e.g. calcium, magnesium, potassium and hydrogen, plus the surplus sodium. The soil can then be flushed with water and/or alcohol to remove all the sodium except that held on the exchange sites. If the sodium-saturated soil is subsequently leached with, say, an ammonium solution the ammonium ions will quantitatively replace the sodium which will be a measure of the CEC of that soil.

In natural soils the composition of the exchange complex will reflect the relative amounts of cations which have been released by weathering, after due allowance for losses by leaching. Thus, for example, soils formed in base-rich parent materials will be dominated by calcium and magnesium, those on base-poor materials by aluminium and hydrogen, and those from recent marine sediments by sodium (Table 1.5). Management practices, especially applications of fertiliser and lime, will, of course, drastically modify the natural composition.

Table 1.5 — Typical composition of the exchange complex (me/100 g) for various topsoils (see also Tables 1.1 and 1.6)

	CEC	Ca	Mg	K	Na	BS[2]
Podzol (Scotland)	39.1	0.6	0.7	0.2	tr.	3.8
Luvisol (England)	28.0	22.8	0.6	0.3	0.1	85.0
Acrisol (USA)	2.1	0.3	0.1	0.1	tr.	23.8
Chernozem (USSR)	33.0	30.5	1.8	0.5	0.2	100.0
Ferralsol (Thailand)	9.6	4.8	1.2	0.3	0.2	67.7
Planosol (Argentina)	22.8	13.4	5.6	0.7	0.3	87.7
Arenosol (Senegal)	9.2	1.5	0.5	0.1	0.1	23.9
Anidosol (Philippines)	61.4	7.8	1.4	0.2	0.2	15.6
Histosol (England)	131.0	85.0	3.7	1.7	1.1	69.8
Thionic fluvisol (Guinea)	17.5	3.2	6.2	0.7	24.7	n.a.

[a] Named according to the FAO/UNESCO system (see Chapter 4).
[b] Per cent base saturation.

One of the cations which can help to balance the negative charges on the soil exchange complex is hydrogen, and hydrogen-dominated soil colloids are sometimes likened to weak acids, dissociating into clay and humus anions and hydrogen cations. The activity of these hydrogen ions in the soil solution can be measured as the soil pH or **soil reaction**. The base cations tend to balance this acidity; so, as the proportion of these on the exchange complex rises (the so-called **base saturation**), the pH also rises, i.e. the soil becomes less acid. Because it is so easily measured, soil pH is frequently recorded. It provides an indication of the base saturation of the soil and hence is a measure of soil fertility since the bases are important plant nutrients.

In very acid soils the clay minerals themselves start to dissociate, releasing aluminium, so that a hydrogen-dominated clay becomes a mixed aluminium and hydrogen clay. It is this phytotoxic aluminium which can be the main problem in highly acid soils so that plants are killed at pH levels which they would be able to tolerate in nutrient solutions when only hydrogen ions were present. Acid conditions also affect the availability of most plant nutrients and it is generally considered that the optimum pH is about 6.0–6.5 in temperate region soils and about 5.0–5.5 in tropical soils for most crop plants. Crops vary widely in their sensitivity to soil acidity and natural vegetation still more.

In humid climates soils generally tend to become more acid with time because of additions of hydrogen ions in rainfall and release of hydrogen from plant roots in exchange for the soil bases they absorb. Soils with a source of bases by weathering, e.g. those on base-rich or calcareous parent materials, tend to resist this process as do soils with a high CECs. Soils containing free calcium carbonate characteristically have a pH in the range 7–7.5 but usually no higher than this because of the buffering effect of the carbonic acid produced from the carbon dioxide evolved in the soil. Conversely, highly permeable and so easily leached soils, especially intrinsically base-poor sands with low CEC, become acid very rapidly, and pH values down to as low as 3 are not uncommon (Table 1.6).

Table 1.6 — Typical values of pH for a range of soils[a], measured in H_2O (see also Table 1.1 and 1.5)

	Topsoil	Subsoil
Podzol (Scotland)	4.1 (humose sl)	4.6 (s)
Luvisol (England)	6.2 (scl)	6.0 (cl)
Acrisol (USA)	4.7 (ls)	4.7 (sc)
Chernozem (USSR)	7.0 (l)	7.3 (l)
Ferralsol (Thailand)	5.9 (sl)	4.7 (scl)
Planosol (Argentina)	6.9 (l)	6.4 (zc)
Arenosol (Senegal)	7.4 (ls)	7.2 (ls)
Andosol (Philippines)	5.3 (humose l)	5.7 (zl)
Histosol (England)	6.9 (peat)	—
Thionic Fluvisol (Guinea)	4.7 (sl)	3.2 (sc)

[a]named according to the FAO/UNESCO system (see Chapter 4).
Textures (given in brackets) are abbreviated: cl — clay loam; l — loam; ls — loamy sand; s — sand; sl — sandy loam; sc — sandy clay; scl — sandy clay loam; zc — silty clay; zl — silt loam.

Natural vegetation will reflect these differences in pH, and farmers can avoid the consequences of low or high pH by growing only crops tolerant of the pH conditions in their soils. pH is, however, easy to change and so liming to raise pH values is a common agricultural practice. Any base would, in fact, do if a change in pH was all that was required, and lime (calcium carbonate, calcium oxide or calcium hydroxide) is used simply because it is the cheapest and most widely available base.

The amount of lime which has to be added depends on the rise in pH required, i.e. the lower the initial pH the more lime is needed. It also depends on the CEC of the soil since the higher the CEC the more the soil is buffered against pH change and so the more lime is needed. Thus high-CEC soils require infrequent liming but then large amounts, whereas sands require more frequent liming but in much smaller amounts. The neutralising value of the liming material also has to be taken into consideration since, for example, calcium oxide is twice as powerful a liming material weight for weight than is calcium carbonate.

Some soils have unusual chemical compositions which cause extreme pH values. When badly drained pyritic alluvium (or coal mine spoil) is oxidised, sulphuric acid is, in effect, produced and pH values as low as 2 have been recorded in the so-called acid sulphate soils. Similarly pH can be deliberately lowered by applying sulphur to a soil, but this is very rarely done.

Salt-affected soils typically have pH values above up to 8.5 but no higher because of the high concentration of neutral soluble salts. If there is a high amount of exchangeable sodium and the soils are subsequently leached, however, e.g. in an irrigation project, the pH can rise to between 8.5 and 10 by the production of sodium carbonate. Such sodic soils (solonetz or slick-spot soils) also have poor physical characteristics since the sodium carbonate makes the clay particles disperse into a slurry-like mass when wet which then dries brick hard. For the same reasons, replacement of sodium on the exchange complex of, for example, a recently sea-flooded soil should use calcium sulphate which will form the relatively harmless sodium sulphate rather than calcium carbonate leading to the production of sodium carbonate.

High concentrations of soluble salts in soils can be injurious to many plants though degrees of tolerance to salinity can be recognised. The salinity of a soil is measured by the **electrical conductivity** of the water extracted from a soil which has just been saturated with water but no more, the so-called **saturation extract.** Typical values are given in Table 1.7. The assessment of saline soils for crop production relies heavily on measurements of electrical conductivity, the **exchangeable sodium percentage** and the **sodium adsorption ratio** which is the ratio of sodium to the square root of the calcium plus magnesium.

Table 1.7 — General interpretation of values of electrical conductivity of saturation extracts of soils (EC).

EC (ms/cm)	Effects on crops
0–2	Salinity effects mostly negligible
2–4	Yields of very sensitive crops may be restricted
4–8	Yields of many crops restricted
8–16	Only tolerant crops yield satisfactorily
>16	Only a few very tolerant crops yield satisfactorily

Source: Richards (1954)

Other chemical reactions which take place in soils include precipitation and solution processes, e.g. reactions between various phosphate anions and calcium, iron and aluminium compounds and some of those involved in the weathering of soil minerals. Oxidation–reduction reactions take place under appropriate conditions often with microbial participation, such as interconversion of various forms of soil nitrogen, phosphorus, sulphur (e.g. the oxidation of pyrite already mentioned), manganese and iron.

1.10 SOIL FERTILITY

Plant roots derive most of their mineral nutrients directly from the soil solution, but this is so dilute that at any given moment it contains far less of each nutrient than is finally found in the plant. Obviously, then, the soil solution is constantly being replenished from 'back-up' sources which thus maintain an approximate equilibrium in the weak concentrations of nutrients of the soil solution.

The advantages of a relatively dilute soil solution is that any losses, e.g. by leaching away in the gravitational water are minimised. The disadvantage is that nutrient concentrations normally found in the soil solution are well below the optimum levels for plant growth. Additions of nutrients not immediately required, and in excess of what the soil solution normally carries, are converted to reserve forms, e.g. during regular soil transformations such as organic matter decomposition, or irregular events such as applications of chemical fertilisers.

In soils the reserve forms of soil nutrients are in a variety of forms which differ in their ease of accessibility and hence availability to the plant within the time scale they are needed. The reserves held on the cation exchange sites of the clay minerals and organic matter are regarded as more or less immediately available. Those bound up in organic matter which has to be decomposed first, or in compounds which are very sparingly soluble and give up their nutrients very slowly, are rather less available. Nutrients available only in the long term are those bound up in the crystalline structures of the soil minerals which have to be weathered and broken down before they are available to the plant, a process which is likely to take many thousands of years before all the nutrients are released.

Thus assessments of the fertility of a soil, i.e. its ability to meet the needs of the vegetation growing in it, involve determinations not just of the amounts of nutrients there are in the soil solution but also the reserves which will replenish this over the time scale (e.g. the growing season) involved. This is the concept of assessment of **available nutrients. Soil testing** for nutrient availability is a largely empirical process though some of the methods do aim for a particular chemical form of the nutrient in question. For example, the soil tests for available potassium by and large measure the exchangeable form plus the small amount currently in the soil solution.

Most soil tests for available nutrients involve shaking a known amount of soil with a known amount of chemical solution for a given time and then measuring the amount of the particular nutrient or nutrients which have been extracted. Table 1.8 lists some commonly used extracting solutions for particular nutrients, the soil-to-extractant ratios employed and the way of subsequently measuring the amounts extracted. All the methods try to reproduce in a short time in the laboratory the complex processes which go to maintain the supply of nutrients to plant roots over the growing season. Different extracting methods will extract different amounts of the nutrient from the same soil and so some means of interpreting the results is required, by comparing them with crop performance and fertiliser response. Thus the choice of a method by a testing laboratory is entirely empirical, and more because it gives results which can be usefully interpreted rather than because it has any theoretical validity.

Table 1.8 — Typical extractants used to determine available nutrients in soils (with names of originators in brackets where appropriate)

Available phosphorus
0.5 M Sodium bicarbonate (Olsen). Useful for soils with pH>7
Dilute hydrochloric acid/ammonium fluoride (Bray No. 2a)
Dilute hydrochloric and sulphuric acids (Nelson)
Dilute sulphuric acid (Truog)
Sodium acetate/acetic acid (Morgan)
Ammonium acetate/acetic acid (MAFF, not now used)

Available potassium
Neutral 1 N ammonium acetate (exchangeable and water-soluble K)
Dilute sulphuric acid (Hunter and Pratt)
Boiling 1 N nitric acid (for non-exchangeable 'reserve' K)

Available magnesium
Neutral 1 N ammonium acetate (exchangeable and water-soluble Mg)

Available sulphur
Ammonium acetate
Sodium bicarbonate

Micronutrients
A very wide range of extractants, often specific to a particular micronutrient

---

Any competent laboratory can produce a set of results labelled available this or that, but they are not worth the paper they are written on unless the method is specified and an interpretation of the results is given. An example of the sort of interpretation required is given in Table 1.9 where the results of a determination of available phosphate by the Agricultural Development and Advisory Service of the Ministry of Agriculture, Fisheries and Food are interpreted by an index system on which fertiliser recommendations can be based.

No extracting method for nitrogen is given in Table 1.8. This is because the supply of nitrogen depends largely on the activities of micro-organisms which cannot reliably be simulated by an extracting procedure. Incubation procedures have been recommended but these are not really suitable for routine analytical purposes. Fertiliser recommendations are often based on the previous cropping history which will partly determine the nature of the decomposing soil organic matter, general soil type and climatic factors such as the amount of rainfall which will have caused leaching of nitrogen (and other nutrients).

The other somewhat difficult nutrient or nutrients are the micronutrients or trace elements such as iron, manganese, copper, zinc, molybdenum and boron. These and related heavy metals can sometimes be present in toxic rather than deficient amounts. They tend to be involved in the enzyme systems of plants and so

Table 1.9— Interpretation of results for available phosphorus extracted with sodium bicarbonate solution according to the procedure used by Agricultural Development and Advisory Service of the Ministry of Agriculture, Fisheries and Food (see section 8.13)

Index	Sodium bicarbonate extract	Index	Interpretation Notes
0	0–9	0	Possibility of failures in arable crops if phosphate not applied
1	10–15	1	Possibility of failures in glasshouse crops if phosphate not applied
2	16–25	2	
3	26–45	3	
4	46–70	4	
5	71–100	5	Phosphate can be reduced below that given in the tables for many field crops
6	101–140		
6			
7	141–200	7	No phosphate required for glasshouse crops
8	201–280	8	Unnecessarily high levels of phosphates; yields
9	>280	9	of many crops may be reduced

(Source: Ministry of Agriculture Fisheries and Food, © Crown Copyright)

deficiencies or toxicities can often give spectacular effects, some of which were thought to be plant diseases. Thus crop appearance, followed by foliar analysis, might be a better route of investigation than soil analysis, where total rather than available (or perhaps more correctly extractable) amounts are sometimes the most reliable indicators.

The chemistry of the individual plant nutrients is a vast and complex subject, but some of the main features are listed below, though these are generalisations and do not cover the situation in every soil.

Nitrogen (N) — The nutrient required to make protein and probably the single most important nutrient in determining plant growth, especially of leaves. Ultimately all derived from atmospheric sources by microbial fixation but recycled through the soil organic matter and undergoing several transformations by microbial action, usually ending up as nitrate in which form it is highly soluble, easily taken up by plants, but readily leached out of the soil. Other losses are by transformation to gaseous forms, and removal in crops. Regarded as a rather ephemeral and highly mobile nutrient necessitating regular large applications of chemical fertilisers to support high-yielding crops.

Phosphorus (P) — Taken up as phosphate anions from solution but very easily fixed by precipitation as calcium compounds or as iron and aluminium compounds in acid soils. These compounds are very insoluble and so the concentration in the soil solution is often well below optimum levels for a crop. Some is recycled in the organic form. Can also be in low total amounts in highly weathered, leached or organic soils.

Sulphur (S) — Occurs mainly as the sulphate anion but some involved in the organic cycle. Can be present in very large amounts in some arid region soils. Mostly added from atmospheric sources, including 'acid rain' or incidentally along with other fertilisers. Deficiencies rather rare.

Calcium (Ca) — The main cation on the exchange complex of most soils and so in effect controls the soil pH. Present in large amounts in calcareous soils or soils derived from base-rich parent materials but can become deficient in highly leached acid soils though often difficult to say whether plants suffer from calcium deficiency *per se* or from some other problem caused by or related to low pH. Often added to soils as lime to raise pH.

Magnesium (Mg) — Behaves somewhat like calcium but usually present in smaller amounts. Sometimes added as a fertiliser or as a magnesian lime.

Potassium (K) — Held on the cation exchange complex and sometimes fixed in a less available form within the lattice of weathered clay minerals. Natural potassium status of soils often related to amount of illitic and similar clay minerals or to micas, felspars, etc., in the sand and silt fraction. Tends to be leached from soils in the long term and so most commonly deficient in acid soils. Commonly added as a fertiliser.

Micronutrients — A complex group but which in general tends to be most available in acid conditions, even to toxic levels, and deficient in calcareous conditions, except molybdenum which has the reverse trend. Deficiencies often because of low total amounts present resulting from nature of parent material, excessive weathering and leaching and in highly organic soils.

1.11   SOIL FORMING PROCESSES

All the soil properties described above are the result of various **soil forming processes** acting over many years. Some of the processes are very slow, but over the thousands or tens of thousands of years available for soil formation they have helped to produce the characteristic soil profiles which are the basis of soil classification and mapping (see Chapters 4 and 5). Some of the processes such as organic matter accumulation and gleying have already been mentioned but will be put into their soil forming context with some of the other main processes which go to form soils.

1.11.1   Organic matter accumulation

In many respects it is the beginnings of organic matter accumulation which differentiates a soil from just a heap of weathered rock. Together with weathering it is the initial soil forming process and continues to a greater or lesser extent throughout the ensuing development of the soil profile. It is convenient to differentiate between situations where fresh organic matter is being actively decomposed so that what is accumulating is the relatively stable humus, usually intimately incorporated with the mineral fraction (e.g. mull), and where such decomposition is inhibited and what builds up is relatively undecomposed material (raw humus, mor or peat). The former tends to have a delaying effect on some of the other soil forming processes by maintaining the fertility and stability of the surface horizons whereas the latter is often associated with more active and spectacular processes such as podzolisation and gleying.

1.11.2   Weathering

This is the general term given to alteration of rocks when exposed to the atmosphere. Three kinds, physical, chemical and biological, can be recognised. Physical weathering includes the mechanical comminution of rock particles by alternate freezing and thawing, wetting and drying, and heating and cooling. It increases the surface area for chemical and biological weathering to act on, reduces particle size towards sand and silt, the ranges more normally considered to be typical of soil, but does not produce clay unless that is already present in the parent rock. Chemical weathering changes the composition and chemical structure of the original (primary minerals) unless like quartz they are resistant and accumulate in the sand and silt fraction. Secondary minerals notably the clays are formed, and ions are released into solution to act as plant nutrients or are leached away. Chemical reactions include solution, hydration, hydrolysis and oxidation. Biological weathering includes the levering apart of rocks by plant roots, mixing and churning activities of various soil animals, and the important production of carbon dioxide which becomes carbonic acid. This, together with other acid exudates, contributes to the chemical weathering processes.

1.11.3   Leaching

In humid areas, especially the humid tropics, large quantities of water flush through the soil and carry away cations and anions dissolved in the soil solution (Fig. 1.6(a)). The removal of weathering products thus encourages further weathering to take place. Leaching losses are delayed, albeit temporarily, by incorporation of ions into organic forms (including uptake into the vegetation) and the retention of cations on the exchange complex of the soil. Some elements are readily leached out, notably sodium, chloride, nitrate and sulphate, while others, such as potassium, magnesium, calcium and phosphate, are lost more slowly. The particular case where free calcium carbonate is removed is called decalcification and changes the pH from alkaline to acid. Some elements, such as silicon and especially iron and aluminium, are removed so slowly that they accumulate as a sort of solution or weathering residue (see ferrallitisation below). In humid regions leaching washes the ions out of the profile but in arid or semi-arid regions there may be deposition lower in the profile, notably of calcium carbonate and calcium sulphate and in extreme cases there may be 'reverse leaching' bringing salts into the profile (see salinisation below).

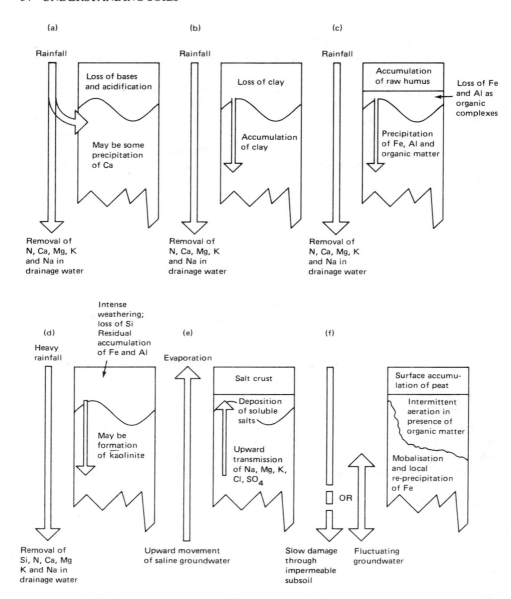

Fig. 1.6 — The soil forming processes of (a) leaching (b) clay translocation (c) podzolisation (d) ferallitisation, (e) salinisation and (f) gleying.

1.11.4   Clay translocation

This very slow process involves the washing out of discrete clay particles in slightly acid conditions and their eventual deposition lower in the profile (Fig. 1.6(b)). The zone from which the clay is washed is called an eluvial horizon which becomes lighter in texture compared with the zone where the clay is deposited, the illuvial horizon, sometimes referred to as a textural B (i.e. subsoil) horizon. The process is sometimes called clay illuviation or lessivage (a French word meaning literally only leaching but usually used specifically for this process).Horizons richer in clay than those above and/or below can arise for reasons other than clay translocation, such as variations in the parent material, superficial deposits of lighter textured materials, and more intense weathering leading to clay destruction nearer the surface of the profile than at depth. Pedologists sometimes have to resort to looking at thin sections of soils under the microscope to prove the process. The clay tends to be deposited in thin skins, called **cutans**, in cracks and on the faces of structural aggregates, sometimes visible to the naked eye. With a special petrographic microscope these cutans exhibit the property of birefringence because the clay particles are laid down in parallel layers thus producing references to 'birefringent clay' as opposed to the more normal 'anisotropic clays'. Soils exhibiting this process are frequently described as 'argillic' e.g. argillic brown earths.

1.11.5 Podzolisation

Russian peasants in the coniferous forest zone noticed that below the surface litter of their soils there was a white horizon, followed at depth by a black one. They thought this black layer was charcoal from past forest fires and that the white layer was ash. They therefore called the soils podzols, literally ash soils. This is, of course, not the explanation for the appearance of the profile. What happens is that organic acids and phenolic compounds from the vegetation and surface organic matter of these very acid soils can form complexes with iron and aluminium and so remove them from the surface, transport them downwards in migrating water and deposit them in the subsoil (Fig. 1.6(c)). The leached eluvial horizon becomes white because the iron which gives most soils their brown colour is removed, while the subsoil becomes black (and brown since there are usually two recognisable zones of deposition) because of the additions of iron and organic matter to the illuvial horizons below. The process removes iron and aluminium preferentially and so silica tends to accumulate in the surface (compare with ferallitisation in which silica is removed preferentially leaving a residue richer in iron and aluminium).

1.11.6 Ferallitisation

Intense leaching and weathering, almost always under humid tropical conditions, give soil horizons depleted of silica and thus high in the relatively silica-poor clay mineral kaolinite and often rich in hydrous iron and aluminium oxides and hydroxides (Fig. 1.6(d)). These are the so-called oxic horizons of the American system of Soil Taxonomy and the FAO–UNESCO classification (see Chapter 4). There may be some localised solution, movement and deposition of these hydrous oxides associated with ground-water fluctuations producing a characteristic mottled horizon called plinthite. When this becomes dry it hardens irreversibly and is called laterite. The term laterite and/or latosol is widely and erroneously used for any red-coloured tropical soil irrespective of whether or not it contains horizons of true laterite or plinthite.

1.11.7 Salinisation

In arid and semi-arid areas saline ground-waters are drawn to the surface, especially in lower-lying areas, and as the water evaporates the salts are precipitated at or near the surface (Fig. 1.6(e)). Thus the process is almost the complete reverse of the leaching process described above. The characteristic soil type is the solonchak.

1.11.8 Gleying

In soils subject to permanent or periodic waterlogging the anaerobic conditions cause chemical reduction of the iron oxides, in which form they become partially soluble and migrate through the soil. Subsequent re-oxidation in less anaerobic parts of the soil or as waterlogging temporarily recedes gives ochreous or reddish brown iron-enriched segregations or concretions (Fig. 1.6(f)). The characteristic mottling in browns and greys is called gleying; in general, the more pronounced it is, the greyer it is and, the nearer it is to the surface, the worse drained the soil is (see section 6.3.4). The gleying can remain as a relict feature in soils long after drainage conditions have improved. It is thought that the gleying process is associated with the presence of organic matter. Typical soils are called gleys or the term gleyic or gleyed is used. Features referred to as 'hydromorphic features' include gleying.

1.11.9 Soil erosion

The processes of soil formation are, to some extent, balanced by erosion, both part of the overall process of landscape development. Erosion is by either wind or water and can reach catastrophic proportions in certain situations, most commonly when the protective covering of vegetation is removed.

1.11.10 Soil additions

This process, the reverse of soil erosion, occurs when fresh material is added to the soil surface. Examples include the additions of silt and clay deposited as alluvium during the periodic flooding of river valleys, cover loams and cover sands which are superficial additions of wind blown material, and colluvium, i.e. material washed downslope by erosion to accumulate in footslope positions. Many soils in both temperate and tropical areas show signs in their profiles of past additions of material, either completely destroying the original profiles or burying them below the new superficial material. Sorting of material during erosion, transport and deposition has given rise to many of the characteristic soil patterns on sloping land.

Not all of these processes occur in every soil, nor do they all occur with the same intensity. Most are very slow processes which cannot actually be seen happening. Nevertheless the wide variety of soil profiles which occur across the earth's surface is testament to their power in turning barren rock into the soils which we are going to encourage you to look at more closely in the rest of this book.

2

Describing a soil sample

2.1 INTRODUCTION

As with most naturally occurring substances, descriptions of soils can be as simple or elaborate as you wish. Some soil properties, however, are so basic that they should always be included in a description, others are very useful (but not absolutely essential) while a few are really for cognoscenti only.

The standard order of describing soil properties tends to reflect the relative importance of the properties, with the most essential given first as in the following example:

> Dark greyish brown (2.5Y 4/2) with many fine prominent yellowish brown (1OYR 5/8) mottles; clay loam, slightly stony (common small angular fragments of limestone); moderately developed fine crumb structure; strongly calcareous.

This describes the five basic properties of colour (and colour mottling), texture (clay loam in the above example), stoniness, structure and presence or absence of calcium carbonate.

For most purposes this degree of detail will suffice, and some of the description can be less elaborate if required. Sections 2.2–2.6 below explain how such a description can be produced for a given sample of soil, e.g. sent to you in a plastic bag, or for a horizon within a soil profile (see Chapter 3).

Additional properties can be described, e.g. porosity, moisture and handling properties, presence and kind of roots, evidence of faunal activity and miscellaneous features. The resulting fuller description then would continue:

> . . . abundant very fine pores; moist; friable; common small and medium live fibrous roots; common earthworm casts; occasional fragments of charcoal.

These additional features are described towards the end of this chapter (see sections 2.8–2.15) and some or all of them can be included as the situation demands.

For example a soil description for a civil engineering project could usefully mention moisture and handling properties, whereas a more biological study might ignore this and dwell on descriptions of the roots and evidence of faunal activities.

As with other scientists, pedologists are only too fond of over-elaborate descriptions in which the important facts are hidden in a morass of fine detail, but hoping that fellow specialists will be duly impressed by their erudition. If you do meet such an elaborate description you might find it useful, at least initially, to score out everything except the account of the five basic properties covered in the first description above and then add back those other items you think might actually be of use to you (if any).

2.2   SOIL COLOUR

2.2.1   The Munsell colour system

Verbal descriptions of colour, e.g. chocolate brown, mean different things to different observers. A standard reference system is therefore necessary and almost invariably uses colour charts based on the Munsell system. These are extremely expensive — over $100 for genuine *Munsell soil colour charts* (1986 prices) or over $50 for a very acceptable Japanese equivalent. You should, therefore, handle them very carefully and avoid letting soil touch the standard colour 'chips'. All 'serious' pedologists have access to such charts. If you are unable to obtain one or cannot afford one, then a subjective but unambiguous description of soil colour will have to suffice but should be recorded as non-Munsell.

In the Munsell system (Fig. 2.1) colour is analysed into three elements: **hue, value** and **chroma**. Hue relates to the basic 'spectrum' colour present. The colours in visible light are divided into ten ranges shown by one or two capital letters, e.g. R for red, YR for yellow-red and Y for yellow. Each range is in turn divided into ten, e.g. 1YR, 2YR, 3YR, up to 10YR, the hue becoming more yellow and less red as the numbers increase but the great majority of soils can be matched with sufficient accuracy using the hues 10R, 2.5YR, 5YR, 7.5YR, 10YR, 2.5Y and 5Y only. The 10 point of each hue corresponds with the zero point of the next yellowest hue.

Value describes the darkness or lightness of the colour, on a scale from 0 to 10, the sort of difference produced by adding black to the colour (low value) or white (high value).

Chroma describes the strength of colour, also on a scale from 0 to 10. You can imagine 10 as the brightest available pigment and adding water progressively to produce successively lower or more 'watery-looking' chromas. At chroma 0 all hues converge on a single scale of neutral greys indexed N0 to N10 (N for neutral) ranging from pure black to pure white.

The full Munsell notation is given thus : hue value, chroma, e.g. 7.5YR 3/2. Standard colour names are suggested opposite each page in the *Munsell soil colour charts* (Fig. 2.1) producing descriptions such as 7.5YR 5/8 (strong brown) — a colour often subjectively described as ochreous or orange, or 10R 3/6 (dark red) — a colour which subjectively might be called reddish brown (the standard Munsell name of which is actually around 5YR 5/4).

Colours can rarely be exactly matched to a Munsell colour chip and some degree of approximation is necessary. A uniform north light is best, with deep shadow or

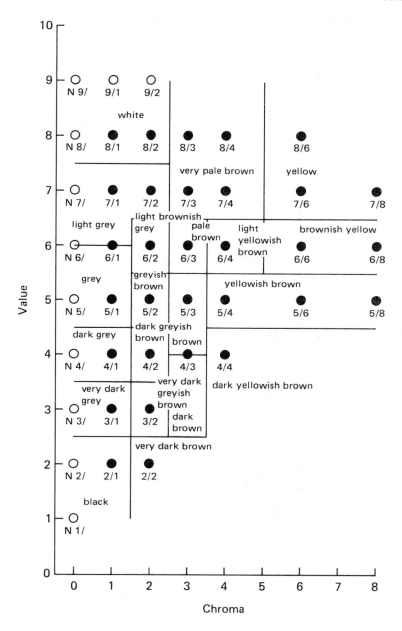

Fig. 2.1 — A typical page from a *Munsell soil colour chart* giving the colour names for the various combinations of value and chroma of the hue 10YR. (Source: Kellogg *et al.* (1951, 1962)).

strong sunlight to be avoided. Colour commonly varies with moisture content and, on the principle that moistening dry soils is easier than drying moist ones, the convention is to give the colour of a moist sample. Sometimes colour contrasts, e.g.

between horizons, are most marked when the soil is dry and it can therefore be permissible (but not usual) to give both dry and moist colours, e.g. light yellowish brown (2.5Y 6/4) dry; olive brown (2.5Y 4/4) moist.

2.2.2   Mottles and other colour variations

It is very important to note any variation in colour in different parts of the soil, especially streaks or mottles of different colours, since this is often a sign of impeded drainage or some other soil forming process.

Mottles should be described according to their abundance, size, contrast (prominence) and colour, in that order. Mottle abundance (you may find Fig. 2.2 useful) is described as follows in percentage of matrix or surface described:

None	0%
Few	<2%
Common	2–20%
Many	20–40%
Very Many	>40%

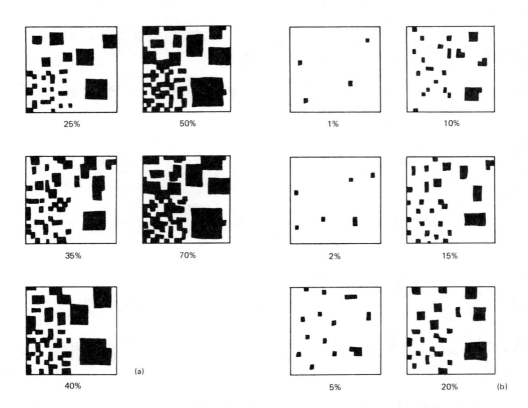

Fig. 2.2 — Chart for estimating the percentage of colour mottles. Each quarter of any one square has the same area of black. The chart can also be used to estimate stones, nodules or similar features (see also Fig. 2.14). Source: USDA

If the mottling is so abundant and/or intricate that it is difficult to decide which colour is mottle and which is matrix then a generalised soil colour description, such as grey (10YR 5/1), reddish brown (2.5YR 5/4) and reddish yellow (7.5YR 7/8) mottled, is permissible.

Mottle size is usually the diameter or the greatest dimension in subcircular examples. Contrasting colours which are in streaks or threads need to be described subjectively, noting their thickness, length, shape and relationship to other soil features. For 'normal' mottles the size scale is as follows:

Extremely fine	>1 mm
Very fine	1–2 mm
Fine	2–5 mm
Medium	5–15 mm
Coarse	<15 mm

Contrast between the mottles and the background matrix or base colour can be described as faint, distinct or prominent according to the scheme.

Faint — Indistinct, evident only on close examination. Often the same colour hue as the matrix and nearly the same chroma and/or value.

Distinct — Not striking, but readily seen. Either the same hue as the matrix but with significantly different value and/or chroma, or more or less the same value and chroma but differing by one hue (2.5 units) from the matrix.

Prominent — Conspicuous, and mottling is one of the outstanding features of the horizon. Hue, chroma and value may be several units apart from the matrix colour.

Examples of typical mottling and other colour variations are:

Greyish brown (10YR 5/2) with common distinct fine mottles of strong brown (7.5YR 5/8).

Greyish brown (10YR 5/2) on ped faces, internally prominent medium mottles of reddish yellow (5YR 6/6) and very dark brown (10YR 2/2); grey (10YR 5/1) along root channels.

Brown (7.5YR 5/4) with common, medium faint light brown (7.5YR 6/4) lime mottles and lime coatings on pebbles.

Very dark grey merging to dark grey (10YR 2.5/1 and 4/1) with common prominent and faint red, dark red, reddish brown, dark reddish brown and dark brown (2.5 YR4/8, 3/6, 3/4, 5YR 3/4 and 10YR 3/3) mottles, redder ones often coarse, sometimes lining small holes.

2.3 SOIL TEXTURE

2.3.1 Particle size classes

Soil texture is probably the single most important soil property, and even if you record nothing else about a soil sample you must describe its texture. Soil texture means the relative proportions of the different-sized particles in the soil. In decreasing size these are the sand, silt and clay. Collectively these constitute the 'fine earth', with particles larger than 2 mm referred to as stones.

The relative proportions of these, or particle size distribution, can be determined in the laboratory (a procedure called particle size analysis or mechanical analysis) but it is laborious and time consuming. In practice, soil texture can be determined sufficiently accurately by a procedure called finger assessment, described below. This is rather messy involving wetting a sample of soil, often by spitting on it, and

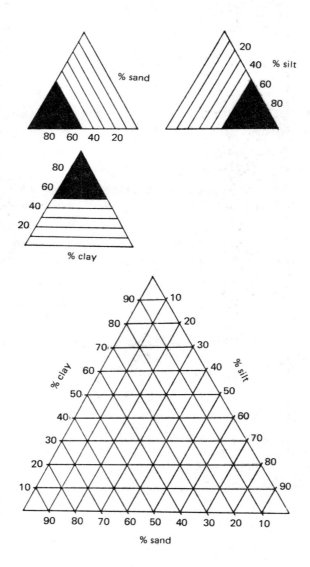

Fig. 2.3 — The construction of the soil textural triangle. The textural triangle really consists of three superimposed triangles, for sand (0% at bottom right-hand corner, 100% on right-hand edge), silt (0% at bottom left-hand corner, 100% on left-hand edge) and clay (0% at top corner, 100% on bottom edge).

manipulating it between the fingers to assess the relative proportions of sand (which feels gritty), silt (which feels smooth and silky, like wet talcum powder) and clay (which is sticky). A soil with approximately equal proportions of each (and which feels doughy) is called a loam.

More elaborate names, 11 or 12 in all such as clay loam, loamy sand and silty clay are used for intermediate textures recognised by finger assessment and these can be correlated with ranges of particle size distribution using a triangular diagram, which is, in effect, three separate superimposed triangles (Fig. 2.3). Fig. 2.4(a) is the full textural triangle based on the USDA particle size classes and Fig. 2.4(b) a much simplified version indicating broad divisions of clays, loams, sands and silts.

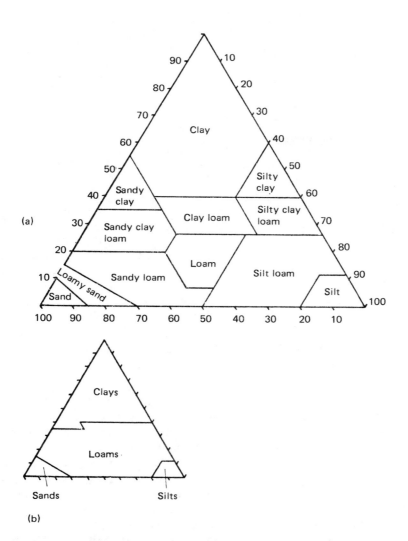

Fig. 2.4 — (a) The soil textural triangle based on USDA size ranges; (b) broad groupings of textural classes.

Unfortunately, there are several particle size definitions (Fig. 2.5). There is almost universal agreement that clay consists of particles less than 0.002 mm (2 μm) in diameter, since this appears to correspond to a mineralogical change with larger particles being common rock forming minerals like quartz, felspar, micas, etc., but those below 0.002 mm being hydrated sheet silicates, the so-called clay minerals. Also, there is fair agreement that the upper size limit for sand is 2 mm (2000 μm) with larger particles being classed as stones. Thus the main disagreement is at the silt–sand division, and in the subdivision of the sand.

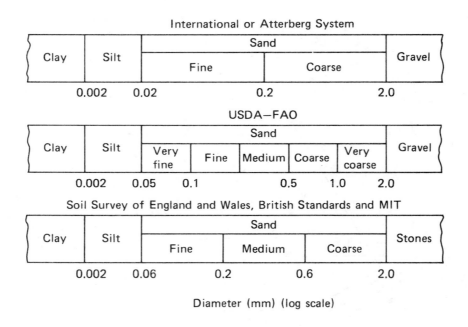

Fig. 2.5 — The particle size ranges used by a number of different systems.

The international system (IS) looks the most logical, with divisions at 2, 20, 200 and 2000 μm but the USDA–FAO system is preferable in practice since the 50 μm sand–silt division corresponds to the point where the fingers can differentiate between grittiness (sand) and silkiness (silt), and to a marked increase in water-holding capacity. The Soil Survey of England and Wales (SSEW)–MIT system, with the silt–sand boundary at 60 μm is, to all intents and purposes, basically the same. Fig. 2.6(a) is the textural triangles based on this, which includes some slightly different names, e.g. **sandy silt loam** for **loam**, and Fig. 2.6(b) shows the broad groupings which are widely used in map legends and bulletins.

The finger assessment procedure given below is based on the USDA system, but an indication is also given of likely IS or SSEW names where they differ.

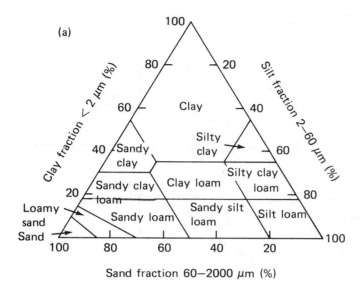

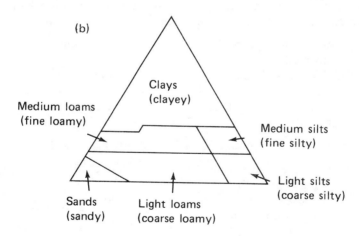

Fig. 2.6 — (a) The soil textural triangle based on Soil Survey of England and Wales size ranges;
(b) broad groupings of textural classes.

2.3.2   Finger assessment procedure

(1) Take about a heaped teaspoonful of soil and moisten it (use saliva or water from a wash bottle if fastidious). Manipulate it to a state of maximum stickiness and plasticity, working out all the lumps. If you encounter any stones (larger than 2000 μm or about the size of a grain of rice) pick them out and discard them. From time to time you may need to add more water to maintain the soil at its maximum plasticity.

Apply the following tests:

(2) What is the predominant feel of the soil?

Gritty	Go to (3)
Silky	Go to (5)
Sticky	Go to (10)
Doughy	Go to(5)
None of these (or not sure)	Go to (3)

(3) Try to make a ball of soil by rubbing between the palms (not moulding it with the fingers):

This is impossible	**Sand**
This can be done only with great care	**Loamy sand**
This is easy	Go to (4)

(4) Try to flatten the ball by pressing it between thumb and forefinger:

The ball collapses	**Sandy loam**
The ball flattens	Go to (5)

(5) Make a ball of soil and try to roll it into a thread, first a thick one (about 1 cm diameter) and then a thinner one (about 0.5 cm in diameter):

Not even a thick thread can be formed	**Loamy sand**
Only a thick thread can be formed	**Sandy loam**
A thick and a thin thread can be formed	Go to (6)

(6) Try to bend the thin thread of soil into a horseshoe shape:

The thread cracks while this is being attempted	Go to (7)
A horseshoe shape can be formed without cracks developing	Go to (9)

(7) Manipulate the soil between the fingers and judge the general feel of the soil:

Soil feels only rough and gritty	**Loam (SSEW sandy silt loam)**
Soil feels silky	**Silt loam** or silt
Soil feels sticky, rough and gritty	Go to (9)

The silt loam may include a few soils which are SSEW **sandy silt loam** or IS **(fine) sandy loam or silty loam.**

(8) Remoistening as necessary, make a thin thread of soil (about 0.3 cm in diameter) and bend into a horseshoe shape. Go to (9).

(9) Try to make the horseshoe shaped thin thread of soil into a ring about 2.5 cm in diameter by joining the two ends of the thread, without cracks forming:

This can be done	Go to (10)
This cannot be done	Go to (12)

(10) Mould the soil into a ball and rub between thumb and index finger to produce a smeared surface:

The smeared surface is smooth with only a few irregularities	Go to (12)
The smeared surface is polished but a few gritty particles stand out	**Sandy clay**
The smeared surface is polished with no (or very few irregularities**)**	Go to (11)

(11) Manipulate the soil between the fingers and judge the general feel of the soil:

Soil feels like soap and takes a high polish	**Clay**
Soil feels like silk and takes a dull polish	**Silty clay**

(12) Form the soil back into a ball and manipulate between the fingers to judge the general feel of the soil:

Soil feels very gritty	**Sandy clay loam**
Soil feels moderately gritty	**Clay loam**
Soil feels doughy and smooth	**Silty clay loam**

When you have decided what texture you think the soil is, find it on the textural triangle (Fig. 2.4). Check that it is not in one or other of the adjoining textural classes by re-applying the appropriate test across the dividing line. If you are still undecided you can 'split the difference' between two but only two adjacent classes, e.g. sandy loam to sandy clay loam.

You may have particular problems with some soils:

(a) Clays and adjacent classes can often be difficult to get completely wetted and free of lumps especially if they are very dry to start with. Thus they often appear sandier than they really are. Gentle grinding in a mortar is helpful, although a finely ground-up clay often feels silty when dry but becomes sticky when wetted.

(b) Soils with many small stones, just over $2000 \mu m$ in size can 'confuse' the fingers which tend to sense a much sandier soil than is really the case. It can be worth while actually picking these small stones out first.

(c) Soils with organic matter, e.g. topsoils, often feel loamier than they really are and it might be advisable to move towards one of the apexes of the textural triangle. For example, if your sample is a topsoil and your first estimate is that it is on the sand–loamy sand boundary then it is probably actually a sand.

(d)   Soils with much organic matter can be qualified as, for example, humose clay loam or peaty sand (see Chapter 4 for a strict definition). Soils which consist of more than about 20–30% organic matter have a separate nomenclature. A humose soil has a distinctive smeary feel and a strong tendency to dirty the fingers. It is dark in colour (Munsell value of 3 or less). When relatively dry a humose soil is softer and more friable than a non-humose soil of corresponding texture. Organic horizons are those in which organic matter seems equal in volume to mineral particles. If materials formed under waterlogged conditions are pre-dominantly gritty and lacking in cohesion, they are described as peaty sand and, if the feel is doughy with not more than moderate grittiness, as peaty loam.

(e)   Finely divided calcium carbonate is often silt sized and so strongly calcareous soils often feel silkier than equivalent non-calcareous soils, and textural classes containing the words silt or silty are common.

2.3.3   Subdivision of the sand fraction
The names sand, loamy sand and sandy loam used on their own imply a more or less even distribution of sand sizes. If, however, you think the sand is predominantly towards the upper or lower ends of the range then you can add qualifying terms, e.g. loamy coarse sand or fine sandy loam. A more precise allocation to one of these categories would need a full or partial particle size analysis.

2.3.4   Abbreviations and groupings
Texture names are often abbreviated using c for clay(ey), z for silt(y), s for sand(y) and l for loam(y), e.g. scl is sandy clay loam. Confusingly c (for coarse) and f (for fine) can also be used if the predominant size of the sand has to be recorded so that, e.g., csl is coarse sandy loam (not clayey sandy loam — which is not a recognised texture class name).

Groupings of textural classes have been indicated in Figs 2.4(b) and 2.6(b). You will probably also encounter the imprecise terms heavy texture (high proportion of clay), light texture (high proportion of sand) or medium texture (loams) but these should really be avoided unless very generalised concepts are being used.

2.4   STONINESS
By definition, stones are the soil particles larger than 2 mm in diameter (or longest dimension) with terms such as rocks or boulders used for very large stones, e.g. above 6000 mm in diameter (or longest dimension).

You should always record the abundance of stones (often called stone content or simply stoniness), but thereafter your description (if any) can be as elaborate as you wish. It is often useful to record the size of the stones, and/or their shape and/or their lithology (if you are geologically inclined or you are interested in the geological origin of the soil parent material).

2.4.1   Stone abundance (stone content or stoniness)
This is usually assessed visually as the percentage volume of stones and reported

using the following scale of stone abundance. Sometimes you might encounter, or wish to use, the alternative terms also listed below in parentheses.

Stoneless *stony*		>1%
Very slightly (or few stones)		1–5%
Slightly stony (or common stones)		6–15%
Moderately stony (or many stones)		16–35%
Very stony (or abundant stones)		36–70%
Extremely stony (or extremely abundant stones)		<70%

Visual assessment of stoniness can be difficult. A rough method of measuring stone content is to dig out a sample of soil and to measure the volume, e.g. by filling it with small plastic balls whose number or weight is calibrated against volume. The stones are then sieved out and their volume determined, conveniently done by a water displacement technique. You may wish to use this procedure if only to 'calibrate' your eyes on a few chosen examples. Soils with large stone contents need large volumes of soil for accurate measurements.

Recently cultivated topsoils where the stones are coated with soil can look less stony than they really are, while conversely a soil surface exposed to rain which has washed finer particles away can often look more stony than it really is. Beware also of concentrations of stones within the profile (stone lines) as a result of cultivations or soil erosion. Stoniness can also be judged roughly by the ease or difficulty of digging through the soil when preparing an inspection pit or hand augering into a soil.

2.4.2 Stone size

The size of stones can be described using the following scale for diameter (or longest dimension):

Very small stones	2–6 mm
Small stones	6 mm–2 cm
Medium stones	2–6 cm
Large stones	6–20 cm
Very large stones	20–60 cm
Boulders	>60 cm

2.4.3 Stone shape

Stone shape is determined by the two properties of roundness and sphericity as shown in Fig. 2.7. If the stones are approximately equal in size in all three dimensions, then the terms **rounded, subrounded, subangular** or **angular** alone can be used, depending on how rounded or angular are the edges of the stones. If the stones have one axis longer than the others then the additional terms **tabular** or **platy** can be used.

2.4.4 Stone lithology

The extent of the description of stone lithology depends on how extensive is your knowledge of geology. However, even the non-geologist could reasonably be expected to record whether the stones were, for example, calcareous or not (they effervesce with dilute acid if calcareous), whether they are of one kind or a mixture of

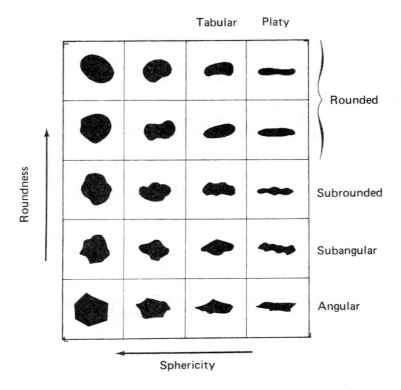

Fig. 2.7 — Stone shape. (Source: Soil Survey of England and Wales)

several kinds of rock and whether they are the same kind as, for example, the bedrock of any soil profile you may be describing.

Examples of some typical descriptions of soil stoniness, combined with soil textures are:

Very stony sandy loam; entirely small to medium rounded flints.

Clay loam, with many medium tabular subrounded fragments of limestone, common small rounded flints and few large subangular fragments of weathered igneous rock.

In very specialised instances you may wish to record whether the stones have any preferred orientation, have cappings or coatings of silt, clay or organic matter, etc.

2.5 SOIL STRUCTURE

In most soils the individual particles of sand, silt and clay (whose proportions determine the soil texture) stick together or aggregate into larger compound units to produce the soil structure. Natural, relatively permanent aggregates are called **peds** while less permanent ones such as those caused by cultivation or frost action are called **fragments** or **clods**. The general term **structural aggregates** covers both.

Soil structure should be described in terms of its degree of development and the size and shape of the aggregates. You will need to examine both the undisturbed soil and how the soil behaves as it is loosened.

2.5.1 Soil structure development

The first step is to determine whether the soil has a recognisable structure and, if so, how well developed it is on a scale of **weakly, moderately** or **strongly developed**. Some soils are structureless (apedal) and can be either **single grain** or **massive**. Single-grain soils (usually sands) have no observable aggregation, as in a sand dune. Massive soils, on the other hand, are a coherent mass with no orderly arrangement of natural planes of weakness defining structural units, e.g. in recently deposited alluvium.

A **weakly developed** structure is not easy to see in undisturbed soil but, if it is loosened, some but by no means all of the material is seen to consist of aggregates (entire or broken) but there is much unaggregated material.

A **moderately developed** structure is visible in the undisturbed soil and loosened material largely consists of entire aggregates. A **strongly developed** structure is very obvious in undisturbed soil; the aggregates do not stick together and are readily detached intact.

The next step is to classify the aggregates according to their shape and size (Fig. 2.8). You will probably find this easiest to do on loosened soil and, depending on the degree of development, you will find this consists of whole aggregates, broken aggregates and unaggregated material. Concentrate on the whole aggregates, ignoring the rest of the material, and classify the predominant aggregates according to the scheme given below. You will often find there is a range of sizes in the aggregates you are examining but, again, try to ignore the extremes and classify according to the predominant size.

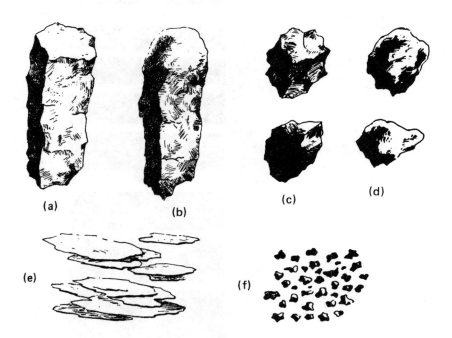

Fig. 2.8 — Soil structure shapes: (a) prismatic; (b) columnar; (c) angular blocky; (d) subangular blocky; (e) platy; (f) granular. (Source: Kellogg *et al.* (1951, 1962)).

The relative size of aggregates is given on a scale from **very fine, fine, medium, coarse** to **very coarse**. Note that the dimensions you measure and the size ranges differ considerably for the different shaped aggregates. Figs 2.9–2.12 will prove helpful.

2.5.2   Size and shape of aggregates

Platy — Plate-like aggregates flat, with well-developed horizontal faces;

<2 mm thick	**Fine**
2–5 mm thick	**Medium**
5–10 mm thick	**Coarse**
>10 mm thick	**Very coarse**

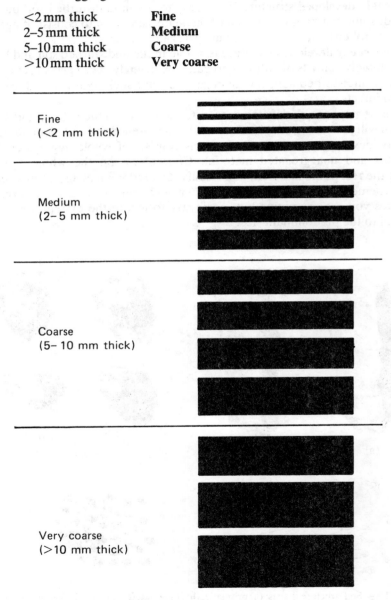

Fine
(<2 mm thick)

Medium
(2–5 mm thick)

Coarse
(5–10 mm thick)

Very coarse
(>10 mm thick)

Fig. 2.9 — Size ranges for platy peds. (Source: USDA)

If the plates are thick in the middle and thin at the edges, the term **lenticular** can be used. Also the terms **thin** and **thick** can replace **fine** and **coarse**.

Prismatic — vertically elongated peds with well-developed vertical faces:

<20 mm wide	**Fine**
20–50 mm wide	**Medium**
50–100 mm wide	**Coarse**
100 mm wide	**Ver coarse**

Prismatic structure is commonest in subsoils especially if they are of a clayey texture. If the top of the prisms are rounded the term **columnar** is used, such structures being limited essentially to the subsoils of sodium-affected soils in arid and semi-arid regions.

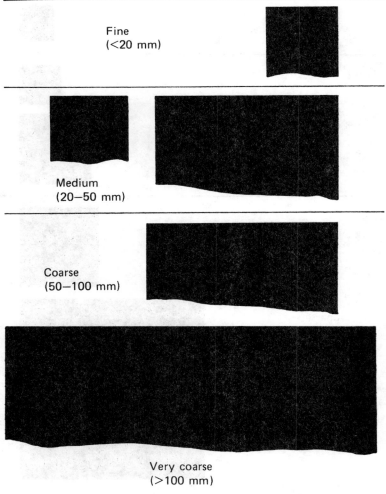

Fig. 2.10 — Size range for prismatic and columnar peds. (Source: USDA)

Blocky — irregular polyhedra of roughly equal dimensions the surfaces of which fit into neighbouring peds as into a mould. Where the faces are flattened and the angles sharply angular the term **angular blocky** is used, but **subangular blocky** where more angles are rounded and the faces typically curved or irregular:

<10 mm across	**Fine**
10–20 mm across	**Medium**
20–50 mm across	**Coarse**
50 mm across	**Very coarse**

Blocky structures are very common especially in subsoils and where the textures are fine loamy or clayey. It is best seen in an undisturbed sample. If loosened, it looks (wrongly) like a granular structure.

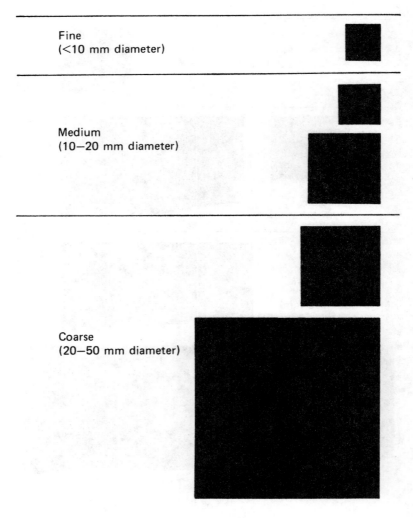

Fine
(<10 mm diameter)

Medium
(10–20 mm diameter)

Coarse
(20–50 mm diameter)

Fig. 2.11 — Size ranges for blocky peds. (Source: USDA)

Granular — Irregular spheres or polyhedra, which do not fit the faces of neighbouring aggregates, although they are often held together by fine roots.

<2 mm across	**Fine**
2–5 mm across	**Medium**
5–10 mm across	**Coarse**
10 mm across	**Very coarse**

Granular structures are usually the result of faunal activity (earthworm casts, etc.) and so are commonest in the topsoil. The term granular implies that the aggregates are non-porous, while similar but porous aggregates, usually in the very fine to medium size range are referred to as **crumb** structure.

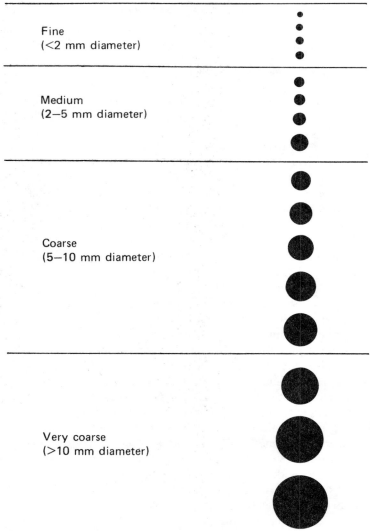

Fine
(<2 mm diameter)

Medium
(2–5 mm diameter)

Coarse
(5–10 mm diameter)

Very coarse
(>10 mm diameter)

Fig. 2.12 — Size ranges for granular peds. (Source: USDA)

2.5.3   Some practical points

It is allowable but not really desirable to give transitional classifications, e.g. fine and medium crumb. Sometimes, however, there is a compound structure consisting of one structure in the undisturbed soil but breaking into different units when loosened. Such structures are described as, for example, well-developed coarse prismatic structure breaking to moderately well-developed medium blocky.

The structure of many topsoils, especially if recently cultivated is often temporary, e.g. in large clods or compacted by passage of machinery, and your description of the structure should reflect this.

Examples are:

Large clods up to 250 mm in diameter due to recent ploughing, breaking to moderately developed medium subangular blocky structure.

Frost-produced, well-developed very fine angular blocky structure on the surface, massive below.

Capped surface, well-developed fine platy structure below.

A capped surface occurs where the surface structure has collapsed or slaked because of heavy rainfall sometimes aided by compaction due to machinery, to form a thin structureless layer.

You will have noted from the above examples that, by convention, structure is described in the order degree of development, size and shape. The shape term can be either an adjective or a noun, so that the descriptions 'weakly developed coarse prismatic structure' or 'weakly developed coarse prisms' are equally acceptable. There are no standard abbreviations (as for texture, for example) but if you want you can invent your own shorthand notation or coding.

2.6   CARBONATES

A useful test for the presence of calcium carbonate in soils is to apply dilute (2 N or 10%) hydrochloric acid and observe the reaction. (Be careful; 2 N or 10% hydrochloric acid will sting the fingers, be extremely painful on open cuts or sores and will slowly destroy clothing or other fabrics with which it comes into contact.)

The descriptive scale and corresponding approximate content of calcium carbonate given in Table 2.1 are used. Note that the term calcareous (said with the second 'c' hard, i.e. 'calkareous') is sometimes used for soils which react with acid irrespective of actual calcium carbonate content and does not imply the 5–10% of the above scale. The test is not reliable for other carbonates, e.g. dolomite.

You may find some soils in which the stones are calcareous but the matrix is not, to be described as non-calcareous matrix with reference under stoniness to the calcareous nature of the stones. If the calcium carbonate is, for example, restricted to the interior of aggregates or occurs as threads or concretions this should be noted, e.g. 'very calcareous, with calcium carbonate depositions in thin threads (about 1 mm in diameter and 5 mm in length), mainly vertically oriented'.

Free calcium carbonate in soils implies a pH of above 7, and usually in the range 7.5–8.0. You can check this, and the pH of non-calcareous soils in the field, by tests with indicators or a portable pH meter. Some pedologists enjoy making such field

Table 2.1 — Descriptive scale and corresponding approximate calcium carbonate content

Description	CaCO$_3$ (%)	Audible effects (hold close to ear)	Visible effects
Non-calcareous	<0.5	None	None
Very slightly calcareous	0.5–1	Just audible fizz	None
Slightly calcareous	1–5	Moderately audible fizz	Just visible effervescence
Calcareous	5–10	Easily audible away from ear	Easily visible small bubbles (up to about 3 mm in diameter)
Very calcareous	>10	Easily audible away from ear	Strong effervescence with large bubbles

tests while others consider them messy, frustrating and unreliable. The author tends to the latter view, preferring to take samples back to the laboratory where a simple reliable test can be made (see Chapter 8). All such tests, however, should be made on soil material to which acid has *not* already been added.

2.7 ADDITIONAL PROPERTIES
A basic soil description will usually end at this point, and you should now look through the following items and ask yourself whether you really need to include any of them in your description. These properties, porosity, soil water state, handling properties (consistency) including cementation, roots and other soil flora, plant remains and organic matter, soil fauna and features of pedogenic origin, are discussed further in sections 2.8–2.14.

2.8 POROSITY
Between and within the soil aggregates there is a system of fissures and pores which control the air—water relationships of soils. If a soil is saturated all the voids are filled with water, but as it dries the larger pores become air filled as water drains away under the force of gravity (see Chapter 1). The remaining voids are smaller than approximately 60 μm in diameter and cannot be seen by the naked eye. Thus any field description of porosity can deal only with the larger pores and fissures which are, however, important in determining how quickly water will pass through a soil (its permeability).

Laboratory or field measurements of total void space, pore size distribution and permeability are amongst the most frustrating determinations which the pedologist can be called on to perform. They are really the province of specialists in soil physics and beyond the scope of this book to discuss. Thus you should think long and hard whether you really need the information and about the precision you would accept. Often an estimate of porosity and permeability based on the texture and structural condition of the soil, with some additional information on fissures and macrospores, as described below, and consistency (see section 2.10) will be just as useful for all practical purposes.

2.8.1   Fissures

The pattern, the abundance and degree of development of fissures, and the planar voids between aggregates is usually readily inferred from the description of the soil structure. Thus a moderately developed medium prismatic structure implies a system of moderately developed, closely spaced (20–50 mm apart) vertical fissures. There is thus little point in repeating effectively the same information twice. Another reason why fissures are not often described is that they may alter seasonally, especially in clayey or fine loamy soils or with cultivations. So, unless you are prepared to describe the soil fissures at different times of the year or you think it is worth reporting obvious fissuring in a dry soil even although this will change on wetting, then it is best to ignore fissures. Large channels which are usually the result of faunal activity or roots are best described under those headings.

2.8.2   Macroporosity

Macroporosity, on the other hand, is more permanent and not readily inferred directly from a description of soil structure. It is the visible pores within the aggregates or between the particles in a structureless soil and can include small holes, tubes or burrows. The basic information required is the percentage and diameter of the macropores. You will probably find Figs 2.13 and 2.14 useful. If the macropores

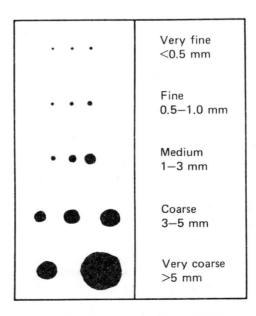

Fig. 2.13 — Macropores. (Source: USDA)

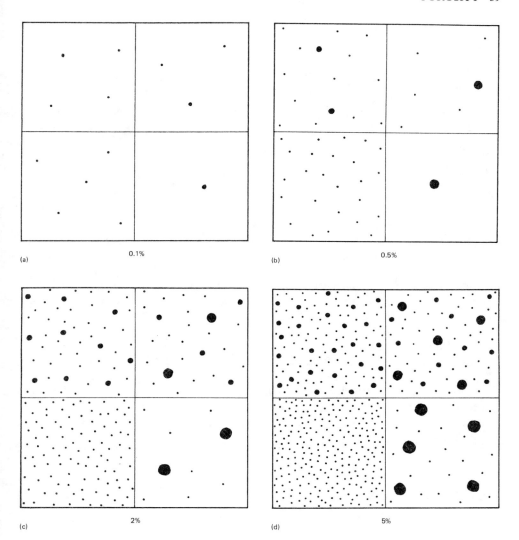

(a)   0.1%

(b)   0.5%

(c)   2%

(d)   5%

Fig. 2.14 — Chart for estimating the percentage of pores (see also Fig. 2.2). (Source: USDA)

are of animal or plant origin, this can be noted at this stage, leaving a more detailed account for the headings Roots and other soil flora (section 2.11) or Soil fauna (section 2.13).

2.9   SOIL WATER STATE

The actual percentage of soil moisture can easily be determined in the laboratory from the loss in weight of a moist soil dried in an oven at 105–110°C. However, it can sometimes be useful to record the soil water state at the time a soil sample is being described. The terms used and how to recognise them are as follows.

Dry — Looks dry, and changes colour if water is added.

Moist — Leaves a slight dampness when squeezed between the fingers; does not change colour on further setting.

Wet — Films of water are visible on the surface of grains and aggregates.

Waterlogged — Water drips out of the soil when it is held up or oozes out of a vertical face in undisturbed soil.

2.10 HANDLING PROPERTIES (CONSISTENCY)

2.10.1 Consistency

This is one of the most subjective assessments you will have to make, relating, as it does, to the feel of the soil and how it behaves when manipulated. The behaviour of the soil is controlled by the kind of cohesion and adhesion, and by the resistance to deformation or rupture. It is very dependent on the soil water state.

Several soil engineering tests such as shear strength, stickiness and plasticity can be approximated by observing, for example, how a prepared soil specimen behaves under pressure, or how it can or cannot be rolled into a thread (procedures very like those used to determine soil texture but at more precise moisture conditions).

A simpler approach is outlined below, assuming that all you wish to do is to report the handling characteristics at the moisture content which obtains at the time the soil is being described. You should combine the description with an assessment of the moisture status (see section 2.9 above). If the soil is dry, slightly moist or moist you may, if you wish, wet it further to see what its handling characteristics are at higher moisture contents.

The descriptive terms are given below separately for dry, moist and wet soil samples.

Dry soils —

Loose — Soil falls apart without handling.

Soft — Soil can be carefully picked up as a mass but falls apart with slight pressure to powder or single grains.

Slightly hard — A structural aggregate can be picked up but breaks with moderate pressure between thumb and forefinger.

Hard — Can just be broken by thumb and forefinger using the strongest pressure you can exert.

Very hard — Cannot be broken between thumb and forefinger and only with difficulty by your hands.

Extremely hard — Requires a hammer or pick to break it.

Moist soils —

Loose — Soil falls apart without handling.

Very friable — Soil crushes under gentle finger pressure, but coheres if pressed together.

Friable — As very friable, but gentle to moderate finger force is needed.

Firm — The soil can be crushed between thumb and forefinger but seems noticeably to resist this.

Very firm — Can only just be crushed between thumb and forefinger but can be broken by hand fairly easily

Extremely firm — The soil can only be broken apart piece by piece and will resist crushing between finger and thumb even if strong pressure is applied.

Wet soils — Both the stickiness (press the wet soil between your thumb and forefinger) and plasticity (try to roll a thread of soil 3 mm in diameter between your fingers or on a glass or plastic surface) have to assessed:

Non-sticky — Almost no soil adheres to finger or thumb.

Slightly sticky — Soil adheres to both finger and thumb but when you pull them apart the soil adheres to only one and does not stretch between them

Sticky — Soil adheres to finger and thumb and when you pull them apart the soil stretches noticeably before breaking, leaving soil adhering to both.

Very sticky — Virtually glues the finger and thumb together and stretches as you pull them apart.

Non-plastic — A thread cannot be formed (soil is drier than the lower plastic limit)

Slightly plastic — A thread can be formed but will break if you try to pick it up or to dangle it from finger and thumb.

Plastic — A thread can be formed which you can pick up or dangle from finger and thumb.

Very plastic — A strong thread can be formed which you can bend and manipulate easily without it breaking.

2.10.2 Cementation

Soil consistency described above is due, in the main, to the clay fraction and depends on the moisture content of the soil. If it is believed that a hard or very hard brittle consistency is due to some other substance and does not change appreciably when the soil is wetted, then the term **cemented** is usually applied instead. This can be qualified as either **weakly cemented** (when the soil can be broken manually) or **strongly cemented** (when the soil cannot be broken manually). Very strongly cemented materials are sometimes referred to as **indurated** and require a sharp hammer blow to break the soil. Soil horizons which are cemented (or compacted or very high in clay) are often called **pans**.

If you can, you should indicate the nature of the cementing material since this can often be useful in classifying the soil profile from which the sample came (see Chapter 4). Common cementing agents in soils and how to recognise them are as follows.

Calcium carbonate — Whitish material which effervesces vigorously when dilute acid is applied (see section 2.5). Sometimes softens slightly when wetted. Common in arid and semi-arid areas and sometimes called caliche if indurated.

Gypsum — Whitish material which can be scratched by a finger nail and does not react with dilute acid. Restricted to arid and semi-arid regions.

Sesquioxides — These are hydrated oxides of iron (brownish) or aluminium (colourless). Terms such as ironstone and, in tropical areas, laterite or plinthite are applied (see Chapter 4). Some podzolised soils have **thin ironpans** a few millimetres thick which can even pass through stones.

Manganese oxides — Black often soft or brittle material which reacts with hydrogen peroxide at normal temperature.

Organic matter — Soft, black, often associated with and masking cementation by sesquioxides in podzolised soils.

2.11 ROOTS AND OTHER SOIL FLORA

It is quite difficult to estimate accurately the amount of roots in a soil, and if you specifically need this information you will need to collect a sample of soil and separate out the roots in the laboratory. It is often useful, however, to make a rough estimate, especially when describing a soil profile since changes in the size abundance or types of roots are usually related to changes in soil properties.

2.11.1 Size and abundance

The use of the descriptive terms *few, common*, etc., varies with the size of the roots (**fine, medium**, etc.) being described as in Table 2.2.

Table 2.2 — Abundance of roots of various sizes

Number of roots per 100 cm^2 for the following root sizes and root diameters

Abundance	Very fine <1 mm	Fine 1–2 mm	Medium 2–5 mm	Coarse 5–10 mm	Very coarse >10 mm
Few		1–10		1 or 2	Describe
Common		10–25		2–5	separately in
Many		25–200		>5	general terms
Abundant		200		—	

2.11.2 Nature of roots

Terms such as **woody, fibrous** and **fleshy** (e.g. tap roots) should be used and you should also try to distinguish living roots from dead ones, though this can be difficult. You should also record special structures, e.g. bulbs or rhizomes, in general terms.

2.11.3   Relationships

It can be particularly important to note whether roots are consistently related to some other feature of the soil either within a given sample of a particular horizon or at boundaries between one soil horizon and another. Things to look for include:

(a)   Are roots restricted to the fissures between soil aggregates?
(b)   Do they grow preferentially along faunal channels?
(c)   Do they change direction, e.g. start to grow sideways at any particular point?

2.11.4   Other soil flora

If you notice any other visible features, especially of fungal mycelia, mycorrhiza or algae, these should be recorded in whatever detail you think appropriate.

2.12   PLANT REMAINS AND ORGANIC MATTER

Dead plant or animal material in or on top of soils is slowly decomposed by soil organisms including the smaller soil fauna and the microflora (bacteria, fungi and actinomycetes). The process is called **humification** and the end product which includes the recycled excreta, bodies and cells of the organisms carrying out the decomposition is called **humus.** It is rare for all the organic material in a soil to have reached the stage of humus, and a general term **organic matter** is generally applied, meaning most of the material which has lost its original structure, including humus.

Organic matter is one of the main colouring agents in soils, imparting a blackish or dark brownish colour. Organic matter is, of course, commonest near the soil surface and description of the topsoil as, e.g., black, dark brown or dark greyish brown compared with a brown or yellowish brown subsoil implies the presence of organic matter. Generally the darker and blacker the colour, the higher the content of organic matter, though in calcareous or salt-affected soils (the so-called black alkali soils) even a very small amount of organic matter produces a very dark colour.

It is thus relatively uncommon to make any comment in a soil description about the presence or absence of organic matter but to leave the reader to imply this from the soil colours. The main exception is where the organic matter is particularly high and is tending to accumulate because its decomposition is being inhibited. Such soils can be qualified by adding the term peaty or humose in front of the soil texture class. When the percentage of organic matter is very high including surface accumulations, then a special description is needed, discussed as part of a soil profile description in Chapter 3 and horizon nomenclature in Chapter 4.

If, however, you notice relatively decomposed plant or animal fragments in a soil, or that there are stains of organic matter where it would not normally be expected, e.g. in the subsoil, then your description can include mention of this. If possible you should note the origin of the material, its state of decomposition and any effect it appears to be having on the surrounding soil.

2.13   SOIL FAUNA

You should record, in general terms, any evidence of faunal activity in soils, e.g. burrows, casts, excreta, nests or signs of mixing or soil separation attributable to soil fauna, and of course, any soil fauna actually seen. Under the same heading you can, if appropriate, mention any signs of human activity both archaeological or due to cultivations or other agricultural operations such as subsoiling or drainage installations.

2.14   FEATURES OF PEDOGENIC ORIGIN

Pedologists interested in the origin of the soil profiles and horizons they are studying have a particular interest in features which will help to shed light on processes of soil formation (pedogenesis). It helps, of course, to know what you are looking for and to have seen such pedogenic features in other profiles or been shown them by a fellow expert, and so mention of such features in a soil description is really for experts, not beginners.

The following list of pedogenic features, then, is meant mainly to help you if you encounter them in someone else's soil description or you happen to be particularly observant.

Pans — These are horizons cemented by, for example, organic matter and/or compounds of iron, aluminium and/or manganese (see cementation above). They are almost always marked by a change in root habit — roots may stop or turn sideways on meeting a pan. Pans can be continuous (even through stones!) or broken.

Coatings — Natural faces in soils, e.g. aggregate faces or faces of stones, can be coated with substances which have usually been washed down from higher in the profile, but occasionally they can result by preferential removal of material. For the nature of the substances involved see the list under Cementation (section 2.10.2 above). The term **cutan** is sometimes used but this can have a quite specific meaning in certain cases and is best avoided as a general term. Coatings of clay, silt, sand, various oxides of iron, aluminium and manganese, organic matter or carbonate are all relatively common.

Crystals — Macroscopic crystals of, for example, calcite and gypsum may occur in some soils. Saline efflorescences can occur in semi-arid regions or in coastal marshland.

Nodules and concretions — These are hard or soft coherent masses which can be detached from the soil matrix but which are not obviously crystalline. Concretions have a concentric appearance when broken; nodules are more irregular. Their composition is commonly of calcium carbonate, gypsum or hydrated oxides of iron and manganese (see section 2.10.2). The soil matrix may be partially included in the nodule or concretion.

Slickensides — These are polished and grooved surfaces produced on adjoining faces of aggregates. They result from stresses caused by repeated expansion and contraction of soils rich in swelling clays such as montmorillonite during wetting and drying. The presence of slickensides is one of the so-called vertic features (see Chapter 5).

2.15   THE FINAL DESCRIPTION

When making soil sample descriptions, especially in the field, most pedologists will use abbreviations and/or use charts on which to record their observations. A completed example (for the basic soil properties only) is given in Fig. 2.15. This would be transcribed in the office to produce the respectable basic description quoted at the beginning of the chapter:

Dark greyish brown (2.5Y 4/2) with many fine prominent yellowish brown(1OYR 5/8) mottles; clay loam, slightly stony (common small angular fragments of limestone); moderately developed fine crumb structure; strongly calcareous.

Having mastered the techniques of describing a given sample of soil, your next step is to describe an entire soil profile, horizon by horizon, and this is the subject of Chapter 3.

Date 31/10/84

Sample Ref.	Basic Colour	Mottles	Texture	Stones	Structure	Others
713/1 Topsoil 0-26cm	2.5 Y 4/2	many fine 1OYR 5/8	cL	Slightly stony ang. ls. frags.	Fine Crumb Mod.	HCl- Strong effer

Fig. 2.15 — Example of a soil description made in the field on a pro forma sheet.

3

Soil profile description

This chapter shows how the descriptions of soil samples, e.g. from soil horizons, can be turned into a complete soil profile description, the naming and classification of which is covered in Chapter 4. It also discusses how to choose and prepare a soil profile for study, and how to complete the description with the relevant site characteristics. Finally, the description of soil auger borings links with a later chapter (Chapter 5) on how to make a soil map.

3.1 EQUIPMENT
You will need some or all of the equipment described in Table 3.1; those marked E are essential, and those marked O optional.

3.2 CHOOSING A SOIL PROFILE FOR STUDY
It is hard work to dig a soil profile pit and so, before you indulge in the backbreaking exercise, you need to be sure the site is truly representative of what you want to describe. Accordingly some preliminary work with a soil auger or even some shallow trial pits are very worthwhile before digging the main pit; or your knowledge of the area and what constitutes a typical soil from your soil mapping work (Chapter 5) will be useful.

You should, of course, avoid obvious atypical areas and keep well away from roadways, ditches, field boundaries, etc., where human disturbance is most likely, i.e. unless you specifically want to see the effects of such disturbance, e.g. in archaeological studies.

Soil exposures, e.g. above a quarry face or in a road cutting or trench save a great deal of work, but again you need to be sure they have not been modified by truncation or by the dumping of spoil on top of them, so that some preliminary investigation in the 'hinterland' is also wise. Long trenches and cuttings can be particularly valuable in showing the likely soil variations and you may want to describe one or more profiles to demonstrate this.

Table 3.1 — Equipment (E, essential; O, optional) required to prepare a soil profile

Essential or optional	Equipment	Use
E	Spade	For pit digging or cleaning down a cutting. You might find a normal square pointed spade and a post-hole spade useful
O	Pickaxe	For stony or cemented soils
O	Saw	For sawing through tree roots if you are in a woodland site
E	Trowel	For profile preparation and sample collecting
E	Knife	To prise out small features
O	Brush	For final cleaning of profile if you are especially fastidious
O	Tarpaulins	To spread on the ground around the profile to help to tidy up the site afterwards
E	Tape measure or ruler	As a photographic scale and to measure horizon depths
E, O	50 m measuring tape	Distance measuring for profile location purposes
E, O	*Munsell Colour Charts* (or equivalent	You may prefer to keep this valuable document in your laboratory or office and to determine colours on samples you bring back
E, O	Magnifying glass (X10)	For small-scale features
E, O	Plastic bags, ties, labels and/or water-proof marker pens	For sample collection
E	Dilute hydro chloric acid	To check for carbonates
E, O	pH test kit	You may prefer to determine pH in the laboratory on samples you bring back
E, O	Supply of water	To wet profile or to supply water for finger assessment of texture
E	Profile recording pro forma sheets	To ensure consistent descriptions
E	Descriptive manual, e.g. this book	
E	Pencils (plenty of spares)	
E	Clipboard	
E, O	Camera and spare film	To record your profile for posterity
E	Whistle	For emergencies
E, O	Abney level and compass	To record site details if necessary
E	Suitable clothing and footwear (spares)	Self-evident
E	Personal comfort and survival kit	

Be very careful, however, in dealing with deep cuttings or quarry faces both about falling and about being buried by a collapse of soil which you yourself might have caused while happily probing and burrowing away at some fascinating pedological feature at the base of the profile. When in doubt, shore up the sides of a pit, and try to avoid working alone if deep pits or cuttings are involved.

Most pedologists like to take a photograph of the soil profile they are interested in, for which a shadow-free bright light is best (though flash can be used). This means careful siting of the profile pit, especially if tree or other shade is nearby. It is usually best to take the photograph before the full profile description is undertaken (which can be rather destructive); so you will have to judge where the sun will be when you are ready to take the photograph.

3.3   SOIL PROFILE PREPARATION

Profile pits are traditionally rectangular in shape with the face being examined about a metre wide and the pit 2—3 m or more long so as to enable easier digging when it becomes deep and to give enough light at the bottom for inspection and photography. Pits should be deep enough to expose the entire profile down to bedrock or relatively unaltered parent material or other substrate. In temperate regions a depth of 1.5 m (unless prevented by rock) is usually enough, but in tropical areas or for special projects (e.g. irrigation investigations) deeper profiles may be necessary. It is often a good idea to auger into the bottom of a pit to see what differences there are below this and whether deepening the pit is desirable.

Most pits are only temporary and have to be filled in afterwards and signs of disturbance minimised. If there is any plant ground cover, e.g. grass, this should be dug out in approximately 0.2 m by 0.2 m sections laid in sequence to one side so the pit can eventually be 're-turfed'. The topsoil should then be separately dug out and placed to one side of the pit, and the lower horizons to the other so that they can be replaced more or less in order. Large stones can usefully be kept separate and labelled with the depth they came from for future identification. Profile digging associated with archaeological work has, of course, to be much more discriminating and excavators either will be aware of the specialist techniques needed or will be carefully supervised and taught.

Purists often insist on sheets of heavy polythene or tarpaulins on each side of the pit on which to pile excavated soil; so the final residue can be put back into the pit leaving the surrounding area uncontaminated. Less fastidious pedologists usually end up kicking residual soil about, hoping to 'lose' it nearby.

However careful you choose to be, what must be observed is the 'sanctity' of the profile face you are about to describe on which the vegetation must be preserved, no spoil placed over it and no observers allowed to trample it.

In wet conditions you may need to dig a drainage ditch or sump and even have to have a helper to bale out the pit to maintain reasonably dry conditions.

When you have dug your pit or found a convenient ready-made trench or cutting the actual preparation of the profile can commence. It sometimes helps to let the face dry out slightly, since this helps to define the soil structure. On the other hand faces which have been exposed for a long time often look unnatural and may have to be wetted. Before you do wet the entire profile, however, try a small strip on a side wall to see the effect — wetting may actually obscure the horizon differentiation you have observed in the dried-out profile. Conversely you must not be misled by apparent horizon differentiation which is, for example, nothing more than the wetting front proceeding downwards after a recent rainfall event.

It is sometimes useful to 'dress' the profile face with a small trowel or knife to encourage the soil to break along natural fissures and so to emphasise the structure, and or to eliminate smearing produced during the digging. Start at the top and work downwards. Do not overdo this, however, or you will end up with an unnatural-looking profile. Try to preserve stones and roots *in situ*, though you may have had to saw through the larger ones during pit digging if you are in woodland.

Finally, and especially before taking a photograph, make sure fragments of higher horizons are not lodged in the lower horizons — some pedologists carry a small brush for such final tidying up or you can use a tyre pump and nozzle. You should also clear the base of the pit of debris so that it exposes a horizontal section through the lowermost horizon or layer. Place your scale (preferably a ruler or tape — see below), and take your photograph using as narrow an aperture as possible to give a good depth of focus. For safety, take three or four shots at different combinations of aperture and speed including one or two which look as if they might be overexposed — they often come out best. You are now ready actually to describe your profile.

3.4 RECOGNISING, DESCRIBING AND SAMPLING HORIZONS

The key task in profile description is recognising how many horizons it contains and which have to be separately described and, if required, sampled for subsequent analysis. Initially, you will notice colour differences, including the appearance of colour mottling, and major differences in, for example, stoniness and soil structure. It is advisable to mark the approximate boundaries between horizons either by scratching a line with a trowel or by driving in pegs (with or without string attached). scale drawing of the profile (e.g. Figs 3.1 and 3.2) can be useful.

Other differences, e.g. in texture, presence or absence of carbonate, or consistency, are much more subtle and often do not become apparent until you are well into describing each horizon in turn. It is a good idea when carrying out the detailed description of what you think is a single horizon to take material for inspection from near the top and near the bottom so that you can check whether the horizon is sufficiently uniform or needs to be subdivided.

There is, however, the danger that you may end up with too many horizons and an overelaborate profile description. As with all natural objects soil horizons are rarely completely uniform throughout, and it is a matter of judgement and experience to decide how much 'within-horizon' variation is acceptable before subdivision into two or more horizons is needed.

When you have decided on the horizons your profile contains you need to measure their depths and to describe the nature of the boundary between them. At this stage (and indeed throughout this chapter) it is wisest to refer to horizons simply by number, consecutively from the surface. Completed profile descriptions allocate, right at the beginning of the individual horizon description, a code or other designation which is linked with the classification of the soil profile. Really, however, you should describe the profile first in 'unbiased' terms before trying to name and classify it — which is why, in this book, the chapter on profile nomenclature and classification (Chapter 5) is separate from and placed after this one on profile description.

It is convention for all profiles to be measured downwards from the surface, excluding living vegetation or leaf litter. Measurements are usually in inches or centimetres and the upper and lower limit of each horizon is given. A very simple description would be:

Horizon 1	0–24 cm	Dark brown sandy loam
Horizon 2	24–85 cm	Brown stony sandy loam
Horizon 3	85+cm	Rock

Boundaries between horizons can be quite distinct or there can be a 'zone of transition' so that one horizon merges into the next. The depth is quoted as the

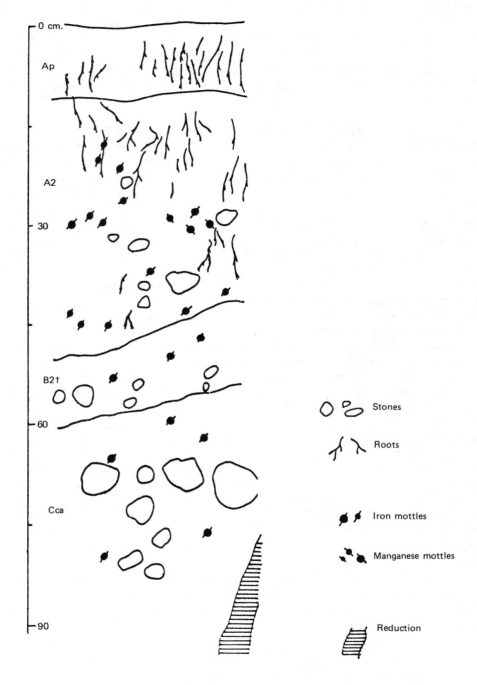

Fig. 3.1 — Scale drawing of a soil profile. See also Table 3.2 (Source: Hammond (1973))

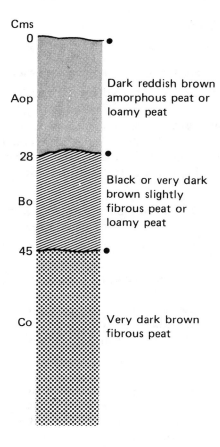

Fig. 3.2 — Diagrammetic representation of a soil profile (Adventurer's series). (Source: Soil Survey of England and Wales)

midpoint of such a zone of transition and you can describe the distinctness of the boundary according to the following scheme of the thicknesses of the transition zone:

Sharp	<0.5 cm
Abrupt	0.5–2.5 cm
Clear	2.5–6.0 cm
Gradual	6.0–13.0 cm
Diffuse	>13.0 cm

If no descriptive term is given it can be assumed that the boundary is sharp, abrupt or clear, while gradual and diffuse boundaries are often described by the non-explicit term 'merging'.

The degree of horizon irregularity (seen as a line in the two-dimensional profile but really a three-dimensional surface) can be described as follows:

Smooth — Nearly a plane.

Wavy or Undulating — If there are pockets which are wider than they are deep.

Irregular — If pockets are deeper than they are wide.

Broken or Discontinuous — If parts of the horizon are unconnected with other parts.

Wavy (undulating) or irregular boundaries need to have the upper and lower limits of the fluctuations denoted, e.g. 10-25/35 cm. The nature of the boundary is conventionally given at the end of the description for the horizon above the boundary thus describing the boundary to the horizon below, e.g.

0–25 cm	Dark brown loam, abrupt smooth boundary to
25–65/85 cm	Brown stony loam, clear, irregular boundary to
65/85+ cm	Rock

Broken horizons need more elaborate treatment, e.g.:

60–75/100 cm	Reddish brown clay, clear broken boundary to underlying rock, the transition zone consisting of fractured and dissolved limestone within which the reddish brown clay occurs as infillings to fissures.

Having recognised the various horizons, you can now turn to describing each using the procedures described for soil sample descriptions given in Chapter 2, using a pro forma profile description sheet, e.g. Fig. 3.3. Some pedologists like to work horizon by horizon describing all the features of one before moving to the next, but it is probably better to do one property, e.g. texture, for all horizons in turn, before moving to the next property. This will help you to recognise changes, if any, more easily from one horizon to the next, which is useful in naming and classifying soil horizons and profiles (Chapter 4) where comparisons of one horizon with the ones above or below are common.

For most of the properties you will need to dig out a sample of the soil and your profile will quickly take on a rather tattered appearance (hence the initial photograph). You will probably also want to take representative samples of each horizon away with you, for subsequent laboratory work or just to have available for future reference. A minimum of about 1 kg of soil from each horizon is recommended, but less will suffice if you simply want to keep samples for reference only. Each sample should be truly representative of the horizon, should be uncontaminated with material from other horizons or chemicals, e.g. dilute acids you may have used to check for the presence of carbonates, and should be stored in stout well-labelled polythene bags.

The importance of clear indelible labelling including your name and the date cannot be overemphasised. These labels should be made out at the time the sample is collected and not on some later occasion when you will discover that human memory is all too fallible.

NAME:

SOIL AND SITE DESCRIPTION

PROFILE NO.:   DATE:

TAXONOMIC UNIT:

LOCATION:

MAP REFERENCE:

TOPOGRAPHY:

Elevation:
Angle of Slope:
Aspect:

CLIMATE:

Recent Weather:

VEGETATION:

PARENT MATERIAL:

DRAINAGE:

Surface:
Soil:

EROSION:

ROCK OUTCROPS:

LAND USE:

MISCELLANEOUS:

(a)

Fig. 3.3 — Pro forma sheet. For soil and site descriptions; (a) front of sheet. (b) reverse of sheet.

SOIL DESCRIPTION

DRAWING OF PROFILE	DEPTH cm	HORIZONS		COLOUR AND ITS DISTRIBUTION	TEXTURE	STONES	STRUCTURE	MACRO POROSITY	HANDLING PROPERTIES	WATER CONDITIONS	ROOTS	ORGANIC MATTER	MISCELLANEOUS
		NAME	DEFINITION & CLARITY OF BOUNDARY										

(b)

3.5 SITE CHARACTERISTICS

The bare minimum which should be recorded is:

(a) location and map reference;
(b) an indication of the landscape, especially slope position, angle and aspect;
(c) a description of vegetation and/or land use.

The location of the profile pit should be given as precisely as possible with a grid reference on a specific map or aerial photograph, the name of the location and the relationship to nearby permanent or semi-permanent landmarks especially if the site has no specific grid or other reference. The name of the person making the description and date should also be recorded.

Landscapes can be described in general terms, but you should always note where in the landscape, e.g. top of slope, or valley bottom, your site lies, and the likely site drainage (e.g. well-drained shedding or flood prone). Give also the height (from a topographic map), the angle of slope, assessed visually or using a small clinometer, and the aspect (i.e. direction the slope faces). Obviously if your pedological investigation is part of a geomorphological study of an area your description of the landscape can be much more elaborate.

Similarly vegetation and land use can be described to whatever degree of detail seems appropriate. Natural or semi-natural vegetation should be described in more detail than a farm crop.

Other information which is commonly reported includes the geology of the site and some climatic information, though in soil survey reports these are often dealt with in separate chapters and site-specific information is not given as part of the site and profile descriptions.

3.6 EXAMPLES

You can judge the sort of descriptions which are acceptable from the examples in Tables 3.2–3.5 (which are real examples taken from various soil survey publications from different parts of the world). For completeness the nomenclature for the soil horizons and classification of the profile has been left in, but you will not be ready to do this for your profile until you have read and understood Chapter 4.

Table 3.2 — A typical soil description form a *Bulletin of the National Soil Survey of Ireland*
(Source: Hammond, 1973)

Horizon	Depth (cm)	Description
Ap	0–12	Dark greyish brown (10YR4/2); loam; fine moderate crumb structure; moist friable; high biological activity; 7% organic matter abundant roots; clear smooth boundary to:
A2	12–42	Light greyish brown (10YR6/3.5); yellow brown (10YR5/8); common, clear, medium to coarse mottles and dark reddish brown (5YR3/3) fine, common manganese mottles; loam; massive apedal structure; compact *in situ*, moist friable, dry slightly firm; less than 1% organic matter; 3% stones exposed surface; common roots to 25 cm sparse below this level; clear, wavy boundary to:
B2t	42–58.5	Greyish brown (10YR5/4); brown (7.5YR5/6); fine, common diffuse mottles; clay loam; massive apedal structure; moist friable to firm; 2–3% stones, shales highly weathered; many fine pores; very sparse, fine rootlets; clear, smooth boundary to:
Cca	>58.5	Light greyish brown (2.5Y5.5/4); yellowish brown (10YR5/6); diffuse, medium coarse mottles; sandy loam; 15–20% stones exposed surface; massive apedal structure; moist friable; compact *in situ*; fine deposition of secondary carbonate; vigorous effervescence; within horizon grey (2.5Y6.5/0) reduction pipe surrounded by olive brown (2.5Y5/6) mottling.

Notes: (1) No site description is given (it appears separately elsewhere in the Bulletin).
(2) The horizon nomenclature of the Irish Soil Survey differs from that described in Chapter 4.
(3) The description corresponds to the profile drawing in Fig. 3.1.

Table 3.3 — A typical profile description from India

Profile 5 — T. R. Bazar	
Classification	Soil taxonomy: Fine, mixed, isomesic, umbric dystochrept FAO: Ferric Luvisol
Location	Wood Broker Tea Estate road cut, between 26 and 27 km stone, 2 km from T. R. Bazar
Elevation	1600 m above mean sea level
Climate	Temperate
Vegetation	Wattle, conifers, eucalyptus and xerophytic shrubs and grasses
Parent Material	Weathered charnockite
Slope	About 15%
Drainage	Well drained, moderate permeability
Land Use	Tea plantation, vegetables and tuber crops
Described By	N. K. Barde, M. Jayaraman and S. R. Naga Bhushana

Horizon	Description
A11	0–10 cm — Very dark brown (10YR 2/2 M), very dark greyish brown (10YR 3/2 R) silty clay loam; weak fine granular structure; very friable; many fine roots inside peds; many micropores; very strongly acid; gradual smooth boundary
A12	10–32 cm — Very dark brown (10YR 2/2 M and R) silty clay loam; weak fine granular structure; very friable; many fine and very fine roots inside peds; many very fine to fine micropores; very strongly acid; gradual smooth boundary
A13	32–66 cm — Very dark brown (10YR 2/2 M and R) silty clay loam; weak fine granular structure; very friable; common very fine to fine roots inside peds; common very fine to fine micropores; very strongly acid; gradual smooth boundary
A14	66–80 cm — Very dark brown (10YR 2/2 M and R) silty clay loam; weak fine subangular blocky structure breaking to weak fine granular; very friable; few to common fine roots inside peds; common fine micropores; few medium-size insect burrows and krotovinas; very strongly acid; clear smooth boundary
B1	80–91 cm — Dark reddish brown (5YR 3/4 M) clay; weak medium subangular blocky structure breaking to weak fine granular; friable, slightly sticky and slightly plastic; common macropores and few micropores; few fine to very fine roots inside peds; very few 2–3 mm size quartz fragments; very strongly acid; clear smooth boundary
B21t	91–106 cm — Dark red (2.5YR 3/6 M and R) clay; weak medium angular blocky structure; friable, slightly sticky and slightly plastic; patchy thin clay cutans; very strongly acid; gradual smooth boundary
B22t	106–139 cm — Red to dark red (10R 3/5 M) clay; weak medium angular blocky structure; friable, slightly sticky and slightly plastic; patchy thin clay cutans; very few 2–3 mm size quartz fragments; few random coarse and fine pores; very strongly acid; clear smooth boundary

Munsell colour codes are for moist (M) and rubbbed (R) samples. Source: ISSS (1982, p. 46).

Table 3.4 — A typical profile description from Iraq

Gypsic yermosol Yy	
Typic gypsiorthid	Iraq
Location	About 50 km north of Baghdad
Altitude	About 250 m
Physiography	Nearly level, high Tigris terrace
Parent material	Gravelly gypsiferous old alluvium
Vegetation	Extensive grazing: *Artemisia scoparia, Plantago ovata, Stipa capenais, Achillea santolina L.* and others
Climate	Mean annual temperature, 23°C; mean annual rainfall, 150 mm

Profile description		
Ah	0–6 cm	Dark brown (7.5YR 4/4) moist; loam; weak medium platy structure; very friable moist; calcareous; little gravel; low organic matter, very many fine roots; clear smooth boundary
Cy1	6–20 cm	Brown (7.5YR 5/3) moist; mixed gypsiferous materials; granular; friable moist; calcarerous; low organic matter; no roots; gradual smooth boundary
Cy2	20–25 cm	Dark brown (7.5YR 4/3) moist; mixed gypsiferous materials; friable moist; granular; calcareous; no roots; diffuse smooth boundary
Cy3	50–80 cm	Brown (7.5YR 5/3) moist; mixed gypsiferous materials; friable moist; granular; slightly calcareous; little gravel; diffuse smooth boundary
Cy4	80–110 cm	Brown (7.5YR 5/3) needle-like mixed gypsiferous materials; very low in lime; about 10% gravel; diffuse smooth boundary
Cy5	110–170 cm	Brown (7.5YR 5/3) moist; needle-like mixed gypsiferous materials; very low in lime; about 20% gravel; diffuse smooth boundary
Cy6	170–500 cm	Brown, mixed gypsiferous soils; about 70% gravel; thin bands of sand

Source: FAO–UNESCO (1977).© UNESCO/FAO. Reproduced by permission of UNESCO and the Food and Agriculture Organisation of the United Nations.

Table 3.5 — A typical profile description from Hawaii in the USDA soil taxonomy

Classification	Typic Eutrandept, medial over cindery, isothermic
Location	Island of Maui, Maui County, Hawaii, Makena Quadrangle, 20°40'00"N latitude and 156°24'10"W longitude. 15 m east of State Highway 37 and 165 m south of Makena Road and State Highway 37 intersection in the northwest corner of pasture number 5 on the Ulupalakua Ranch 7.4 km from Kula
Physiographic position	Midslope of mountainous upland, 550 m elevation
Topography	12% west-facing slope
Drainage	Well drained; medium run-off; moderate permeability
Vegetation	Burclover (*Medicago hispida*), Kikuyu grass (*Pennisetum clandestinum*), plantain (*Plantago lanceolata*), rattail grass (*Sporobolus capensis*), and white clover (*Trifolium repens*).
Parent material	Volcanic ash over cinders
Sampled by	K. Flach, L. Swindale, L. Giese, F. Stephens, and G. Yamamoto, 13 April 1965
Remarks	The soil does not disperse well; hence the field estimate of texture are given in the profile description
Soil No.	S65Ha-4-22

	Colours are for moist soil.
Ap	0–23 cm (0–9 in). Dark brown (7.5YR 3/2) silt loam; moderate fine and very fine granular structure; slightly hard (dry), very friable (moist), slightly sticky and slightly plastic (wet); abundant roots; many pores; clear smooth boundary
A12	23–41 cm (9–16 in). Dark brown (7.5YR 3/2) loam; moderate fine and very fine subangular blocky structure; slightly hard (dry), very friable (moist), slightly sticky and slightly plastic (wet); abundant roots; many fine and very fine pores; gradual wavy boundary
B2	41–63 cm (16–25 in). Dark reddish brown (5YR 3/4) silty clay loam; weak medium and coarse prismatic structure; slightly hard (dry), very friable (moist), sticky and plastic (wet); abundant roots; many pores, worm casts and channels; abrupt wavy boundary.
IIC1	63–76 cm (25–30 in). Black cinders (1–10 mm); single grain; extremely hard and loose (dry); few roots; cinder layers occur intermittently; abrupt smooth boundary
IIIC2	76–99 cm (30–39 in). Dark brown (7.5YR 3/R) loam; massive; slightly hard (dry), friable (moist), slightly sticky and slightly plastic (wet); few roots; many hard earthy lumps; abrupt wavy boundary
IIIC3	99 cm (39 in). Black cinders (1–10 mm); single grain; extremely hard and loose (dry); 10–20% cobble and stone-sized Aa lava by volume

Source: USDA (1975, p. 629).

4

Naming and classifying a soil profile

4.1 INTRODUCTION

Now that you have finished describing a soil profile you would obviously like to classify it and to give it a name. This is not as simple as it might seem, since there are many different systems of naming and classifying soils and, even when you have chosen a system, applying it can be a daunting operation.

The subject of soil classification raises strong emotions amongst pedologists, and each would dearly like to produce his own system which he would undoubtedly consider superior to all others. The range of systems stems from the fact that soil is a continuum with many properties which vary from place to place without any clear cut entities such as a biological species or a chemical compound.

Most pedologists agree that a classification of soil should reflect the processes of soil formation but it is often doubtful what these genetic relationships are or how they can be recognised. Almost everyone agrees that the item to be classified is the soil profile, as seen in a small area such as a soil pit (the American concept of a pedon). Classification of the entire profile (or pedon) depends on recognising and naming the horizons which make up that profile. Particular emphasis is placed on subsoil horizons since surface horizons are frequently so modified that they have little genetic significance.

Most classifications are hierarchical in that they involve successive subdivisions, but the choice of properties used for subdivision and the level in the classification at which each is considered can vary widely between different classifications.

The question of nomenclature is inextricably linked with soil classification since the second main reason for classifying a soil profile, other than attempting to reveal genetic relationships, is to communicate through the name a shorthand impression of the nature of the soil profile. Thus a soil classification serves as a sort of language, and to be of value it should be a language spoken by many other soil scientists. However elegant and logical a language, say Esperanto, might be in grammar and syntax, if few others speak it you would be better off learning English with all its idiosyncrasies.

The same is true of soil classifications. Excellent systems have to be ignored while some which are widely criticised have to be learned because many pedologists use them.

Most national soil surveys have their own classification system. Even in an area as small as Britain the Soil Survey of Ireland, the Soil Survey of Scotland and the Soil Survey of England and Wales each have their own system and within each country there have been changes of system with time. Fortunately most systems have some features in common with others; so the system of the Soil Survey of England and Wales, given as an example of a national system in section 4.2, should be reasonably understandable, at least in broad terms, elsewhere in Britain.

Two systems can claim to have an international status, the FAO–UNESCO Soil Map of the World system (see section 4.3) and the American Soil Taxonomy (formerly referred to as the Seventh Approximation). The Soil Taxonomy has been widely criticised and few pedologists outside the USA or its pedologic sphere of influence would choose to use it. Nevertheless it would be foolish to ignore it since that would deny access to the vast amount of recent American pedological literature, and so a brief account is given in section 4.4. The Soil Taxonomy has replaced an earlier and much copied and understood United States Department of Agriculture (USDA) 'zonal' soil classification system using many of the 'traditional' soil names and so if only to help you in studying older soil literature and maps the chapter closes with a brief description of this in section 4.5.

Academic pedologists trying to unravel the deeper mysteries of soil formation tend to be more interested in the higher categories or levels of a classification system. Another group of pedologists, the soil surveyors, are more concerned with trying to map what they would recognise as different soils within the landscape (see Chapter 5). The *ad hoc* criteria which they use to differentiate their soils and which make it relatively easy to make soil maps are often not the same as those used in the higher levels of the system. The matching of these 'lower levels' with the higher levels is therefore difficult. Units devised initially during mapping will often straddle two or more of the higher classes unless they are carefully defined, bearing in mind the criteria used in the higher levels.

Conversely those who construct the higher levels of the system often fail to recognise that their criteria have to be applied in field conditions. It does not endear them to their more practical colleagues if the latter, for example, have to stand out in a steaming rain forest with insects crawling all over them and to decide whether a particular soil has or has not a cation exchange capacity (CEC) of 1.5 milliequivalents or less per 100 g of clay in at least some part of the subsoil but within 150 cm of the surface (one of the several requirements for an acric ferralsol in the FAO–UNESCO system). The sort of soil classification appropriate to soil mapping will be described further in Chapter 5.

4.2 THE SOIL CLASSIFICATION SYSTEM FOR ENGLAND AND WALES
4.2.1 General Description
This is a hierarchical system, whose structure is shown in Table 4.1. This also gives the approximate conceptual correlation with botanical classification in terms of the levels of the system. The lower levels of soil series and phases, used mainly in soil mapping, are dealt with in section 4.2.5 and Chapter 5.

Table 4.1 — The basic hierarchical structure of the soil classification system of the Soil Survey of England and Wales, and conceptual comparisons with a botanical classification. The number of categories recognised at each level in the soil classification is given in brackets, and the examples show how a three digit code is contructed which locates a given soil within the classification

Soil	Plant
MAJOR GROUP (10), e.g. 5 brown soils	ORDER, e.g. Glumiflorae (sedges, rushes and grasses)
GROUP (43), e.g. 5.7 argillic brown earths	FAMILY, e.g. Graminae (grasses)
SUB-GROUPS (118), e.g. 5.73, gleyic argillic brown earths	GENUS, e.g. *Triticum* (wheat)
SOIL SERIES (1118*), e.g. Waterstock series	SPECIES, e.g. *Triticum aestivum* (bread wheat)
PHASE (of a series), e.g. Waterstock series (stony phase)	VARIETY, e.g. Norman

* The total up to the end of 1983, but only 698 in current use, the rest redundant because of rationalisation of names and definitions.

There are ten major soil groups, as shown in Table 4.2, e.g. **brown soils**. These can be subdivided into 43 soil groups, e.g. argillic brown earths, all of which are given in the table except for seven rare ones. Soil groups are in turn divided into a total of 118 subgroups, e.g. gleyic argillic brown earths.

The systematic coding used also in the national soil map for England and Wales at 1:250 000 is included, and the approximate proportions of the major groups and subgroups in the main legend of that map are indicated. Some major groups and groups are very common, and others very rare. Thirteen of the subgroups are so rare that they are not represented in the main legend of the national soil map. Of the remainder, 17 each occupy 1% or less of the map; so the conclusion is that the vast majority of soils you will encounter will belong to one of the remaining 13 subgroups. The rarer soils may, however, be of local importance, including some of the more 'exotic' environments studied by ecologists.

The classification is based on the recognition of diagnostic horizons, sequences of which help to define the the major groups, groups and subgroups. The full definitions and descriptions of the horizons and the various categories of the system are given in a manual. They are, of course, much more comprehensive but also much more complicated than the treatment below. Nevertheless you should be able to classify most soil profiles you are likely to meet in England and Wales (and similar areas) using the information given. If your classification is critical then of course you should check your conclusions with the full definitions in the manual.

The main diagnostic horizons are described first, with some test profile descriptions for you to allocate horizon names (Table 4.3(a)). The answers are in Table 4.3(b). An explanation of some of the terms used in the nomenclature of the groups and subgroups introduces the full system set out in Table 4.4. By using Table 4.4 and the key in Table 4.5 you should be able to classify a profile at least as far as the group level. Recognition of the subgroup is really a matter of elimination within the various groups using the descriptions in Table 4.4.

Table 4.2 — The major groups and groups of the soil classification of the Soil Survey of England and Wales and their extent on the national soil map

Major groups Number	Name	Extent[a] (%)	Group Number	Name	Extent[a] (%)
1	Terrestrial raw soils	NR		Five, rare	NR
2	Raw gley soils	<1	2.1	Raw sandy gley soils	NR
			2.2	Unripened gley soils	<1
3	Lithomorphic soils	7	3.1	Rankers	1
			3.2	Sand-rankers	NR
			3.3	Ranker-like alluvial soils	NR
			3.4	Rendzinas	5
			3.5	Pararendinas	NR
			3.6	Sand-pararendzinas	<1
			3.7	Rendzina-like alluvial soils	<1
4	Pelosols	5	4.1	Calcareous pelosols	4
			4.2	Non-calcareous pelosols	<1
			4.3	Argillic pelosols	<1
5	Brown soils	33	5.1	Brown calcareous earths	4
			5.2	Brown calcareous sands	<1
			5.3	Brown calcareous alluvial soils	<1
			5.4	Brown earths	14
			5.5	Brown sands	2
			5.6	Brown alluvial soils	1
			5.7	Argillic brown earths	9
			5.8	Balaeo-argillic brown earths	3
6	Podzolic soils		6.1	Brown podzolic soils	5
			6.2	Humic cryptopodzols	NR
			6.3	Podzols	1
			6.4	Gley-podzols	1
			6.5	Stagnopodzols	2
7	Surface water gley soils	26	7.1	Stagnogley soils	23
			7.2	Stagnohumic gley soils	2
8	Ground-water gley soils	8	8.1	Alluvial gley soils	5
			8.2	Sandy gley soils	1
			8.3	Cambic gley soils	NR
			8.4	Argillic gley soils	NR
			8.5	Humic-alluvial gley soils	1
			8.6	Humic-sandy gley soils	<1
			8.7	Humic gley soils	<1
9	Man-made soils	<1		Two, rare	<1
10	Peat soils	3	10.1	Raw peat soils	2
			10.2	Earthy peat soils	1

[a]NR, not recorded.

4.2.2 Nomenclature and Recognition of Soil Horizons

Soil horizons can conveniently be divided into:

(a) topsoil horizons characterised by the presence of organic matter;
(b) subsoil horizons produced by the soil forming processes;
(c) more or less unaltered parent materials;
(d) horizons which are additionally gleyed.

Each horizon is given a 'genetic' symbol. There is also a convention for transitional horizons and horizons developed in multi-origined parent materials.

Topsoil horizons

These come in three main varieties:

(a) surface accumulations of organic matter including peat;
(b) humose mineral topsoils;
(c) non-humose mineral topsoils.

You will probably not have too much difficulty in recognising these but if you have to resort to laboratory work the strict criteria for each are given in Fig. 4.1.

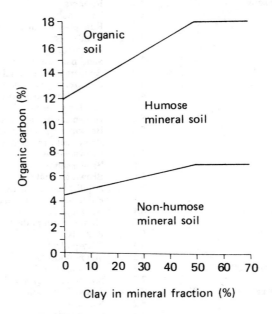

Fig. 4.1 — Limits of organic and humose soil materials (Source: Soil Survey of England and Wales)

Surface accumulations of organic matter

L   Fresh litter, no more than a year old, normally loose and with little altered plant structures; not affected by waterlogging.

F   Partly decomposed or comminuted litter in which some of the original plant structures can still be seen; seldom saturated with water for more than a month at a time; usually dark brown.

H   Well-decomposed organic material with no visible trace of original plant structures; seldom saturated with water for more than a month at a time; usually black and sometimes containing grains of mineral matter, notably white bleached sand grains.

L, F and H horizons occur in that order from the surface and are collectively called **raw humus** or **mor**. Expect them in uncultivated heathland, coniferous forest, uplands and mountains and sometimes in areas of youthful or incipient soils.

O   Peaty horizons continually wet for at least a month in most years or artificially drained.

Various subdivisions are recognised depending on appearance, origin and degree of cultivation including:

Of   Fibrous peat often from Sphagnum or Phragmites.
Om   Semi-fibrous peat.
Oh   Humified peat, uncultivated, usually black. (Compare Of, Om and Oh with L, F and H of raw humus.)
Op   Cultivated (p for ploughed) surface peat.

Fuller descriptions of these and others are in the manual. Expect peat in low-lying waterlogged marshy ground and at high altitudes in high-rainfall areas (blanket peat). The kind of peat often varies with depth.

Humose and non-humose mineral topsoils

A   Surface horizon with incorporated organic matter often by cultivation

The two main varieties are:

Ah   Uncultivated mineral topsoil (with at least 1% organic matter), often merging into the horizon below.
Ap   Cultivated topsoil, usually with a sharp lower boundary.

If these have many ochreous mottles and/or very drab colours due to waterlogging they are designated Ahg and Apg respectively.

These horizons are extremely common and easily recognised by their darker colours (caused by their higher content of organic matter) and clear signs of cultivation in Ap horizons. There is a general lack of surface accumulations of organic debris, except possibly very thin L, F and H horizons overlying an Ah or infertile Ap which has not been recently cultivated. Expect Ah (or Ahg) horizons under natural grassland and deciduous woodland, and Ap (or Apg) horizons in most agricultural soils.

Subsoil horizons

Two main kinds can be recognised: the so-called eluvial or E horizons (formerly thought of as a variety of A horizon) and altered subsoil horizons or B horizons, as distinct from unaltered parent material (or sometimes in practice not so distinct from it).

Eluvial horizons (E horizons)

E   Subsurface non-calcareous horizon which, by paler colour, lower clay content or less evident structure than an underlying B horizon gives evidence that clay and/or sesquioxides have been removed.

The three main varieties are:

Ea   An E horizon from which iron (and aluminium) have been removed by the process of podzolisation. Close inspection of the sand grains normally shows they have been stripped of any surface coatings so that the horizon colour depends on the colours of the bleached grains, often white, especially when dry. Ea horizons usually have a Munsell chroma of 2 or less and a value of 4 or more.

Eb   An E horizon from which clay has been removed by clay translocation but still retaining an overall brownish colour (as compared with an Ea horizon). It usually has a significantly lighter texture, more friable consistence and less evident coarse structure than the horizon (usually a Bt) below.

Eg   A specific kind of gleyed E horizon, best explained below along with other gleyed horizons.

Ea and Eb horizons are best recognised by comparison with the horizons above and below, and it can sometimes be the case that you first recognise one of the associated horizons and then decide to look more closely for an Ea or Eb which you may have already, but mistakenly, identified as, say, a Bw. Ea and Eb horizons can, however, sometimes be missing because of erosion or incorporation into an Ap.

The white bleached Ea horizons of podzolised soils are usually sufficiently conspicuous not to cause much problem in their identification. You will typically find them underlying L, F, H and sometimes Ah horizons in heathland, coniferous woodland and upland especially on sands or other base-poor parent materials. The occurrence of underlying black Bh and very dark brown Bs horizons or a thin Bs ironpan horizon provides almost certain corroboration. The lower boundary of such Ea horizons is frequently very undulating. Podzolised soils are sometimes cultivated and the Ea wholly or partly incorporated into the cultivated Ap which is usually very black, with white speckles of bleached sand grains. Occasionally the Bh and Bf horizons are also partly mixed in.

Eb horizons depleted of clay by the eluviation of clay into the underlying horizons are more difficult to spot, since they are often much the same colour as the underlying horizons. The process of clay illuviation in a formerly uniformly textured parent material will result in an Eb horizon with less clay than the underlying Bt horizon. Such textural variations can result from other causes notably variations in the parent material or multi-origin parent materials giving lighter textured layers over heavier ones. It is not normally possible to identify Eb horizons with certainty unless there are signs of clay illuviation in the underlying Bt horizon (see below) which by implication will suggest you should call the immediately overlying subsoil horizon an Eb. Although clay illuviation is one of the commonest processes in British soils it is also one of the most difficult to recognise. Expect it in almost any medium- to light-textured soil (though it can also occur in heavier-textured soils). Eb horizons are not found or are rare in upland situations, in calcareous soils or in youthful or immature soils.

Altered subsoil horizons (B horizons)

B   A mineral subsoil horizon other than an E horizon (see above), visibly affected by soil forming processes but not solely by gleying.

The problem with this definition, and it is a problem with which pedologists have been grappling with for decades, is what constitutes visible evidence of soil formation, i.e. where does the soil finish and the parent material (C or R horizon) begin? In many cases there is a gradual transition and it is a matter of subjective opinion as to where to draw the line. Some clues that you are still dealing with the soil *per se* would be the presence of roots, any kind of structural development, decomposed or broken-up rock fragments rather than *in situ* rock, and differences in texture, colour, mottling, pH or content of calcium carbonate as compared with deep quarry exposures of the rock or geological specimens of it.

Five kinds of B horizon are recognised:

Bh   A horizon enriched in organic matter (and perhaps iron and/or aluminium) as a result of podzolisation making it darker than an immediately overlying horizon (normally an Ea). Bh horizons normally have Munsell value and chroma of less than 3.

Bs   A strongly coloured subsoil horizon (Munsell chroma 4 or more), which is believed to be enriched in iron translocated from above by podzolisation. This may not necessarily produce the distinctive bleached Ea horizon and chemical analysis may be required to demonstrate the enrichment in iron, and usually also aluminium. The Munsell chroma is usually at least 2 higher than some overlying subsoil horizon (not necessarily the immediately superior horizon).

Bf   A sharply defined black to reddish brown, brittle or cemented B horizon less than 10 mm thick (thin ironpan). It normally lies directly below well-developed A, Ea (normally Eag) or Bh horizon, and directly above an ungleyed Bw, Bs or C horizon.

Bh, Bs or Bf, singly or in combination, are often referred to as podzolic B horizons (but see manual for exact definitions).

Bt   A subsoil B horizon believed to contain clay translocated from above and so originally overlain by an Eb horizon, which may have been lost by erosion or incorporated into an Ap. It should contain noticeably more clay than the horizon above (but see caveats discussed for Eb horizons) and shiny clay coatings, normally slightly redder than the rest of the horizon should be visible by eye or hand-lens, lining fissures and/or bridging sand or gravel particles. It is often referred to as an argillic B horizon of which a variant is referred to as palaeo-argillic (see below and manual for more precise definitions).

Bw   A weathered subsoil horizon showing the effects of weathering, leaching or soil structure development but which does not qualify as one of the other B horizons (or, of course, one of the E horizons). It usually has a Munsell value and chroma of 3 or 4.

Most soils will contain one or more of the above B horizons except very shallow or immature soils and very badly drained soils including peat. Look for the characteristic sets of eluvial on illuvial horizons, i.e. a podzol Ea with Bh, Bs or Bf horizons below, or an Eb above a Bt. If none of these applies then you are probably dealing with a Bw unless it is very strongly mottled (see gleyed horizons below). Some Bs horizons which are not overlain by bleached Ea horizons are difficult to identify and may need chemical analysis, but they tend to occur in upland areas, often on steep slopes and have bright reddish colours which often leave a stain on the skin or fabric and a rather greasy feel (see discussion on brown podzolic soils below).

Parent materials

The simplest distinction, and acceptable in most cases, is the threefold division into:

C   Comparatively unaltered substratum, soft and unconsolidated (Use this without any suffixes when in doubt or if it is not important.) Varieties include Cu (ordinary), Cr (dense and difficult to dig), Ck (with deposited calcium carbonate), Cg (gleyed, but see CG below), Cgk (both gleyed and calcareous), Cgy (containing gypsum) and Cgf (containing abundant ferruginous material).

R   Bedrock too hard to dig with a spade when moist.

CG   Intensely gleyed horizon with Munsell chroma 1 or less in yellowish, greenish or bluish hues which change colour on exposure to air; the characteristic substrate of unripened alluvium, e.g. in estuarine marshes (see manual for fuller treatment of unripened horizons).

Gleyed horizons (g and G horizons)

As explained in Chapter 1 gleying is the name given to the process which occurs in waterlogged soils whereby iron oxides are reduced, usually in the presence of organic matter, and migrate to form re-oxidised brown iron-rich mottles, segregations or nodules, sometimes accompanied by similar but black manganese oxides.

A gleyed horizon is indicated by common or abundant ochreous or rusty and/or greyish mottles or alternatively by a dominant Munsell chroma of 1 or less on ped faces or in matrix. The manual gives more elaborate criteria and you should consult it if in doubt.

Horizons with conspicuous gleying as described above are given the suffix g or, if more subdued, (g), but with the following exceptions.

(1)   L, F, H and O horizons do not use the suffixes even if (very rarely) you find mottles.

(2)   Eag horizons may have few or no mottles but have a dominant Munsell chroma of 2 or less (i.e. greyish). They normally underlie O horizons and overlie a horizon richer in iron.

(3)   An Eb horizon with slight gleying is denoted Eb(g). If the gleying is more pronounced the notation Eg is used. It has a dominant Munsell chroma of less than 3 (i.e. greyish) or a chroma of 3 or 4 and distinctly higher value (i.e. paler) or a yellower hue than the main colour of the underlying horizon. It usually overlies a relatively impervious Bg (see below) or Btg horizon. Like an Ea or Eag it is sometimes called an albic horizon (but see manual for exact definition).

(4)   In B horizons, only Bs(g), Btg or Bt(g) are permitted. Otherwise use simply Bg. Note in particular that Bwg and Bw(g) are not strictly permitted though you sometimes see the latter.

(5)   C horizons (see above) have a separate system, but also based on mottles and grey colours.

Examples of gleyed horizons include Apg or Ap(g) for mottled cultivated topsoils often under grass in low-lying or other wet locations. Eag horizons typify the upland soils with thin ironpans (Bf horizons). Gleyed subsoil horizons such as Eg, Bg or Btg are widespread in soils in low-lying sites and/or with heavy impermeable textures. It it quite common to have, say, a Bw or Bt(g) horizon passing down to a Bg or Btg with the only real difference being an intensification of mottling with depth. It is relatively uncommon, but by no means impossible, to have a horizon with a g or (g) suffix overlying an unmottled B or C horizon.

The term **gleyic (or stagnogleyic)** is frequently used in the definitions of groups and subgroups. Both refer to signs of waterlogging but **gleyic** is used for situations where waterlogging is caused by a high but usually fluctuating water table, and usually in permeable materials, whereas **stagnogleyic** refers to waterlogging caused by slowly permeable subsoil. To be described as gleyic (or stagnogleyic) a soil should have:

(1) an Eg, Bg, Btg or Cg horizon starting between 40 and 80 cm of the surface but not above this in which case the soil is a true gley (or stagnogley) and/or
(2) ochreous mottles and low Munsell chroma, i.e. pale matrix colours within 60 cm.

More precise definitions which vary between soil groups and subgroups are given in the manual.

Additional subscripts
Mineral B or C horizons (except Cr) which are cemented are suffixed m, e.g. Bhm. Compact but brittle horizons some of which probably mark the occurrence of previous permafrost and called indurated horizons or fragipans carry the suffix x, e.g. Cx, but their definition is somewhat contentious.

Transitional and intermixed horizons
Horizons of transitional character are designated by combining the separate horizon letters, e.g. BC, but not involving any subscripts so that, for example, BtC is invalid. Note, however, the particular use of CG described above. You should really try to avoid using such terms since they tend to imply you cannot make up your mind as between two alternatives, though the temptation to do this as a beginner is great. Horizons which have intermixtures of discrete patches of the horizons above and below are indicated as, for example, E & B, but situations requiring this terminology are rare.

Subdivisions of horizons
In very detailed profile descriptions some horizons may be subdivided by using arabic numerals after the horizon designation, e.g. Bw1 and Bw2. You might have to use this if you have several horizons in your profile and you think, say, two or more are simply Bw horizons with no feature such as gleying by which you could annotate them separately.

Multiple parent materials
Many soil profiles in Britain and many other parts of the world are developed in more than one parent material. Examples include a superficial loamy drift (or Head for those with a geological background) over an outcrop of clay, layers of alluvium of different textures, or 'cover loams' of silty wind-blown dust added to the surface

horizons. If you can recognise these differences (and you have not confused them with some of the effects of soil formation) then you can add arabic numerals before the horizon designation for each of the presumed parent materials. The designator 1 for the uppermost material is omitted so that a typical horizon sequence might be Ap, Ea, Bt, 2Btg, 3C. Some early soil survey publications used Roman numerals, e.g. IIC, since discontinued.

Some examples

You will probably need much practice before you become familiar with horizon nomenclature, and you will have continually to refer back to the descriptions given above or those in the manual. To start you off, however, four abbreviated profile descriptions are given in Table 4.3 but with enough information for you to work out the horizon names. Profiles 1 and 2 are fairly straightforward, but profile 3 has at least one case of a horizon subdivision, while profile 4 has multiple parent materials and perhaps some other traps as well. The answers are given at the bottom of the table which you might like to obscure while you are attempting the exercise.

Table 4.3(a) — Four brief profile descriptions for derivation of horizon symbols (answers on next page)

Horizon symbol	Profile description	Horizon symbol	Profile description
Profile 1: Newport series		*Profile 2: Shirrell Heath series*	
1/1	0–25 cm — Dark brown, slightly stony sandy loam or loamy sand	2/1	0–10 cm — Very dark greyish brown or black, slightly stony humose sand, with common bleached grains
1/2	25–55 cm — Brown, slightly stony loamy sand or sand; weak subangular blocky structure	2/2	10–30 cm — Dark reddish grey, slightly stony sand; single grain structure
1/3	55–120 cm — Yellowish red or brownish yellow, slightly stony sand; single-grain structure	2/3	30–50 cm — Dark reddish brown, slightly stony, humose loamy sand or sand; single-grain structure
		2/4	50–80 cm — Yellowish red, slightly stony sand; single-grain structure
		2/5	80–120 cm — Reddish brown or light yellowish brown, soft sandstone
Profile 3: Dale series		*Profile 4: Swanwick series*	
3/1	0–20 cm — Dark greyish brown, slightly mottled, stoneless clay or clay loam	4/1	0–25 cm — Dark greyish brown, sandy loam or sandy silt loam
3/2	20–50 cm — Grey, mottled, stoneless clay; strong coarse prismatic structure	4/2	25–70 cm — Grey, mottled, slightly or moderately stony sandy loam; weak or moderate medium subangular blocky structure
3/3	50–100 cm — Grey with many ochreous mottles, stoneless clay; strong coarse prismatic structure	4/3	70–85 cm — Grey, mottled slightly stony sandy loam or sandy clay loam; weak or moderate coarse subangular blocky structure
3/4	100–120 cm — Grey, mottled, clay; massive or coarse platy structure	4/4	85–100 cm — Grey, mottled, stoneless to very stony sandy loam or loamy sand

Table 4.3(b) — Answers to the horizon symbols in Table 4.3(a)

Horizon symbol	Horizon nomenclature	Horizon symbol	Horizon nomenclature
1/1	Ap	3/1	Apg
1/2	Bw	3/2	Bg1
1/3	Cu	3/3	Bg2
		3/4	BCg
2/1	Ah		
2/2	Ea	4/1	Ap
2/3	Bh	4/2	Eg
2/4	Bs	4/3	Btg
2/5	Cr	4/4	2Cg

4.2.3 Major groups and groups

In the naming of the groups, and also the subgroups, there are a number of recurrent terms such as sandy, pelo- and calcareous. Some, e.g. podzolic, have obvious genetic connotations while others are everyday words but used in this context with a specific meaning. These terms are set out below.

Alluvial — Developed in a parent material of recent alluvial, i.e. water-laid, origin; often clayey but can be loamy or silty; sandy alluvium is sometimes classed along with other sandy parent materials.

Argillic — A soil or horizon (a Bt horizon) characterised by the accumulation of clay translocated from above.

Brown — Used in a few subgroup names and implying simply a change in subsoil colour due to weathering under well-aerated conditions.

Calcareous or Calcaro — Containing free calcium carbonate which effervesces on application of dilute acid, usually because the soil is formed over a calcareous parent material such as chalk, limestone or marl; when used for a profile it implies such conditions within at least 40 cm of the surface but in some groups not until 80 cm so long as the overlying subsoil has a pH above 6.

Cambic — Altered but not highly weathered and usually of a loamy texture; a term used extensively in some classifications wherein it has a specific definition, but in Britain it normally implies a loamy Bg.

Colluvial — Formed in recently eroded material which has accumulated in footslopes and valley bottoms; used in subgroup names only.

Ferri- or ferric — Containing appreciable and visible iron compounds; usually used in connection with the podzolisation process; used in subgroup names only.

Ferritic — Rich in iron; usually for horizons and soils from iron-rich parent materials, e.g. ironstones; used in subgroup names only.

Gleyic — A soil or horizon with obvious gley features (see above) due to the influence of a high and usually fluctuating ground-water table (as opposed to Stagnogleyic where gleying is caused by a slowly permeable subsoil).

Humic or humo- — Having a peaty (O horizon) or humose topsoil (see Fig. 4.1).

Man-made — With obvious signs of disturbance by man other than normal cultivations, e.g. deep incorporation of organic and other wastes, and usually containing artefacts, e.g. brick and pottery fragments.

Palaeo- — Used for ancient soil forming processes particularly clay translocation thought, on the evidence of brighter or redder colours, to have taken place under former warmer climatic conditions.

Pelo- — Used for clayey soils or horizons which lack an overlying loamy or sandy horizon more than 15 cm thick and usually exhibit marked shrinkage and swelling on drying and wetting leading to marked vertical fissuring in dry conditions (so-called vertic features).

Podzolic — Showing some or all of the features of podzolisation, the process of mobilisation, migration and deposition of iron and aluminium as organic complexes.

Sand or sand- — When used in group and subgroup names it refers specifically to textures of sand or loamy sand for at least 40 cm of the uppermost 80 cm of a profile.

Stagno- — Used in conjunction with gley, gleyic and humo- (q.v.) when the waterlogging is due to a slowly permeable subsoil rather than to a near-surface water table and so most commonly used in clayey or fine loamy soils.

Sulphuric — Used for soils, almost always in estuarine alluvium containing suphides which, on oxidation, produce very acid soil conditions. Used in subgroup names only.

Typical — A common term used for subgroups and implying either the central concept of the group or the lack of any distinctive features which would allow allocation to any other subgroup.

The full classification system with all ten major groups, 43 Groups and 118 subgroups is set out, somewhat dauntingly, in Table 4.4. The author and his colleagues have, over the years, tried to devise an algorithmic system that would 'key out' the correct subgroup but have come to the conclusion that a satisfactory key is impossible to devise. This is because some differentiating criteria are used in separations at both the group and the subgroup level and cause almost endless backtracking through a key or require unreasonably complicated criteria. It is possible to devise a key (Table 4.5) for allocation of a profile as far as the soil group level, however. You may care to try out the key by classifying the four profiles which were used for the exercise in horizon names (Table 4.3).

You should first 'tidy up' any profile description by amalgamating subdivided horizons. For example Bw1 and Bw2 would become a single Bw. Also eliminate any transitional horizons or multiple-parent-material designations so that a horizon sequence such as A Bw BC C 2C becomes simply A Bw C. Then start at the beginning of the key and work through the alternatives until you come to one which appears to correspond to the profile you are attempting to classify. Refer to the appropriate description in Table 4.4 to check whether the profile fits the more detailed description given there. You will probably have to go back to the original profile description to check the depths at which certain horizons or features first appear.

Table 4.4 — The soil classification of the Soil Survey of England and Wales

Major soil group		Soil group		Soil subgroup	
Number	Name and description	Number	Name and description	Number	Name and description
1	**Terrestrial raw soils:** Mineral soils in very recently formed material, with no soil horizons other than a superficial organic or organo-mineral layer less than 5 cm thick, unless buried beneath a recent deposit more than 30 cm thick	1.1	**Raw sands:** Non-alluvial sandy soils found mainly on dune sands		Not subdivided below group level
		1.2	**Raw alluvial soils:** In recent alluvium		
		1.3	**Raw skeletal soils:** With bedrock or very stony rock rubble at 30 cm or less		
		1.4	**Raw earths:** In unconsolidated, non-alluvial loamy or clayey deposits		
		1.5	**Man-made raw soils:** In artificially disturbed materials such as mining spoil		
2	**Raw gley soils:** Mineral soils in material that has remained waterlogged since deposition. Prominently mottled or greyish above 40 cm depth. Mainly confined to intertidal flats and saltings that represent stages in the development of mature salt marshes	2.1	**Raw sandy gley soils:** In sandy material with no distinct topsoil		Not subdivided below group level
		2.2	**Unripened gley soils:** With permanently waterlogged loamy or clayey alluvium (soft mud) at 20 cm or less		
3	**Lithomorphic (A/C) soils:** Shallow, with a distinct, humose or peaty topsoil, but no subsurface horizons more than 5 cm thick (other than a bleached horizon). Normally over bedrock, very stony rock rubble or little altered soft unconsolidated deposits within 30 cm depth	3.1	**Rankers:** Loamy or clayey, with non-calcareous topsoil over bedrock (including massive limestone), non-calcareous rock rubble or soft non-calcareous deposits	3.11	**Humic rankers** (with humose or peaty topsoil)
				3.12	**Gleyic rankers:** (faintly mottled and permeable)
				3.13	**Brown rankers:** (distinct topsoil and unmottled subsoil — if present)
				3.14	**Podzolic rankers:** (with bleached subsurface horizon)
				3.15	**Stagnogleyic rankers** (faintly mottled over slowly permeable material)
		3.2	**Sand rankers:** In non-calcareous unconsolidated soft non-alluvial sandy deposits	3.21	**Typical sand-rankers** (unmottled with no bleached subsurface horizon)
				3.22	**Podzolic sand-rankers** (with bleached subsurface horizon)

Table 4.4 (*Contd.*)

Major soil group	Soil group	Soil subgroup
Number Name and description	Number Name and description	Number Name and description
		3.23 **Gleyic sand-rankers** (faintly mottled)
	3.3 **Ranker-like alluvial soils:** In non-calcareous recent alluvium	3.31 **Typical ranker-like alluvial soils** (unmottled)
		3.32 **Gleyic ranker-like alluvial soils** (faintly mottled)
	3.4 **Rendzinas:** Calcareous, over chalk, or extremely calcareous rock rubble or soft unconsolidated deposits	3.41 **Humic rendzinas** (with humose or peaty topsoil)
		3.42 **Grey rendzinas** (with distinct topsoil that is extremely calcareous or greyish)
		3.43 **Brown rendzinas** (with brownish distinct topsoil that is not extremely calcareous)
		3.44 **Colluvial rendzinas** (in colluvium more than 40 cm thick)
		3.45 **Gleyic rendzinas** (mottled with distinct topsoil over permeable material)
		3.46 **Humic gleyic rendzinas** (mottled with humose or peaty topsoil over permeable material)
		3.47 **Stagnogleyic rendzinas** (mottled over slowly permeable material)
	3.5 **Pararendzinas:** Loamy or clayey over moderately calcareous (1–40% $CaCO_3$) non-alluvial material	3.51 **Typical pararendzinas** (unmottled with distinct topsoil)
		3.52 **Humic pararendzinas** (unmottled with humose or peaty topsoil)
		3.53 **Colluvial pararendzinas** (in colluvium more than 40 cm thick)
		3.54 **Stagnogleyic pararendzinas** (faintly mottled over slowly permeable material)
		3.55 **Gleyic pararendzinas** (faintly mottled over permeable material)

3.6 **Sand-pararendzinas:** In calcareous unconsolidated soft sandy deposits other than alluvium (normally dune sands)

3.61 **Typical sand-pararendzinas** (unmottled)
3.62 **Gleyic sand-pararendzinas** (faintly mottled)

3.7 **Rendzina-like alluvial soils:** In little altered calcareous alluvium, lake marl or tufa, at least 30 cm thick

3.71 **Typical rendzina-like alluvial soils** (unmottled)
3.72 **Gleyic rendzina-like alluvial soils** (mottled with distinct topsoil)
3.73 **Humic gleyic rendzina-like alluvial soils** (mottled with humose or peaty topsoil)

4 **Pelosols:** Non-alluvial clayey soils that crack deeply in dry seasons, but are slowly permeable when wet. They have a coarse blocky or prismatic structure and no prominently mottled non-calcareous subsurface horizons within 40 cm depth

4.1 **Calcareous pelosols:** With calcareous subsoil and no clay-enriched subsurface horizon

4.11 **Typical calcareous pelosols**

4.2 **Non-calcareous pelosols:** Non-calcareous to at least 80 cm depth and no clay-enriched subsurface horizon

4.21 **Typical non-calcareous pelosols**

4.3 **Argillic pelosols:** With a clay-enriched subsurface horizon

4.31 **Typical argillic pelosols**

5 **Brown soils:** With dominantly brownish or reddish subsoils and no prominent mottling or greyish colours (gleying) above 40 cm depth. They are developed mainly on permeable materials at elevations below about 300 m OD. Most are in agricultural use

5.1 **Brown calcareous earths:** Non-alluvial, with calcareous loamy or clayey subsoils without significant clay enrichment

5.11 **Typical brown calcareous earths** (unmottled)
5.12 **Gleyic brown calcareous earths** (faintly mottled with permeable subsoil)
5.13 **Stagnogleyic brown calcareous earths** (faintly mottled with slowly permeable subsoil)
5.14 **Colluvial brown calcareous earths** (in colluvium more than 40 cm thick)

5.2 **Brown calcareous sands:** Non-alluvial, with calcareous sandy subsoils without significant clay enrichment

5.21 **Typical brown calcareous sands** (unmottled)
5.22 **Gleyic brown calcareous sands** (faintly mottled)

Table 4.4 (*Contd.*)

Major soil group		Soil group		Soil subgroup	
Number	Name and description	Number	Name and description	Number	Name and description
		5.3	**Brown calcareous alluvial soils:** In calcareous recent alluvium more than 30 cm thick	5.31	**Typical brown calcareous alluvial soils** (unmottled)
				5.32	**Gleyic brown calcareous alluvial soils** (faintly mottled with permeable subsoil)
				5.33	**Pelogleyic brown calcareous alluvial soils** (faintly mottled and clayey with slowly permeable subsoil)
		5.4	**Brown earths:** Non-alluvial, with non-calcareous loamy and clayey subsoils without significant clay enrichment	5.41	**Typical brown earths** (unmottled)
				5.42	**Stagnogleyic brown earths** (faintly mottled with slowly permeable subsoil)
				5.43	**Gleyic brown earths** (faintly mottled with permeable subsoil)
				5.44	**Ferritic brown earths** (unmottled with bright ochreous iron-rich subsoil)
				5.45	**Stagnogleyic ferritic brown earths** (faintly mottled with bright ochreous iron-rich slowly permeable subsoil)
				5.46	**Gleyic ferritic brown earths** (faintly mottled with bright ochreous iron-rich permeable subsoil)
				5.47	**Colluvial brown earths** (in colluvium more than 40 cm thick)
		5.5	**Brown sands:** Non-calcareous sandy or sandy gravelly	5.51	**Typical brown sands** (unmottled with no clay-enriched subsoil)
				5.52	**Gleyic brown sands** (faintly mottled with permeable subsoil without significant clay enrichment)
				5.53	**Stagnogleyic brown sands** (faintly mottled with slowly permeable subsoil)
				5.54	**Argillic brown sands** (unmottled with clay-enriched subsoil)
				5.55	**Gleyic argillic brown sands** (faintly mottled with permeable clay-enriched subsoil)

5.6 Brown alluvial soils: In non-calcareous loamy or clayey alluvium more than 30 cm thick

5.61 **Typical brown alluvial soils** (unmottled)

5.62 **Gleyic brown alluvial soils** (faintly mottled with permeable subsoil)

5.63 **Pelogleyic brown alluvial soils** (faintly mottled and clayey with slowly permeable subsoil)

5.7 Argillic brown earths: Loamy or clayey with an ordinary clay-enriched subsoil

5.71 **Typical argillic brown earths** (unmottled)

5.72 **Stagnogleyic argillic brown earths** (faintly mottled with slowly permeable subsoil)

5.73 **Gleyic argillic brown earths** (faintly mottled with permeable subsoil)

5.8 Palaeo-argillic brown earths: Loamy or clayey, with an ancient, reddish or reddish mottled, clay-enriched subsoil formed, at least in part, before the last (Devensian) glacial period

5.81 **Typical palaeo-argillic brown earths** (unmottled)

5.82 **Stagnogleyic palaeo-argillic brown earths** (faintly mottled with slowly permeable subsoil)

5.83 **Gleyic palaeo-argillic brown earths** (faintly mottled with permeable subsoil)

6 Podzolic soils: With black, dark brown or ochreous humus and iron-enriched subsoils formed as a result of acid weathering conditions. Under natural or semi-natural vegetation, they have an unincorporated acid organic layer at the surface

6.1 Brown podzolic soils: With a dark brown ochreous, iron-enriched subsoil and no overlying bleached horizon

6.11 **Typical brown podzolic soils** (unmottled with distinct topsoil)

6.12 **Humic brown podzolic soils** (unmottled with humose or peaty topsoil)

6.13 **Palaeo-argillic brown podzolic soils** (unmottled with an ancient, reddish clay-enriched subsoil)

6.14 **Stagnogleyic brown podzolic soils** (faintly mottled with slowly permeable subsoil)

6.15 **Gleyic brown podzolic soils** (faintly mottled with permeable subsoil)

6.2 Humic cryptopodzols: With humose or peaty topsoil over thick humose, humus-enriched subsoil and no bleached subsurface horizon

6.21 **Typical humic cryptopodzols** (with no iron-enriched subsurface horizon)

6.22 **Ferri-humic cryptopodzols** (with an iron-enriched subsurface horizon)

Table 4.4 (*Contd.*)

Major soil group		Soil group		Soil subgroup	
Number	Name and description	Number	Name and description	Number	Name and description
		6.3	**Podzols:** Well drained, with a bleached subsurface horizon and no thin ironpan	6.31	**Humo-ferric podzols** (with black or dark brown humus and iron-enriched layer beneath the bleached horizon)
				6.32	**Humus podzols** (with black humus-enriched layer containing little iron, below the bleached horizon)
				6.33	**Ferric podzols** (with a dark brown or ochreous, iron-enriched layer containing little humus, below the bleached horizon)
				6.34	**palaeo-argillic podzols** (with ancient, reddish clay-enriched subsoil)
		6.4	**Gley-podzols:** With a bleached subsurface horizon over a dark-coloured humus or iron-enriched subsoil directly over a periodically wet, prominently mottled or greyish horizon	6.41	**Typical gley-podzols** (with humus-enriched subsoil containing little iron)
				6.42	**Humo-ferric gley-podzols** (with black or dark brown humus and iron-enriched subsoil)
				6.43	**Stagnogley-podzols** (with slowly permeable subsoil)
		6.5	**Stagnopodzols:** With a peaty topsoil and periodically wet bleached subsurface horizon over an iron-enriched subsoil. Mainly found in uplands	6.51	**Ironpan stagnopodzols** (with a thin ironpan)
				6.52	**Humus-ironpan stagnopodzols** (with humus-enriched subsurface horizon over a thin ironpan)
				6.53	**Hardpan stagnopodzols** (with a bleached hardpan)
				6.54	**Ferric stagnopodzols** (with dark brown or ochreous iron-enriched subsoil containing little humus)

7 **Surface-water gley soils:** Non-alluvial, seasonally waterlogged slowly permeable soils, formed above 3 m OD and prominently mottled above 40 cm depth. They have no relatively permeable material starting within and extending below 1 m of the surface

7.1 **Stagnogley soils:** With a distinct topsoil. They are found mainly in lowland Britain

7.11 **Typical stagnogley soils** (with ordinary clay-enriched subsoil)
7.12 **Pelo-stagnogley soils** (clayey)
7.13 **Cambic stagnogley soils** (with no clay-enriched subsoil)
7.14 **Palaeo-argillic stagnogley soils** (with ancient, reddish or reddish mottled clay-enriched subsoil)
7.15 **Sandy stagnogley soils** (with sandy topsoil)

7.2 **Stagnohumic gley soils:** With a humose or peaty topsoil. They are mainly upland soils, intermediate between stagnogley soils and peat soils

7.21 **Cambic stagnohumic gley soils** (with no clay-enriched subsoil)
7.22 **Argillic stagnohumic gley soils** (with ordinary clay-enriched subsoil)
7.23 **Palaeo-argillic stagnohumic gley soils** (with ancient, reddish or reddish mottled, clay-enriched subsoil)
7.24 **Sandy stagnohumic gley soils** (with sandy subsurface horizon)

8 **Ground-water gley soils:** Seasonally waterlogged soils affected by a shallow fluctuating ground-water table. They are developed mainly within or over permeable material and have prominently mottled or greyish coloured horizons within 40 cm depth. Most occupy low-lying or depressional sites

8.1 **Alluvial gley soils:** With distinct topsoil, in loamy or clayey recent alluvium more than 30 cm thick

8.11 **Typical alluvial gley soils** (loamy with non-calcareous subsoil)
8.12 **Calcareous alluvial gley soils** (loamy with calcareous subsoil)
8.13 **Pelo-alluvial gley soils** (clayey with non-calcareous subsoil)
8.14 **Pelo-calcareous alluvial gley soils** (clayey with calcareous subsoil)
8.15 **Sulphuric alluvial gley soils** (extremely acid subsoil within 80 cm)

8.2 **Sandy gley soils:** Sandy, with distinct topsoil and no clay-enriched subsoil

8.21 **Typical sandy gley soils** (with non-calcareous subsoil)
8.22 **Calcareous sandy gley soils** (with calcareous subsoil)

8.3 **Cambic gley soils:** Non-alluvial, loamy or clayey with a distinct topsoil and no clay-enriched subsoil

8.31 **Typical cambic gley soils** (loamy with non-calcareous subsoil)
8.32 **Calcaro-cambic gley soils** (loamy with calcareous subsoil)
8.33 **Pelo-cambic gley soils** (clayey)

Table 4.4 (*Contd.*)

Major soil group		Soil group		Soil subgroup	
Number	Name and description	Number	Name and description	Number	Name and description
		8.4	**Argillic gley soils:** With a distinct topsoil and a clay-enriched subsoil	8.41	**Typical argillic gley soils** (with loamy topsoil)
				8.42	**Sandy argillic gley soils** (with sandy topsoil)
		8.5	**Humic-alluvial gley soils:** With a humose or peaty topsoil in loamy or clayey recent alluvium more than 30 cm thick	8.51	**Typical humic-alluvial gley soils** (with non-calcareous subsoil)
				8.52	**Calcareous humic-alluvial gley soils** (with calcareous subsoil)
				8.53	**Sulphuric humic-alluvial gley soils** (with extremely acid subsoil within 80 cm)
		8.6	**Humic sandy gley soils:** Sandy, with humose or peaty topsoil and no clay-enriched subsoil. Intermediate between sandy gley soils and lowland peat soils	8.61	**Typical humic-sandy gley soils** (with non-calcareous subsoil)
				8.62	**Calcareous humic-sandy gley soils** (with calcareous suboil)
		8.7	**Humic gley soils:** Non-alluvial loamy or clayey with humose or peaty topsoil. Intermediate between cambic and argillic gley soils and lowland peat soils	8.71	**Typical humic gley soils** (with non-calcareous subsoil lacking significant clay enrichment)
				8.72	**Calcareous humic gley soils** (with calcareous subsoil lacking significant clay enrichment)
				8.73	**Argillic humic gley soils** (with clay-enriched subsoil)
9	**Man-made soils:** With a thick man-made topsoil or a disturbed subsurface layer (containing disturbed fragments of soil horizons) to at least 40 cm depth. They result from the addition of earth-containing manures, or the restoration of soil material after mining or quarrying	9.1	**Man-made humus soils:** With a thick man-made topsoil	9.11	**Sandy man-made humus soils** (sandy or sandy skeletal)
				9.12	**Earthy man-made humus soils** (loamy or clayey)

9.2 **Disturbed soils:** With a distinct topsoil and a disturbed subsurface layer to at least 40 cm depth — Not subdivided below group level

10 **Peat soils:** With more than 40 cm of organic material in the upper 80 cm or with more than 30 cm of organic material over bedrock or very stony rock rubble

10.1 **Raw peat soils:** In undrained organic material that has remained wet to within 20 cm of the surface

10.11 **Raw oligo-fibrous peat soils** (mainly fibrous or semi-fibrous with pH less than 4.0 throughout)

10.12 **Raw eu-fibrous peat soils** (mainly fibrous or semi-fibrous with pH 4.0 or more in some part)

10.13 **Raw oligo-amorphous peat soils** (mainly humified with pH less than 4.0 throughout)

10.14 **Raw eutro-amorphous peat soils** (mainly humified with pH 4.0 or more in some part)

10.2 **Earthy peat soils:** Normally drained, with a well-aerated and well-structured earthy topsoil or ripened mineral surface layer

10.21 **Earthy oligo-fibrous peat soils** (mainly fibrous or semi-fibrous with pH less than 4.0 throughout)

10.22 **Earthy eu-fibrous peat soils** (mainly fibrous or semi-fibrous with pH 4.0 or more in some part)

10.23 **Earthy oligo-amorphous peat soils** (mainly humified with pH less than 4.0 throughout)

10.24 **Earthy eutro-amorphous peat soils** (mainly humified with pH 4.0 or more in some part)

10.25 **Earthy sulphuric peat soils** (with an extremely acid subsurface horizon containing pale yellow crystals or streaks, above 80 cm)

(Source: Soil Survey of England and Wales)

Table 4.5 — Key for identifying soil groups in the classification system of the Soil Survey of England and Wales

Description	Soil group
Man-made soils	
A horizon more than 40 cm thick	Man-made humus soil
Horizons of former profile mixed	Disturbed soil
Material not soil material, e.g. mine or quarry waste	Man-made raw soil
Natural raw soils: Natural surface materials with little or no soil formation	
Sand (usually dunes)	Raw sand
Incompletely vegetated, regularly waterlogged unconsolidated tidal flats	Raw gley soil (undifferentiated)
Bedrock, or its detritus, screes, shingle	Raw skeletal soil
Peat soils: More than 40 cm of organic material (O horizon) in the upper 80 cm, excluding fresh litter or living moss	
Undrained or incompletely drained	Raw peat soil
Surface peat altered following thorough drainage	Earthy peat soil
Lithomorphic soils: Other soils with profiles less than 40 cm thick to a C or R horizon, lacking Bw, Bt, Bf, Bh or Bs horizons or a gleyed subsoil layer	
On hard non-calcareous rock or its detritus or gravel	Ranker
On recent non-calcareous alluvium	Ranker-like alluvial soil
On recent calcareous alluvium	Rendzina-like alluvial soil
On other calcareous materials	Rendzina (includes pararendzinas and sand pararedzinas)
On other loose material	Lithomorphic soil (undifferentiated)
Pelosols: Soils clayey within 15 cm of the surface, which have no non-calcareous gleyed horizon within 40 cm which extends below 40 cm and no subsoil colours with chromas of 5 or more in hues of 7.5YR or redder unless inherited from unaltered geological material, e.g. Keuper Marl	
Calcareous within 80 cm of the surface and all non-calcareous layers with a pH >6	Calcareous pelosol
Other pelosols	Pelosol (undifferentied)
Podzolic soils: Soils with a Bf, Bh or Bs horizon	
With a Bf below one or more of the following O, Ea, Eag, Eg, Bh horizons or with an Eag or Eg directly underlain by a Bs or Bsg	Stagnopodzol
With EaBhBs, EaBh, EaBs, BhBs profiles and no gleyed layer immediately below the Bh or Bs	Podzol
With EaBhBs, EaBh, EaBs or BhBs profiles and a gleyed layer immediately below the Bh or Bs	Gley-podzol
With a Bs but no Ea, Eag, Bf, gleyed layer or prominent Bh	Brown podzolic soil

Table 4.5 (*Contd.*)

Description	Soil group
Gley soils: Other soils with a gleyed horizon within 40 cm. Prefixed 'humic' in all cases if there is an O horizon or humose A horizon	
In recent alluvium	Alluvial gley soil; Humic-alluvial gley soil
Other gley soils with a slowly permeable subsoil	Stagnogley soil Stagno-humic gley soil
Other gley soils, sandy in more than half of uppermost 80 cm	Sandy gley soil Humic-sandy gley soil
Other gley soils	Ground-water gley soil (undifferentiated) (includes cambic gley soils and argillic gley soils) Humic gley soil
Brown soils: Other soils which have a Bw or Bt at least 5 cm thick and no gleyed layer within 40 cm. The groups lacking a Bt horizon are prefixed **Calcareous** if they have no horizon with a lower pH than 6 and are calcareous within the depth noted in parentheses	
(a) *Groups with Bw and no Bt* (5 cm thick in depth range 25–120 cm)	
Sandy texture in at least half of the topmost 80 cm	Brown sand Brown calcareous sand (80 cm)
From recent loamy or clayey alluvium	Brown alluvial soil Brown calcareous alluvial soil (40 cm)
Others	Brown earth Brown calcareous earth (40 cm)
(b) *Groups with Bt* (at least 5 cm thick in depth range 25–120 cm)	
Bt has chroma of 5 or more in hues of 7.5YR or redder not inherited from unaltered geological material	Palaeo-argillic brown earth
Bt does not meet this colour requirement	Argillic brown earth

Use of the above key with the four profile descriptions given in Table 4.3 should produce the following: —

Profile 1 Newport series	— brown sand	(typical)
Profile 2 Shirrell Heath series	— podzol	(humo-ferric)
Profile 3 Dale series	— stagnogley	(pelo-)
Profile 4 Swanwick series	— argillic gley soil	(typical)

In most cases intelligent application of this approach will yield the correct group or at worst, a classification that would not be disgracefully wrong. Some groups are rather rare as can be seen from Table 4.2. and you might like to think especially carefully if first approximation indicates one of these.

4.2.4 Subgroups

All the recognised subgroups are listed in Table 4.4 with brief definitions of each. When you have decided the group to which a soil belongs you should then allocate it to its appropriate subgroup by reference to this table. Again the profiles given in Table 4.3 could serve as examples for this exercise.

One is tempted to say that when in doubt the 'typical' subgroup is the safest subgroup to use — most groups offer one. 'Gleyic' or 'stagnogleyic' are reasonable offerings for soils mottled at depth, which may well be correct, for subgroups in the **lithomorphic soils, brown soils** and **podzolic soils**, though you should check in Table 4.4 that such a subgroup is valid for your particular group.

Subgroups often indicate a transition from one group or even major group to another. Consider, for example, the sequence 5.41 typical brown earths, 5.42 gleyic brown earths, 8.41 typical argillic gley soils, 8.71 typical humic gley soils, 10 peat soils. These could all form on much the same parent material, in close proximity to each other, with the only significant difference their drainage status, getting progressively worse down the sequence. You should, therefore, always look at the definitions of 'related' subgroups in other groups or even major groups. The subgroup name will be an indication of where to look as in the above example.

4.2.5 Lower levels of classification (soil series)

When soil mapping first began, soil surveyors would recognise different soils on a more or less *ad hoc* basis and name them after the locality near which they were first encountered. For example a common soil around Hamble in Hampshire was a deep well-drained silty soil developed in brickearth. This soil was then called the Hamble series, and the name was applied whenever similar soils were found elsewhere. Soils which the surveyor considered were sufficiently different were given a different name, e.g. Hook series which were like the Hamble series but showed signs of significant drainage impedance, and so had a different horizon sequence. Thus the definition of a soil series became 'a grouping of soils with similar horizons developed in lithologically similar parent materials and named after the locality where first described'.

These series were often only loosely defined and where they were more rigorously defined it tended to be on the basis of properties which enabled the surveyor to recognise different soils and hence to make a map. He or she was not usually too concerned with the niceties of the higher levels of a soil classification system. Thus, as already noted, it was frequently found that a useful soil series for mapping did not conveniently fit into the higher categories of the system. Moreover soil surveyors in different parts of the country often used their own local series names for a soil which had already been described and named elsewhere.

Following the introduction of the soil classification system for England and Wales the opportunity was taken to rationalise and redefine the various series and so make them 'fit' the classification. The new definition of the soil series is 'a subdivision of a subgroup based on narrowly defined diagnostic properties inherited from the soil parent material'. Soil series are defined using a combination of the broad type of parent material, the texture(s) of the soil profile and the presence or absence of material with distinctive mineralogy. To some extent making these new definitions fit the higher categories is achieved at the expense of easy recognition in the field which was the basis of the original concept of a soil series.

A manual describing the criteria for differentiating soil series has been published. It is of Byzantine complexity and is most definitely not for the beginner. Even those who would claim some pedological expertise find it difficult if not downright impossible to use. There is, however, a much easier way in practice to end up with either the correct series name for your soil profile or at least a series which is closely related to the correct one. This is to use the keys provided for most of the soil associations in the bulletins accompanying the national soil map. This approach 'short-cuts' you past all the main complexities of the criteria for differentiating soil series, but it does require you to have some idea of the soil environment in which you are working.

Let us assume, for example, that you have been describing soils in an upland area of Wales. On the national soil map you might find the area you are working in labelled, say, 611c. Reference to the legend would tell you this was the Manod Association, a group of geographically related soils in which the Manod series was the commonest, but where several other series were also likely to be found (see Chapter 5). If you look up the regional bulletin for Wales under the Manod Association you will find a key to the component series such as Table 4.6.

Table 4.6 — A typical key to component series within a soil association in the national soil map for England and Wales

	Description	Series
	Shallow soils, rock within 30 cm; fine loamy	Powys
	Deeper soils	1
1	Rock within 80 cm	2
	Deeper soils; brightly coloured subsoil, fine loamy	Meline
2	With dark, humose or peaty topsoil; fine loamy	Parc
	With thin, surface leaf mould or brown, distinct topsoil	3
3	With brightly coloured subsoil	4
	With brown suboil	5
4	Fine loamy	Manod
	Coarse loamy	Withnell
5	Fine loamy	Denbigh
	Fine silty	Barton

Source: Rudeforth *et al.* (1984).

Your profile (actually Table 4.3, Profile 1) is briefly as follows:

0 –22 cm Ap	Dark brown, slightly stony, clay loam
22–70 cm Bw	Brown, moderately stony, clay loam
70 -100 cm Cu	Yellowish brown weathering siltstone, very stony with matrix of clay loam.

You should be able to 'key out' your soil as likely to belong to the Denbigh series by following the route 'deeper soils, go to 1', '1 Rock within 80 cm, go to 2', '2 With brown distinct topsoil, go to 3', '3 With brown subsoil, go to 5', and finally, '5. Fine loamy Denbigh'. As confirmation you could read the description given for a typical Denbigh soil and see whether 'your' Denbigh is essentially the same. As further confirmation you could look up the index where you would discover that there is an association dominated by and so named after the Denbigh soil. Under the heading for this association (actually No. 541j) you will find a slightly different key to component soils, but which will still 'key out' your profile as Denbigh series. This method is not infallible, but you stand more chance of getting the correct series or an sensible 'near miss' than if you tried to use the main manual.

You may have also noticed that there is the possibility of some mild cheating. You need not have annotated the horizons in your profile nor worked out its name in the higher categories of the system to apply the keys. When you have discovered a series name, in this case the Denbigh, you will see in the extended legend for the national map (a slim brown booklet) that each series has a three digit code which actually gives its full classification in the higher levels. The Denbigh series is coded 541 which means (see Table 4.4) that it is a typical brown earth.

4.3   LEGEND OF THE FAO/UNESCO SOIL MAP OF THE WORLD
4.3.1   General description
In 1974 FAO–UNESCO published the Legend volume for the 1:5 000 000 Soil Map of the World, intended as a means of describing the dominant and subsidiary map units, but which is effectively a soil classification system. It is probably the only classification which is both truly international and capable of universal application, though advocates of the USDA Soil Taxonomy would also claim it was capable of universal application.

There are 26 soil groups, conveniently one for each letter of the alphabet, e.g. P for podzols, C for chernozems, Z for solonchaks as set out in Table 4.7. One hundred and six soil units are recognised, denoted by a lower-case letter, e.g. Pg for gleyic podzols. The groups and units are defined by the assemblage of characteristic soil horizons and these too have upper- and lower-case letter notation. You should therefore be careful when dealing with the FAO–UNESCO system not to confuse, for example, Cg which may mean an entire soil unit, a glossic chernozem, or alternatively a horizon of gleyed (g) parent material (C).

As with other soil classifications, reference has to be made to the manual (in this case called the *Legend*) for the full definitions of the horizons and soil groups and units. The account given below is necessarily abbreviated but should be sufficient to enable you to give a reasonably accurate FAO–UNESCO name to any soil profile you have to deal with, if used in conjunction with the key in Table 4.8.

Table 4.7 — The soil groups and units of the FAO/UNESCO Soil Map of the World Legend
(Source: adapted from Dudal *et al.*, 1974)

A	**ACRISOLS**	**G**	**GLEYSOLS**	**N**	**NITOSOLS**	**U**	**RANKERS**
Af	Ferric Acrisols	Gc	Calcaric Gleysols	Nd	Dystric Nitosols		
Ag	Gleyic Acrisols	Gd	Dystric Gleysols	Ne	Eutric Nitosols	**V**	**VERTISOLS**
Ah	Humic Acrisols	Ge	Eutric Gleysols	Nh	Humic Nitosols	Vc	Chromic Vertisols
Ao	Orthic Acrisols	Gh	Humic Gleysols			Vp	Pellic Vertisols
Ap	Plinthic Acrisols	Gm	Mollic Gleysols	**O**	**HISTOSOLS**		
		Gp	Plinthic Gleysols	Od	Dystric Histosols	**W**	**PLANOSOLS**
B	**CAMBISOLS**	Gx	Gelic Gleysols	Oe	Eutric Histosols	Wd	Dystric Planosols
Bc	Chromic Cambisols			Ox	Gelic Histosols	We	Eutric Planosols
Bd	Dystric Cambisols	**H**	**PHAEOZEMS**			Wh	Humic Planosols
Be	Eutric Cambisols	Hc	Calcaric Phaeozems	**P**	**PODZOLS**	Wm	Mollic Planosols
Bf	Ferralic Cambisols	Hg	Gleyic Phaeozems	Pf	Ferric Podzols	Ws	Solodic Planosols
Bg	Gleyic Cambisols	Hh	Haplic Phaeozems	Pg	Gleyic Podzols	Wx	Gelic Planosols
Bh	Humic Cambisols	Hl	Luvic Phaeozems	Ph	Humic Podzols		
Bk	Calcic Cambisols			Pl	Leptic Podzols	**X**	**XEROSOLS**
Bv	Vertic Cambisols	**I**	**LITHOSOLS**	Po	Orthic Podzols	Xh	Haplic Xerosols
Bx	Gelic Cambisols			Pp	Placic Podzols	Xk	Calcic Xerosols
		J	**FLUVISOLS**			Xl	Luvic Xerosols
C	**CHERNOZEMS**	Jc	Calcaric Fluvisols	**Q**	**ARENOSOLS**	Xy	Gypsic Xerosols
Cg	Glossic Chernozems	Jd	Dystric Fluvisols	Qa	Albic Arenosols		
Ch	Haplic Chernozems	Je	Eutric Fluvisols	Qc	Cambic Arenosols	**Y**	**YERMOSOLS**
Ck	Calcic Chernozems	Jt	Thionic Fluvisols	Qf	Ferralic Arenosols	Yh	Haplic Yermosols
Cl	Luvic Chernozems			Ql	Luvic Arenosols	Yk	Calcic Yermosols
		K	**KASTANOZEMS**			Yl	Luvic Yermosols
D	**PODZOLUVISOLS**	Kh	Haplic Kastanozems	**R**	**REGOSOLS**	Yt	Takyric Yermosols
Dd	Dystric Podzoluvisols	Kk	Calcic Kastanozems	Rc	Calcaric Regosols	Yy	Gypsic Yermosols
De	Eutric Podzoluvisols	Kl	Luvic Kastanozems	Rd	Dystric Regosols		
Dg	Gleyic Podzoluvisols			Re	Eutric Regosols	**Z**	**SOLONCHAKS**
		L	**LUVISOLS**	Rx	Gelic Regosols	Zg	Gleyic Solonchaks
E	**RENDZINAS**	La	Albic Luvisols			Zm	Mollic Solonchaks
		Lc	Chromic Luvisols	**S**	**SOLONETZ**	Zo	Orthic Solonchaks
F	**FERRALSOLS**	Lf	Ferric Luvisols	Sg	Gleyic Solonetz	Zt	Takyric Solonchaks
Fa	Acric Ferralsols	Lg	Gleyic Luvisols	Sm	Mollic Solonetz		
Fh	Humic Ferralsols	Lk	Calcic Luvisols	So	Orthic Solonetz		
Fo	Orthic Ferralsols	Lo	Orthic Luvisols				
Fp	Plinthic Ferralsols	Lp	Plinthic Luvisols	**T**	**ANDOSOLS**		
Fr	Rhodic Ferralsols	Lv	Vertic Luvisols	Th	Humic Andosols		
Fx	Xanthic Ferralsols			Tm	Mollic Andosols		
		M	**GREYZEMS**	To	Ochric Andosols		
		Mg	Gleyic Greyzems	Tv	Vitric Andosols		
		Mo	Orthic Greyzems				

1985 REVISED LEGEND

A Revised Legend was introduced in 1985 (FAO, 1985), but the original legend remains the one to be used for reading and interpreting the 1:5 000 000 FAO/UNESCO Soil Map of the World. The Revised Legend will be used, however, for updating the maps and for the preparation of all new maps at the same or larger scale. The main changes to the Soil Groups are given below but there are numerous minor changes also.

E	RENDZINAS	
I	LITHOSOLS	now amalgamated as a new group I LEPTOSOLS
U	RANKERS	
X	XEROSOLS	deleted since main justification was the non-soil property of arid climate. Arid region soils
Y	YERMOSOLS	now to be named according to intrinsic soil properties. See C CALCISOLS below
L	LUVISOLS	split into those with high clay activity which remain L LUVISOLS and those with low clay activity which form a new Group E LIXISOLS
A	ACRISOLS	split into those with high clay activity which remain A ACRISOLS and those with low clay activity which form a new Group U ALISOLS
C	CALCISOLS	a new Group for soils whose dominant soil forming process is the accumulation of calcium carbonate and/or gypsum
X	PLINTHOSOLS	a new Group for soils containing plinthite (formerly grouped with F FERRALSOLS)
*	ANTHROSOLS	a new Group for soils strongly influenced by human interference

There are also important changes to the definitions of some diagnostic horizons and properties notably the argillic and oxic B horizons and introduction of new terms such as 'fimic A horizon' (equivalent to the plaggen and anthropic epipedons of Soil Taxonomy) and 'fluvic properties' to improve the definition of Fluvisols.

Table 4.8 — A key to the groups of the FAO–UNESCO Soil map of the World, Legend

Description	Soil group
1. *Soils characterised by very weak profile development (a weak A horizon directly on C)*	
On hard rock	Lithosol I
On loose materials	Regosol R
2 *Soils linked to specific parent materials and with relatively limited profile development*	
Peat, more than 40 cm deep	Histosol O
On alluvium (AC soils)	Fluvisol J
On highly calcareous materials (AC soils)	Rendzina E
On sand (AC or ABwC soils)	Arenosol Q
On volcanic ash (AC or ABwC soils)	Andosol T
3 *Other AC soils with a umbric A horizon*	Ranker U
4 *Soils with permafrost within 2 m of the surface*	gelic cambisol
	gelic gleysol
	or gelic histosol
5 *Soils of desert and semi-desert climate which have horizons due to diffgerential weathering or movement of clay, calcium carbonate or sulphate*	
With an A horizon having more than 1% organic matter on average in the top 40 cm	Xerosol X
With A horizon lower in organic matter	Yermosol Y
6 *Soils with a mollic A horizon, with or without a Bt horizon*	
No subsoil accumulation of secondary carbonate and/or sulphate	Phaeozem H
With subsoil accumulation of secondary carbonate and/or sulphate	
Very dark A horizon	Chernozem C
Brown A horizon	Kastanozem K
7 *Soils with high salinity in some part of the profile*	
With natric B horizon	Solonetz S
Without natric B horizon and not on recent alluvium	Solonchak Z
Without natric B but with planosol features (see below)	Solodic planosol
8 *Clayey soils with vertic features indicating strong swelling and shrinking*	Vertisol V
9 *Soils gleyed within 50 cm but lacking Bt, Bs, Bf or Bh horizons, other than recent alluvial soils*	Gleysol G
10 *Soils with Bs, Bf, and/or Bh horizons*	Podzol P
11 *Soils with an oxic B horizon and usually no Bt horizon*	Ferralsol F
12 *Soils characterised by the presence of a Bt horizon*	
With a bleached E horizon, gleyed at least in part and with abrupt lower boundary and with a slowly permeable horizon within 125 cm of the surface (not a spodic B)	Planosol W
With a bleached E horizon, often gleyed, deeply tongued into the Bt	Podzoluvisol D

Table 4.8 (*Contd.*)

Description	Soil group
With a dark A horizon and bleached ped surfaces beneath	Greyzem M
Other soils without a very dark A but with a very thick Bt (clay content does not decrease much from maximum within 150 cm of surface	Nitosol N
Other soils without a very dark A but with a high base content (over 50% saturated) in the Bt	Luvisol L
Other soils without a very dark A and with a lower base content in the Bt	Acrisol A
13 *Other soils with A and Bw horizons*	Cambisol B

Some of the full definitions are a little vague and require some subjective judgement while conversely others have strict criteria which involve quite detailed laboratory analysis and are not suitable for immediate decisions in the field. In this latter case most pedologists will base their initial classification on other signs in the profile and await later confirmation or denial by the laboratory staff.

4.3.2   Master and diagnostic soil horizons
The master horizons are listed below followed by an explanation of the suffixes which can be applied to them. Some combinations of master horizon and suffix(es) together with some additional criteria make up the so-called **diagnostic horizons** by means of which the groups and units are defined. Attention is drawn to these diagnostic horizons such as mollic A, oxic B and albic E in the summary which follows. Note that the precise definitions of the horizons, especially the diagnostic ones (e.g. cambic or umbric) are complex and the following is much abbreviated. You should refer to the full legend as necessary.

The FAO–UNESCO horizon nomenclature is as follows.

H   Peat.
A diagnostic histic horizon is an H horizon 20–40 cm thick (or thicker if very loose) *or* at least 25 cm of ploughed or mixed topsoil of high organic content depending on texture (from at least 14% in non-clayey soils to at least 28% in clays).

O   Surface organic horizon other than peat.
A   Organo-mineral topsoil.
A diagnostic mollic A horizon is a well-structured, deep or moderately deep, ploughed or mixed topsoil which has not enough organic matter to be histic but is usually significantly darker than the subsoil though fairly dull in colour (not high Munsell chroma). It must have a base saturation above 50%. The precise criteria including thickness minima are complex.

A diagnostic umbric A horizon is similar but has a base saturation of less than 50%. Again the precise criteria are complex.

A diagnostic ochric A horizon is too light in colour, has too high a Munsell chroma (i.e. too brightly coloured), too little organic matter or is too thin to be a mollic or umbric horizon, or it is hard and massive when dry.

E   Eluvial horizon (material removed).

A diagnostic albic horizon is a 'bleached' E horizon whose colour is determined by the primary silt and sand (not the clay and iron compounds as is usual) and is hence usually whitish in colour.

B   Weathered subsoil or an illuvial horizon (material washed in).

A diagnostic cambic B horizon is a weathered Bw horizon without accumulations of illuviated clay (see argillic and natric below) or illuviated organically complexed iron and aluminium compounds (see spodic below). It excludes very sandy or stony horizons. It must have significant amounts of weatherable minerals (cf. oxic below) and evidence of weathering.

A diagnostic oxic B horizon is a highly weathered Bw horizon with low CEC and with no more than traces of primary aluminosilicate minerals such as felspars, micas, ferromagnesian minerals, etc. It lacks argillic or natric features (see below).

A diagnostic argillic B horizon (Bt) has an accumulation of clay washed in from above, but no natric properties. There are precise and complex requirements for qualification as an argillic B horizon based on:

(a) the increase in clay content as compared with overlying horizons;
(b) the thickness of the horizon compared with the rest of the profile;
(c) the presence of clay skins (cutans or other evidence for clay illuviation).

A diagnostic natric B horizon (Btn) has the properties of an argillic B horizon but in addition has high exchangeable sodium or magnesium and usually a marked columnar or prismatic structure in some part.

A diagnostic spodic B horizon (Bs and Bh) has accumulated sesquioxides (extractable with solutions of pyrophosphate or dithionite–citrate) and/or organic matter illuviated from above. The precise criteria are particularly tortuous and complex, requiring detailed laboratory analyses.

C   Soft geological material, little altered (other than by reduction).
R   Hard geological material.

Diagnostic horizons also include those which would classed (see below) as calcic (suffix k), gypsic (suffix y) or sulphuric. These are usually B horizons but can be C or even A horizons.

The suffixes applied to the horizon designations are listed below. Usually only one or at most two are applied.

b   Buried or bisequel soil horizon, e.g. Btb.
c   Concretionary; normally used in combination, e.g. Bck or Bcs.
g   Gleyed, i.e. mottled, normally due to seasonal waterlogging.
h   Humus accumulation in mineral horizons, e.g. Ah; used in topsoils only if unploughed; so h and p suffixes are mutually exclusive.
k   Accumulation of calcium carbonate. This constitutes a diagnostic calcic horizon, subject to minimal requirements of 15 cm thickness, at least 15% calcium carbonate, and at least 5% more calcium carbonate than in the C horizon.
m   Strongly cemented, consolidated or indurated; usually used in combination with a suffix indicating cementing material, e.g. Bms, an ironpan.

n   Accumulation of sodium.

p   Ploughed or tilled; see h above.

q   Accumulation of silica, e.g. Cmq silcrete in a C horizon.

r   Strongly reduced as a result of ground-water influence, e.g. Cr.

s   Accumulation of sesquioxides (hydrous oxides of iron and aluminium).

t   Accumulation of illuviated clay, e.g. Bt or Btn.

u   Unspecified; used where a meaningless symbol is required as in horizon subdivisions to give for example Bu1 and Bu2 rather than B1 and B2 which can have erroneous connotations from other classification systems.

w   *In situ* alteration or weathering

x   compact and brittle but not strongly cemented; a fragipan.

y   Accumulation of gypsum. This constitutes a diagnostic gypsic horizon, subject to minimal requirements of 15 cm thickness, at least 5% more gypsum than in the C horizon and a product of the thickness (in centimetres) and percentage gypsum of 150 or more.

z   Accumulation of salts more soluble than gypsum.

Horizons can be subdivided by numeral suffixes placed after the letter suffixes, e.g. Bt1, Bt2.

Where the profile contains lithological discontinuities Arabic numerals are prefixed, e.g. A,B,2C, where the C horizon differs from the material in which the soil is presumed to have formed.

Other terms used in describing horizons and profiles but for which there are no specific suffixes include the following:

Base saturation — The proportion of the exchange complex of the soil (see Chapter 1) saturated with bases. A distinction is drawn between high- and low-base status depending as the base saturation is above or below 50%.

Fragipan — A special kind of compact but brittle subsoil horizon (precise definition complex).

Gelic — The presence of permafrost.

Hydromorphic properties — Features indicating waterlogging such as a histic H, gleying (see suffix g above), plinthite, or evidence based on observations in boreholes. The precise definitions are complex.

Plinthite — A soft iron-rich humus-poor clay usually occurring in tropical soils as red mottles, in platy, polygonal or reticulate patterns and which dries irreversibly to hard ironstone (or laterite).

Sulphidic and Sulphuric — Sulphidic horizons are waterlogged horizons containing material which, on drainage and oxidation form sulphuric acid and produce highly acid sulphuric horizons. The two can be jointly referred to as thionic.

Vertic — Refers to features associated with dark swelling tropical clays, including hummocky 'gilgai' microrelief and deep shrinkage cracks.

Slickensides — Polished and grooved surfaces usually on ped faces caused by one mass sliding past another, e.g. in swelling clays (see vertic).

4.3.3 Soil groups

The summary below gives brief descriptions and requirements for the FAO–UNESCO soil groups, with some of the 'traditional' though often ill-defined names which pedologists are likely to have used previously.

A   Acrisols — Soils with an argillic Bt horizon, acid and low- base status; often with brightly coloured subsoil (red–yellow podzolic soils).

Must have umbric or ochric A and a Bt with less than 50% base saturation. No features diagnostic of groups D, N or W.

Compare with luvisols (Bt with more than 50% base saturation) and ferralsols (with oxic rather than argillic B).

Units are orthic, ferric, humic, plinthic and gleyic

B   Cambisols — Soils with main feature a cambic B (brown earths).

Must have cambic B (unless umbric A is thicker than 25 cm). Can have ochric or umbric A, or a calcic or gypsic horizon. Can have hydromorphic features below 50 cm. No features diagnostic of groups T, V or Z.

Compare with acrisols, ferralsols, luvisols.

Units are eutric, dystric, humic, gleyic, gelic, calcic, chromic, vertic or ferralic.

C   Chernozems — Black steppe soils with thick mollic A horizons rich in organic matter.

Must have a dark mollic A at least 15 cm deep. Must have one or more of calcic B, gypsic B or lime accumulation within 125 cm of surface. Can have hydromorphic properties below 50 cm; can have Bt. No features diagnostic of groups E, S, T, V, W or Z.

Compare with greyzems (similar but with bleached coatings on ped surfaces and usually a Bt), phaeozems (lacking calcic or gypsic features within 125 cm of surface) and kastanozems (paler coloured mollic A).

Units are haplic, calcic, luvic and glossic (with tonguing of A into B or C).

D   Podzoluvisols — Soils with argillic Bt and deep tonguing of E into Bt, or having iron nodules over Bt (Intermediate between podzols and luvisols, sod-podzolic soils).

Must have argillic Bt and features described above. No mollic A. Can have hydromorphic features below 50 cm.

Compare with luvisols (Bt with no tonguing, etc.).

Units are eutric, dystric and gleyic.

E   Rendzinas — Shallow soils in highly calcareous material (other than recent alluvium).

No diagnostic horizons other than mollic A horizon directly over highly calcareous material. No vertic features.

Compare with rankers (similar but non-calcareous).

Not subdivided into units.

F   Ferralsols — Strongly weathered soils of the humic tropics characterised by an oxic horizon (latosols, lateritic soils, ferralitic soils, oxisols).

Must have an oxic B. Can have plinthite within 125cm of surface.

Compare with acrisols (less weathered).

Units are Orthic, xanthic, rhodic, humic, acric and plinthic.

G   Gleysols — Soils with hydromorphic (i.e. gley) features above 50 cm. (Ground-water gleys.)

Units are eutric, calcaric, dystric, mollic, humic, plinthic and gelic (tundra soils).

No diagnostic horizons (except buried ones). Can have A, histic H, cambic B and calcic or gypsic horizons. No features diagnostic of groups J, S, V or Z.

Compare with fluvisols (non gleyed in alluvium) and gleyic units of other groups.

Units are eutric, calcaric, dystric, mollic, humic, plinthic and gelic (tundra soils).

H   Phaeozems — Like chernozems but without a calcic or gypsic horizon or an accumulation of lime within 125 cm (Prairie soils).

Must have a mollic A. Can (and usually does) have a Bt. No features diagnostic of groups E, G, S, T, V or W.

Compare with chernozems (lime and/or gypsum accumulations within 125 cm) and greyzems (bleached coatings on peds).

Units are haplic, calcaric, luvic and gleyic.

I   Lithosols — Very shallow soils (less than 10 cm thick) over rock.

J   Fluvisols — Soils in recent alluvium or colluvium (alluvial soils).

No diagnostic horizons (except buried ones). Can have ochric or umbric A, histic H or sulphuric horizon. Profile features due more to depositional history than to pedogenesis.

Compare with gleysols (diagnostic gleyed horizons), lithosols (incipient soils not in alluvium) and more mature soils in the area.

Units are eutric, calcaric, dystric and sulphuric or thionic (acid sulphate soils).

K   Kastanozems — Similar to chernozems but paler mollic A horizon, shallower horizons and calcic and/or gypsic B horizons (chestnut soils).

Horizons like chernozems but mollic A having a Munsell chroma of more than 2. No features diagnostic of groups E, S, T, V, W or Z.

Compare with chernozems, phaeozems, greyzems (see comparisons under chernozems).

Units are haplic, calcic and luvic.

L   Luvisols — Soils with an argillic Bt horizon of high-base status (argillic brown earths, grey–brown podzolic soils).

Must have a Bt horizon with base saturation at least 50% within 125 cm of the surface (cf. acrisols). No mollic A. No features diagnostic of groups D, N or W.

Compare with cambisols (lack Bt), planosols (more extreme textural profiles of albic E horizons over slowly permeable Bt), nitosols (tropical soils usually over basic rocks with high organic matter in Bt) or podzoluvisols (E tonguing into Bt).

Groups are orthic, chromic, calcic, vertic, ferric, albic, plinthic and gleyic.

M   Greyzems — Like phaeozems but with bleached coatings on ped surfaces (grey forest soils of cool temperate zones).

Must have dark mollic A at least 15 cm thick and bleached coatings on ped surfaces. Usually with Bt. Can have hydromorphic features below 50 cm. No features diagnostic of groups E, S, T, V or W.

Compare with phaeozems (no bleached ped surfaces) and chernozems and kastanozems (with lime and/or gypsum accumulations).

Units are orthic and gleyic.

N   Nitosols — Soils with a thick argillic Bt with a clay content which does not decrease much from maximum within 125 cm of surface.

Must have Bt as specified above, and usually with high organic matter. No mollic A or albic E. No features diagnostic of groups D or V.

Compare with ferralsols, vertisols (with vertic features) and planosols (with marked textural variation down the profile).

Units are eutric, dystric and humic.

O   Histosols — Peats or organic soils.

Must have a histic H.

Compare with humic units of other groups.

Units are eutric, dystric and gelic.

P   Podzols — Soils characterised by the removal of iron and aluminium compounds from an E horizon, their migration as organic complexes and deposition in a spodic B horizon.

Must have a spodic B horizon. Can have an E, thin ironpan or hydromorphic properties within 50 cm of the surface.

Compare with podzoluvisols.

Groups are orthic, leptic, ferric, humic, placic and gleyic.

Q   Arenosols — Soils in coarse-textured unconsolidated material (other than recent alluvium).

Must have recognisable B horizon though too sandy to qualify as argillic, cambic or oxic, or at least 50 cm albic material. Can have ochric A.

Compare with fluvisols (in recent alluvium including sandy) and less sandy soils of the area.

Units are cambic, luvic, ferralic and albic.

R   Regosols — Soils with weak profile development (AC soils) in loose materials (other than recent alluvium).

No diagnostic horizons. Lacking features diagnostic of other groups. Can have ochric A.

Compare with lithosols (similar over hard rock), arenosols (on sand with cambic or oxic B), andosols (on volcanic ash), rendzinas (on highly calcareous deposits) and vertisols (vertic features).

Units are eutric, calcaric, dystric and gelic.

S   Solonetz — Sodic and alkaline soils with a natric B horizon.

Must have Btn (natric horizon). Can have hydromorphic properties below 50 cm. Must not have albic E showing hydromorphic properties and abrupt textural change (both characteristic of planosols). No vertic features.

Compare with planosols (see above) and solonchaks.

Units are orthic, mollic and gleyic.

T   Andosols — Soils on recent volcanic ash (at least 60% volcanic material).

Must have mollic or umbric A. Can have Bw in which case ochric A also allowed. Must have bulk density less than 0.85 g/cm. No vertic features.

Compare with regosols (can include incipient soils on volcanic ash) and Ferralsols (more highly weathered).

Units are ochric, mollic, humic and vitric.

U Rankers — Shallow soils over rock (AR soils).

No diagnostic horizons other than umbric A horizon less than 25 cm thick. No features diagnostic of groups T or V.

Compare with rankers (similar but calcareous), andosols (over volcanic ash) and regosols (over unconsolidated material).

Not subdivided into units.

V Vertisols — Dark clays rich in swelling clay minerals giving marked shrink—swell (vertic) features, especially deep shrinkage cracks, gilgai microrelief and subsoil structures characteristic of shrink—swell clays.

No diagnostic horizons but must have more than 30% clay to a depth of 50 cm and vertic features as above.

Compare with some clayey fluvisols (no vertic features).

Units are pellic and chromic.

W Planosols — Soils with an albic E horizon having hydromorphic properties and a slowly permeable B horizon.

Must have an argillic or natric B showing an abrupt textural change, a heavy clay or a fragipan creating a slowly permeable horizon, overlain by an albic E with hydromorphic properties in at least part of the horizon.

Compare with luvisols, gleysols and nitosols; none with abrupt textural changes.

Units are eutric, dystric, mollic, humic, solodic and gelic.

X Xerosols — Soils of arid and semi-arid climates (sierozems or semi-desert soils).

Must have a very weak ochric A but usually with more than 0.5% organic matter. Can have cambic B, argillic B, calcic or gypsic horizons. No features diagnostic of groups V or Z.

Compare with yermosols (similar but ochric A has less than 0.5% organic matter) and some arenosols (in sand).

Units are haplic, calcic, gypsic and luvic.

Y Yermosols — Soils of arid and semi-arid climates (desert soils).

Must have a very weak ochric A with less than 0.5% organic matter. Can have cambic B, argillic B, calcic or gypsic horizons. No features diagnostic of groups V or Z.

Compare with xerosols (similar but ochric A has 0.5–1.0% organic matter) and some arenosols (in sand).

Units are haplic, calcic, gypsic, luvic and takyric (see Solonchaks).

Z Solonchaks — Saline soils (other than in recent alluvium).

No diagnostic horizons. Can have A, histic H, cambic B, calcic or gypsic horizons and hydromorphic features.

Compare with solonetz.

Units are orthic, mollic, takyric (drying to hard crust with polygonal cracks) and gleyic.

Table 4.9 — A key to descriptive adjectives used for FAO–UNESCO soil units

Adjective	Symbol	Major property[a]	A Acrisols	B Cambisols	C Chernozems	D Podzoluvisols	F Ferralsols	G Gleysols	H Phaeozems	J Fluvisols	K Kastanozems	L Luvisols	M Greyzems	N Nitosols	O Histosols	P Podzols	Q Arenosols	R Regosols	S Solonetz	T Andosols	V Vertisols	W Planosols	X Xerosols	Y Yermosols	Z Solonchaks
Acric	a	Weathered; CEC<1.5 milliequivalents per 100 g of clay in B horizon					X																		
Albic	a	Containing albic material															X								
Calcaric	c	Accumulation of $CaCO_3$						X	X	X	X							X							
Calcic	k	Having a calcic horizon									X												X	X	
Cambic	c	Having a cambic B horizon		X	X																				
Chromic	c	High chromas		X								X									X				
Dystric	d	Low-base status — low fertility bulk sodium percentage <50%	X	X		X		X	X	X				X	X			X				X			
Eutri	e	High-base status — moderate to high fertility bulk sodium percentage >50%		X		X		X	X	X				X	X			X				X			
Ferralic	f	Showing ferralic properties (high sesquioxides)	X														X								
Ferric	f	Showing ferric properties		X										X		X	X								
Gelic	x	Containing permafrost	X	X				X	X	X					X			X							
Gleyic	g	Showing hydromorphic features	X	X	X	X	X	X	X	X			X	X	X	X			X			X			X
Glossic	g	Having an umbric A or histic B horizon			X						X								X						
Gypsic	y	Having a gypsic horizon																					X	X	X
Haplic	h	Unit with normal horizon sequence	X	X	X			X	X		X	X		X		X		X	X				X	X	

Term	Code	Description
Humic	h	Having an umbric A horizon
Leptic	l	Weakly developed; see FAO–UNESCO (1974, p. 39)
Luvic	l	Having an argillic B horizon
Mollic	m	Having a mollic A horizon
Ochric	o	Having an ochric A horizon
Orthic	o	Most commonly occurring; 'typical' unit
Pellic	p	Low moist chromas of <1.5
Placic	p	Thin ironpan over spodic B horizon
Plinthic	p	Containing plinthite
Rhodic	r	Red to dusky red oxic B horizon
Solodic	s	>60% exchangeable sodium in slowly permeable horizon
Takyric	t	Barren, showing takyric features
Thionic	t	Having a sulphuric horizon
Vertic	v	Showing vertic properties
Vitric	v	Lacking a smeary consistence
Xanthic	x	Yellow to pale yellow oxic B horizon

[a] Highly abbreviated; full definitions are given in FAO–UNESCO (1974, pp. 32–41).
[b] Lithosols (I), rendzinas (E) and rankers (U) are not listed, since they are not subdivided.
Source: Landon (1984).

4.3.4   Naming a soil profile

In order to give a FAO–UNESCO name to a soil you should start with the key in Table 4.8 which is intended to guide you towards the correct group. Start at the beginning and compare your soil with the first group description. If the soil does not match this group description then pass on to the next group in the list until you find a match. At this stage you should then consult the summary of groups given above and check that the soil conforms to the requirements set out for that group.

Check also the requirements for the groups mentioned for comparison, and in particular any subgroup whose name indicates a transition towards the group you have chosen, using Table 4.9. For example if you thought the soil was a gleysol you should also look at the descriptions of the gleyic units in other groups. Finally you may want to refer to the full legend for the exact definitions of the group and unit. You may care to try to derive the FAO–UNESCO group and unit for the examples given in Table 4.10(a) (answers are given in Table 4.10(b)

Table 4.10(a) — Typical soil profiles for FAO/UNESCO system.

Soil 1
Saskatchewan, Canada; rolling glacial till landscape, grassland

0–24 cm	Black, ploughed, well structured slightly calcareous sandy clay loam with about 5% organic matter
24–72 cm	Brown sandy clay loam, weak blocky structure, slightly calcareous
72+ cm	Light brown sandy clay loam, weak blocky structure very calcareous (about 10–15%), with some of the calcium carbonate in fine threads and coatings along fissures
	Hint: the kind of A horizon is important.

Soil 2
India; flat alluvial plain; crop stubble

0–22 cm	Brownish grey, weakly structured humus deficient sandy loam, pH 6.4.
22–70 cm	Dark brown sandy clay, well developed columnar structure with rounded tops, fissures filled with pale grey clay, pH 8.5
70+ cm	Light brown, dense, poorly structured sandy clay with greyish and reddish brown mottles, pH 9.0, saline

Soil 3
Scotland, hollow in glacial till landscape, arable (but crop poor)

0–18 cm	Black, sandy clay loam, pH 3.6
18–30 cm	Greyish brown clay loam with grey and brown mottles
3–50 cm	Grey, greyish brown and strong brown mottled clay loam
50+ cm	Massive grey and brown mottled clay

Soil 4
South East England, steeply sloping chalk escarpment, scrub woodland

0–15 cm	Black, humose silt loam, very calcareous, well structured, abundant small lumps of chalk
15+ cm	Hard fissured chalk

Table 4.10(b) — Answers to Table 4.10(a)

Soil 1 Haplic chernozem. The A horizon is mollic and there is evidence for accumulation of calcium carbonate, though the amount in the subsoil is not enough to constitute a calcic horizon. The Group is Haplic, i.e. 'normal', since there is no evidence for clay accumulation either.

Soil 2 Gleyic solonetz. The characteristic columnar structure with rounded tops is diagnostic of the natric horizon of a Solonetz; the mottling at depth constitutes hydromorphic features, hence the Group is Gleyic.

Soil 3 Humic gleysol. The profile is strongly gleyed, hence Gleysol and the topsoil with its low pH is umbric rather than mollic; there is insufficient organic matter to constitute a histic horizon hence Humic Gleysol rather than Histosol.

Soil 4 Rendzina. Very calcareous, with A horizon directly over chalk, i.e. limited profile development and linked to a specific parent material; no Group separation.

4.4 THE SOIL TAXONOMY

4.4.1 General description

In the 1950s dissatisfaction with the soil classification systems then in use led pedologists of the USDA to devise a completely new system. At six points in the development of the scheme a draft was given limited circulation for comments, and in 1960 the Seventh approximation appeared, by which name it subsequently became widely known. Further revisions then took place culminating in the definitive system, called the Soil Taxonomy. USDA published the handbook *Soil Taxonomy* in 1975.

Previous soil names and assumed relationships were set aside and a completely new nomenclature was devised. This nomenclature is regarded as either one of the best or one of the worst features of the system. Its advocates point out the logic of the names and the use of formative elements whereby the place of any soil in the system can be easily established. Its detractors bemoan the loss of old familiar (but often badly and/or ambiguously defined) names such as solonetz and their replacement by new discordant names such as natrixeralf.

The second contentious feature of the system is that it is based on observed soil properties rather than on assumed genetic relationships, which annoys pedologists who have spent their lives studying how soils form and trying to divine an underlying rationale. The system claims to be able to allocate any profile unambiguously to a class, but in order to achieve this the definitions are lengthy, complex and with a style reminiscent of legal jargon. Many of the definitions involve laboratory analyses or long-term observations which makes the system difficult to apply in the field unless you are prepared to make some inspired guesses to be confirmed or revised later. Other criticisms include inadequate treatment of tropical and some desert region soils and the relegation of any consideration of hydromorphic soils to lower levels of the classification.

The Soil Taxonomy is based partly on on the recognition of diagnostic horizons, partly on other soil properties and partly on climatic criteria. A brief description of the main diagnostic horizons is given in Table 4.11 but of course the full definitions are much more elaborate and the handbook should be referred to as necessary.

Table 4.11 — The diagnostic horizons of the USDA Soil Taxonomy

Name	Description
Surface horizons (epipedons)	
Histic epipedon	More than 20–30% organic matter (sliding scale with clay content) averaged to 20 cm depth if unploughed. More than 14–28% organic matter if ploughed. Less than 30 cm thick if drained; 45 cm if undrained
Mollic epipedon	More than 1% organic matter, moist value and chroma both <3.5, not hard and massive when dry, more than 50% base saturated, less than 250 ppm citric-soluble P_2O_5. Minimum thickness, 10 cm on rock, 25 cm in deep soils
Anthropic epipedon	Similar to mollic, but more than 250 ppm citric-soluble P_2O_5
Umbric epipedon	Similar to mollic, but less than 50% base saturated
Ochric epipedon	Under 1% organic matter, or else other properties exclude from other epipedons
Plaggen epipedon	A man-made surface layer more than 50 cm thick
Sub-surface illuvial horizons	
Agric horizon	Layer with lamellae of accumulated clay and humus directly below the plough layer
Argillic horizon	(Enriched in clay) contains $>1.2 \times$ clay in horizon above (minimum 3% difference; 8% is always enough), changing within 30 cm vertically. Thickness is $>0.1 \times$ sum of overlying horizons or >15 cm, and contains illuviation argillans (void or grain)
Natric horizon	Similar to the argillic but has 15% + of CEC saturated with sodium
Spodic horizon	Cemented over >2.5 cm thickness with organic matter and iron and/or aluminium oxides and/or has distinctive micromorphology and/or is enriched in amorphous constituents soluble in hot sodium dithionite–pyrophosphate solution
Placic horizon	A thin cemented ironpan
Calcic horizon	(Secondary carbonate accumulation) >15% $CaCO_3$ equivalent (5% more than in C), 15 cm thick
Petrocalcic horizon	As calcic but hard
Gypsic horizon	Secondary $CaSO_4$ accumulation in a horizon >15 cm thick
Petrogypsic horizon	As gypsic but hard
Salic horizon	Accumulation of salts more soluble than calcium sulphate in a horizon >15 cm thick
Duripan	A hard horizon, cemented by silica which does not slake in water
Other horizons	
Cambic horizon	An altered, but not highly weathered, horizon with a texture finer than loamy fine sand
Oxic horizon	A highly weathered horizon, finer than loamy fine sand, with a CEC of less than 16 milliequivalents per 100 g of clay, and with not more than traces of weatherable minerals. Clay not water dispersible
Albic horizon	A bleached horizon with uncoated grains
Fragipan	A horizon with high bulk density; hard when dry but brittle when moist
Plinthite	Soft highly weathered mottled clay. The iron-rich parts harden to give ironstone or concretions when repeatedly wetted and dried
Sulphuric horizon	With yellow jarosite mottles and a pH below 3.5
Sombric horizon	Dark, base-rich subsurface horizon of high-altitude tropical soils with illuvial humus

Source: Adapted from USDA (1975).

Many of the terms used in Soil Taxonomy are similar to those in the FAO–UNESCO system (see above) and for most purposes can be regarded as synonymous. The precise definitions are often different, however, though what each group of workers is trying to define is conceptually the same thing.

The system is hierarchical with ten orders, each with a name containing a formative element which is used in the ensuing names of the suborders, great groups and subgroups. Families and series are defined on properties important to the growth of plants and on properties which help to identify different soils in the field during soil survey. An example of the nomenclature is given in Table 4.12.

Table 4.12 — Examples of the nomenclature of the USDA Soil Taxonomy

Level	Example
Order	Inceptisol (formative element -ept)
Suborder	Ochrept
Great group	Xerochrept
Subgroup	Typic xerochrept
Family	Coarse-loamy, mixed, thermic typic xerochrept
Series	Escondido

4.4.2   Orders and suborders

The list of the ten orders is given in Table 4.13 together with the formative element derivation and indications as to what each order is trying conceptually to define. A brief summary of the orders and suborders is given below but is, of course, highly abbreviated. This is one system where you really do need the full 754–page manual before you can confidently derive the classification of a soil.

A summary of the USDA Soil Taxonomy is as follows.

Entisols (-ent) — May have ochric, anthropic, albic or agric horizons but no others.

Aquents	— Hydromorphic (low chromas).
Arents	— Strongly disturbed by man.
Fluvents	— Alluvial.
Psamments	— Loamy fine sand or coarser to 1 m.
Orthents	— Other entisols.

Vertisols (-ert) — More than 30% clay to 1 m; shrinkage cracks 1 cm wide to 0.05 m; gilgai and/or slickensides and/or strong skew planes.

Torrerts	— Usually dry.
Uderts.	— Usually moist.
Usterts	— Dry for 3 months or more (tropical).
Xererts	— Dry for 3 months or more (subtropical).

Table 4.13 — The nomenclature of the USDA soil taxonomy

Order	Formative element			Main soil types
	Derivation	Mnemonic	Connotation	
Entisol (-ent)	Nonsense symbol	Recent	Young soils	Azonal soils
Vertisol (-ert)	Latin *verto*, turn	Invert	Self-mulching or mixing	Swelling clays
Inceptisol (-ept)	Latin *inceptum*, beginning	Inception	Slightly developed	Brown earths and related soils
Aridisol (-id)	Latin *aridus*, dry	Arid	Arid soils	Desert and semi-desert soils
Mollisol (-oll)	Latin *mollis*, soft	Mollify	Organic rich	Base-rich soils of steppe and grassland
Spodosol (-od)	Greek *spodos*, wood ash	Podzol	Spodic horizon	Podzolised soils
Alfisol (-alf)	Nonsense symbol	Pedalfer	Aluminium and iron	Soils with clay illuviation
Ultisol (-ult)	Latin *ultimus*, last	Ultimate	Weathered	Well-weathered soils of humid subtropics
Oxisol (-ox)	French *oxide*, oxide	Oxide	Oxic horizon	Red tropical soils (latosols)
Histosol (-ist)	Greek *histos*, tissue	Histology	Organic soils	Organic soils peat

Source: Adapted from USDA (1975).

Inceptisols (-ept) — Have a cambic horizon or a fragipan or duripan or a histic or umbric epipedon or are low-bulk-density soils dominated by amorphous materials; no spodic, argillic, gypsic or oxic horizons; no plinthite; no sulphidic material within 50 cm; no salic or natric horizons but includes soils with exchangeable sodium percentage above 15% within 50 cm.

Andepts	— With allophane and/or volcanic ash.
Aquepts	— Hydromorphic (low chromas).
Plaggepts	— With plaggen epipedon.
Tropepts	— Low seasonal temperature variation.
Umbrepts	— With umbric horizon.
Ochrepts	— Other inceptisols.

Aridisols (-id) — Contain salts or are usually dry.

Argids	— With natric or argillic horizon.
Orthids	— Other aridisols.

Mollisols (-oll) — Have a mollic horizon and base saturation above 50%.

Albolls	— Have albic and argillic or natric horizons, both somewhat gleyed.

Aquolls	— Other hydromorphic mollisols.
Borolls	— Mean annual soil temperature below 8°C.
Rendolls	— More than 40% calcium carbonate in C horizon.
Udolls	— Other mollisols, usually moist.
Ustolls	— Dry a total of 90 days or more but not consecutively.
Xerolls	— Dry 60 or more days consecutively.

Spodosols (-od) — Have a spodic horizon or a placic horizon and a fragipan.

Aquods	— Hydromorphic..
Ferrods	— Ratio of free iron to carbon in B is more than 6.
Humods	— Part of B horizon is not redder when ignited.
Orthods	— Other spodosols.

Alfisols (-alf) — Have an argillic or natric horizon or a fragipan with clay skins with a base saturation of 35+%, without an overlying spodic or oxic horizon.

Aqualfs	— Hydromorphic (low chroma).
Boralfs	— Mean annual soil temperature below 8°C.
Udalfs	— Other alfisols, usually moist.
Ustalfs	— Dry a total of 90 days or more but not consecutively.
Xeralfs	— Dry 60 or more days consecutively.

Ultisols (-ult) — Soils with a warm-temperature regime. They have an argillic horizon or a thick fragipan with clay skins, a base saturation of less than 35% but no overlying spodic or oxic horizon.

Aquults	— Hydromorphic (low chroma).
Humults	— High organic content.
Udults	— Other ultisols, usually moist.
Ustalts	— Dry a total of 90 days or more but not consecutively.
Xerults	— Dry 60 or more days consecutively.

Oxisols (-ox) — Must have an oxic horizon, or waterlogged and reduced plinthite.

Aquox	— Hydromorphic (histic epipedon or low chroma).
Humox	— Oxisols with base saturation less than 35%, usually moist, with high organic content.
Orthox	— Other oxisols, usually moist.
Ustox	— Dry 60 or more days consecutively.
Torrox	— Usually dry.

Histosols (-ist) — Have over 20–30% organic matter to 30+ cm if drained, or to 45+ cm if undrained.

Folists	— Not water saturated.
Fibrists	— Have more than two-thirds weakly decomposed plant remains.
Hemists	— Have between one-third and two-thirds weakly decomposed plant remains.
Saprists	— Have less than one-third weakly decomposed plant remains.

If you feel initially more at home with one of the systems already described or with the 'old faithful' zonal system (see section 4.5 below) Table 4.14 will be useful. It gives some of the approximate correlations between different classification systems. Other correlations are given in other manuals (see bibliography in Chapter 9).

Table 4.14 — Approximate equivalent names in different classification systems

Soil Taxonomy	FAO–UNESCO	Soil Survey of England and Wales	Others
Entisols	Lithosols, regosols, some arenosols, fluvisols and gleysols	Some terrestrial raw soils, raw gley soils, lithomorphic soils and brown soils	Azonal soils, some low humic gleys
Vertisols	Vertisols	No equivalents	Grumosols, regurs, black cotton soils, tropical black clays
Inceptisols	Rankers, cambisols, andosols, many gleysols, some solonchaks and fluvisols	Many brown soils, pelosols, surface-water gley soils and ground-water gley soils	Some latosols, brown earths (non-argillic), gleys and andosols
Aridisols	Xerosols, yermosols, some solonchaks, solonetz and planosols	No equivalents	Desert and semi-desert soils, sierozems, solonchaks and solonetz
Mollisols	Chernozems, kastanozems, phaeozems, greyzems, some rendzinas, gleysols, solonchaks, solonetz and planosols	Some rendzinas	Chernozems, chestnut soils, brunizems (prairie), some rendzinas, brown earths, gleys, solonchaks and solonetz
Spodosols	Spodosols	Podzolic soils	Podzols, brown podzolic, ground-water podzols
Alfisols	Luvisols, podzoluvisols and planosols, some nitosols	Argillic groups (e.g. argillic brown earths), some surface-water gley soils	Grey–brown podzolic, grey wooded, non-calcic brown, some chernozems, planosols, terra rossa, latosols and lateritic soils
Ultisols	Acrisols, some nitosols	No equivalents	Red–yellow podzolic, reddish brown lateritic, some planosols, latosols, lateritic soils and terra rossa
Oxisols	Ferralsols	No equivalents	Various lateritic soils, latosols, some terra rossa
Histosols	Histosols	Peat soils	Peat, bog soils, organic soils, muck

4.5   THE USDA ZONAL SOIL CLASSIFICATION SYSTEM

4.5.1   General description

In the 1900s Russian pedologists began to recognise that characteristic soil profiles were associated with certain aspects of the environment, notably climate and natural vegetation. They devised classification systems which depended not only on the morphological properties of the profile but also on the assumed main environmental factors which had produced these. This Russian concept of soils linked to broad climatic–vegetational zones was slow to emerge from that country and it was not until 1927 following the translation into English of a Russian textbook that the concept of soil zonality became known internationally.

This concept was embraced enthusiastically and formed the basis of the standard USDA soil classification system until the arrival of the Soil Taxonomy in the 1960s. The system also influenced the classification systems of many other countries, including Britain.

The system is set out in Table 4.15. An initial, rather subjective division is made

Table 4.15 — The USDA zonal soil classification system

Order	Suborder	Great soil group
Zonal soils	1 Soils of the cold zone	Tundra soils
	2 Light-coloured soils of arid regions	Desert soils, red desert soils, sierozem, brown soils, reddish brown soils
	3 Dark-coloured soils of semi-arid, subhumid and humid grasslands	Chestnut soils, reddish chestnut soils, chernozem soils, prairie soils, reddish prairie soils
	4 Soils of the forest–grassland transition	Degraded chernozem, non-calcic brown soils
	5 Light-coloured podzolized soils of the timbered regions	Podzol soils, gray wooded or gray podzolic soils, brown podzolic soils, grey-brown podzolic soils, red–yellow podzolic soils
	6 Lateritic soils of forested warm-temperature and tropical regions	Reddish brown lateritic soils, yellowish brown lateritic soils, laterite soils
Intrazonal soils	1 Halomorphic (saline and alkali) soils of imperfectly drained arid regions and littoral deposits	Solonchak soils, solonetz soils, soloth soils
	2 Hydromorphic soils of marshes, swamps, seep areas and flats	Humic gley soils, alpine meadow soils, bog soils, half-bog soils, low-humic gley soils, planosols, ground-water laterite soils
	3 Calcimorphic soils	Brown forest soils, rendzina soils
Azonal soils		Lithosols, regosols, alluvial soils

into zonal, intrazonal and azonal soils. Zonal soils include those soils having well-developed soil characteristics that reflect the assumed influence of the active factors of soil formation, i.e. climate, and living organisms, chiefly vegetation. These characteristics are best developed on gently undulating but not perfectly level upland, with good drainage, from parent material not of extreme texture or chemical composition that has been in place long enough for the biological forces to have expressed their full influence. In effect these are the mature well-drained soils on average parent materials where regional climate and associated vegetation has apparently controlled their formation. Intrazonal soils have more or less well-developed soil characteristics that reflect the dominating influence of some local factor of relief or parent material over the normal effect of the climate and vegetation. Azonal soils lack well-developed soil characteristics because either conditions of parent material or relief have prevented the development of definite soil characteristics (i.e. immature soils).

The most important level of classification in this system is the great soil group and, until fairly recently, this could be considered the main vocabulary of all Western soil scientists, with modifications to suit local purposes. Teachers of soil science often use the zonality concept and great soil group names when first introducing students to pedology. Most soil scientists can visualise typical profiles of these groups and would carry in their mind their basic properties and the generally accepted explanation of their formation. They would also expect to find them in particular geographical zones (the suborder concept) and within those zones would know the set of conditions likely to produce the soils (the zonality concept). This makes it relatively easy to give at least a reasonably acceptable name for a soil profile under consideration without having to resort to the complexities of the newer systems. The difficulties come at borderlines between different classes, or where unexpected soils turn up, or where the pedologist is working in an unfamiliar area.

Many pedologists would still secretly admit to thinking in terms of great soil groups (at least initially to help to narrow down the possibilities) before translating to a more modern system. If you like this approach you will, however, have to learn some theoretical pedology so that you too can become familiar with the soil forming processes and conditions which produce these characteristic great soil group profiles. Some useful textbooks to study are given in the bibliography in Chapter 9.

5

Making a soil map

5.1 INTRODUCTION

The aim of this chapter is to turn you into a soil surveyor by showing you how to make a detailed soil map for a chosen site. This kind of map is produced by traversing the area on foot and making a record of the soils at appropriate intervals. It is helpful to begin with a description of a map which has already been made so that you can appreciate some of the concepts and nomenclature. This will be followed by a discussion of map scales and the purposes for which maps at different scales are produced.

Preparations for a soil survey (background information, equipment, etc.) are then dealt with before guidance is given on the steps and thought processes involved in making an actual soil map. Suggestions are given on the topics to be covered in a report accompanying a completed map, followed finally by a discussion of the somewhat different procedures needed for making maps at a smaller (more detailed) or larger (reconnaissance) scale.

5.2 A BASIC SOIL MAP

Fig. 5.1 shows a detailed soil map for an imaginary area of about 100 ha in England at a scale of 1:25 000. Soil series names (see Chapter 4) such as Hanslope, Faulkbourne and Chelmer have been chosen as the basis for the **mapping units**. Areas of each mapping unit are annotated with a **mapping symbol** (e.g. Hn) which is explained in the accompanying **legend** (Table 5.1). Most of the mapping units are simple, i.e. they are named after a single soil series but one (bN/HV) is composite. This is because in this part of the area the surveyor was unable to map the different soils separately at the chosen scale. The lines between the mapping units are called **soil boundaries.**

The map was produced by the surveyor making observations at various points as shown on the field sheet (Fig. 5.2). Field sheets, as in this case, are normally at a larger scale (i.e. more detailed) than the final published map (Fig. 5.1). Each observation point is numbered on the field sheet to allow reference to profile descriptions held in a separate notebook and each point is annotated with the symbol

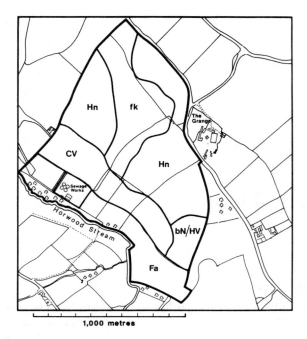

Fig. 5.1 — Detailed soil map for an imaginary area in England (1:25 000).

for the soil series to which the soil at that point belongs. The final map rarely, if ever, shows the positions of the actual observation points; so the user of the map does not really know the evidence on which the map was compiled.

In an ideal world it would be possible to draw boundaries on soil maps so that the mapping units contained only a single kind of soil, in this example a single soil series. At the extreme northern end of the site, Fig. 5.2 (the field sheet) shows that on the basis of the observations made it has been nearly but not quite possible to delineate a fairly large area where only Hanslope soils (Hn) were encountered. One observation (No. 53) within the area, however, belongs to another series, the Faulkbourne series (fK).

The surveyor then had a choice. He could have tried to delineate a separate area of Faulkbourne soils, in which case he would probably have felt it necessary to make additional observations in the vicinity to check how extensive this soil was. The end result would be a more precise map, but more complicated and requiring extra effort. Instead he chose the alternative of ignoring the single isolated observation of the Faulkbourne series and, on the final map, has shown the whole area as Hanslope series. The final map, of course, does not indicate that there was another kind of soil present and that the map unit is not 100% pure. In fact map units are never 100% pure and so a map unit labelled, for example, Hn really means 'the commonest or dominant soil in this map unit is the Hanslope (Hn) series but there are likely to be other soil series represented as well'.

Table 5.1 — Legend for the 1:25 000 soil map of Fig. 5.1

Soil group	Soil subgroup	Texture and parent material	Soil series	Map symbol
Calcareous pelosols	Typical calcareous pelosols	Clayey; chalky till (Chalky Boulder Clay)	Hanslope	Hn
Argillic pelosols	Typical argillic pelosols	Clayey; chalky till (Chalky Boulder Clay)	Faulkbourne	fK
Brown sands	Argillic brown sands	Sandy-skeletal; flinty glaciofluvial drift	St Albans	SA[a]
Paleoargillic brown earths	Typical paleoargillic brown earths	Flinty fine loamy or fine silty over clayey; head or till	Bengeo	bN[a]
	Gleyic paleoargillic brown earths	Flinty loamy; head over glaciofluvial deposits	Chelmer	cV
	Stagnogleyic paleoargillic brown earths	Flinty fine loamy or fine silty over clayey; head or till	Hornbeam	HV[a]
Stagnogley soils	Pelo-stagnogley soils	Clayey; chalky till (Chalky Boulder Clay)	Ragdale	Rg[b]
	Paleoargillic stagnogley soils	Flinty fine loamy or fine silty over clayey; head or till	Oak	Oq[b]
Alluvial gley soils	Pelo-alluvial gley soils	Clayey; riverine alluvium	Fladbury	Fa
	Pelo-alluvial gley soils	Clayey or peaty; riverine alluvium over peat	Midelney	Ma[b]

[a] Occurs only in Bengeo–Hornbeam Complex.
[b] Does not occur as separate mapping unit.

The question then is: how reliably pure are the map units shown on a soil map? The answer depends both on scale (see later) and on whether the surveyor was a 'lumper' or a 'splitter'. Lumpers tend to ignore atypical observations and so can quickly produce maps which are relatively simple but whose map units are relatively impure. Splitters often come close to a nervous breakdown worrying about finer and finer shades of difference between the soils being encountered. Their eventual product is a highly intricate map with many map unit delineations of greater within-unit purity.

It is rarely possible to tell except by intuition what kind of surveyor produced any particular map. Sometimes the legend or the accompanying memoir indicate the degree of map unit purity, e.g. Table 5.2. You may be alarmed to read that, in this example, even map units labelled as a single series (the Bursledon series) may only contain 47% of that series and hence 53% of assorted other soils; yet this is quite normal.

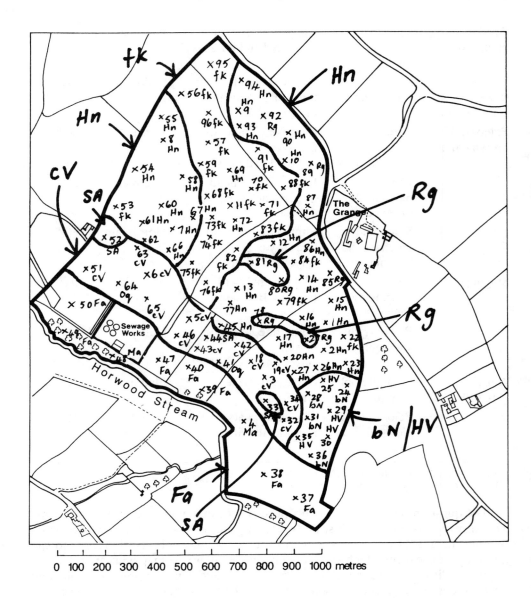

Fig. 5.2 — Field sheet for part of the area shown in Fig. 5.1. Original at 1:10 000 but reduced in scale in this reproduction.

Table 5.2 — Average homogeneity of main mapping units in a 1:25 000 soil map in eastern England

Mapping unit	Average homogenity		Inclusions in mapping unit		
Name	Dominant series	Proportion of profiles (%)	Chief included series	Proportion of profiles (%)	Other series (%)
Fladbury	Fladbury	100	—	—	—
Enborne	Enborne	90	Fladbury	9	1
Windsor	Windsor	76	Wickham	13	11
Essendon	Essendon	76	St Albans	8	16
Oak	Oak	72	Ragdale	7	21
Chelmer	Chelmer	69	Oak	8	23
Hanslope	Hanslope	66	Ragdale	20	14
Ragdale	Ragdale	60	Hanslope	19	21
Titchfield	Titchfield	60	Windsor	13	27
Wickham	Wickham	56	Windsor	16	28
Curdridge	Curdridge	56	Swanwick	11	33
Bursledon	Bursledon	47	Shedfield	31	22

Source: Sturdy (1971).

Map unit purity tends to decrease as the map scale decreases. Map units have to cover larger areas on the ground and so encompass greater amounts of soil variability. Table 5.3 and the discussions later in the chapter cover this.

A range of properties is normally allowed for each category of a soil classification system (Chapter 4) including the soil series used in detailed mapping. Thus the soils at the various observation points of a soil survey will never be exactly identical with each other even if they are given the same series name. The intention is, however, that they will be more similar to one another than they will to the soils appearing in another map unit. In the early days of soil mapping soil series were often recognised on somewhat *ad hoc* criteria which served to differentiate soils in the field. The problem of reconciling these 'definitions' with those in the higher levels of a soil classification has already been discussed in Chapter 4.

A positive indication of impurity is given where a surveyor uses a composite map unit. On the scale of map currently being discussed, i.e. a detailed map at about 1:25 000 to 1:63 360, the composite unit would be called a **soil complex**. Areas thus annotated would contain an intricate mixture of different soils within which the surveyor either could not discern any mappable pattern or thought it was not worthwhile to try to show whatever pattern existed. The representation of soil complexes varies. Sometimes just the dominant soil series appears in the name and symbol, e.g. Berkhampsted complex (bK'), sometimes two or more series names are used e.g. Ford End/Thames (FE/Ts), or, as in the Soil Survey of Scotland, a completely different name (not in itself a series name) is used, e.g. Queensferry complex (Qn), which is made up of a mixture of the Darleith, Macmerry and other series.

The second major problem faced by a soil surveyor, which is linked to the problem of map unit purity, is how to draw boundaries between areas of different soils. In reality different soils merge into one another often over considerable

Table 5.3 — Soil maps: factors related to scale

Type of map	Scale	Typical soil mapping units	Typical land capability mapping units	Smallest area conveniently shown (planning unit)	Typical purpose of map
Very detailed	1:10 000 or larger	Types, variants and phases of soil series	Capability unit	0.2 ha (plot)	Detailed planning within project area, e.g. for civil engineering
Detailed	1:25 000	Soil series and phases	Capability unit	1.2 ha (field)	Planning within farm or project; land reapportionment; land taxation
Semi-detailed	1:50 000	Soil series and complexes	Capability subclass	5 ha (farm)	Maps of extensive projects; detailed regional planning; guide to advisory officers
Reconnaissance	1:200 000	Associations of series	Dominant capability class or subclass	80 ha (village or large farm)	Broad region planning (e.g. location of projects)
National	1:1 000 000	Associations of major groups	Associations of capability classes or subclasses	20 km² (region)	National land planning; education

Source: McRae and Burnham (1981).

distances. In this transition zone there will be found soils, called **intergrades**, with similarities to both kinds of soils being mapped. On the field sheet (Fig. 5.2) near The Grange, for example, the surveyor has marked some of the observations HV/fK or fK/HV showing he was not really sure to which series the soils at these points belonged. In such a case he would almost certainly draw the boundary between the two map units more or less through the middle of the transition zone. As with map unit purity, however, the final map (Fig. 5.1) on which none of the raw data is shown gives a misleading sense of accuracy by simply showing a sharply drawn line.

The surveyor may be guided by some physical feature such as a break in slope, a change in the vegetation or a variation in soil surface appearance, e.g. stoniness, in where to locate his soil boundaries but mostly he has to interpolate between observations. If he is indulging in what is called **free survey**, where he can make observations where they seem to be most useful, then he may choose to make extra observations near a suspected boundary, perhaps going back on himself, e.g. observations 41–44 in Fig. 5.2. Again there is no indication of the thought processes on the final published map. Indeed there is usually no indication of whether he has been using free survey or alternatively has used a **grid survey** with observations restricted to a regular grid when the location of soil boundaries is probably even more conjectural than in a free survey.

A soil surveyor should of course try to locate all soil boundaries as accurately as possible but especially those between contrasting soil types. Great care should also be taken where the map is likely to be subjected to particular scrutiny and where the relationship between soil boundaries and landmarks, e.g. roads, makes any error particularly obvious.

One final piece of nomenclature remains to be explained, the **soil phase**. Sometimes the surveyor wants to make a subdivision of one or other of his mapping units to take account of some special property he thinks is worth recognising. This can be a non-soil feature such as slope or flood risk, or a soil-based property such as surface texture or stoniness whose variation is, however, not sufficient to merit recognition of a separate soil series. In such cases he can define various phases of particular series. Phases are commonly represented on soil maps by a numerical subscript to the series symbol, e.g. hL_1 and hL_2 denoting the normal and stony phases respectively of the Hamble (hL) series, but such a distinction may well not be made on other maps with the Hamble series or the subscripts may have different meanings.

Thus to recap, on soil maps at scales of around 1:25 000 to 1:63 360 which have been made mainly as a result of fairly detailed field work:

(a)   map units are usually based on soil series, complexes, or phases;

(b)   the final map is usually at a smaller scale than the field sheet and will not show the individual observation points or what was found at each;

(c)   map units are never 100% pure and there may be little if any indication of their actual purity;

(d)   soil boundaries are usually drawn approximately at the midpoint of a transition zone from one kind of soil to another and seldom represent a sharp change;

(e)   the observation points may have been chosen at what the surveyor considered to be the most informative locations (free survey) or may have been located on a predetermined grid.

5.3   SCALES AND MAP UNITS

The kind of map discussed above would be called a detailed soil map (see Table 5.3) for which the surveyor might typically make about 100 observations per square kilometre, i.e. about one observation per hectare. As a result the completed map when reduced to the final production scale of 1:25 000 would have a resolution of about 1.5 ha, i.e. areas of different soils any smaller than this would have to be included as an impurity within a larger map unit as already described. Such a resolution would be more than sufficient for a farmer whose separate fields or other management blocks are likely to be much larger than this. Indeed, a farmer might well criticise a soil map as having too much detail, showing little patches of different soils which in practice he would simply ignore.

On the other hand if any portion of the area surveyed was required for trials or experiments then a resolution of 1.5 ha would probably be inadequate. A more detailed map would be required and might entail several hundreds or even thousands of observations per square kilometre. This will clearly involve much more effort and hence expense.

A soil surveyor, working hard and making fairly complete descriptions of the soils at each observation point, could be expected to make about 50–70 observations in a full working day under relatively easy conditions. The work rate will be slower if the terrain is difficult and if a small-scale map is being prepared with substantial journey time between observation points. Conversely a faster work rate can be expected in large-scale mapping with closely spaced observations and perhaps with relatively little variation in the soils being encountered.

It is possible to economise in the descriptions of the observations. For example it may simply be sufficient just to record the soil series (or other classification unit in use) perhaps with a comment such as 'slightly more stony than usual'. The danger in this approach is that if the definitions of the soil categories are subsequently modified then it might not be possible to re-assign the original observations to the new nomenclature and the whole area would have to be resurveyed.

For the same reason making single-factor soil maps, i.e. recording only a single property such as depth of topsoil, is a waste of opportunity. Much surveying time is taken up in getting to the observation points. Once there, it is foolish to record only a single factor or losing the soil information by, e.g. allocating a land classification grading to the point and recording only that.

A basic rule of soil mapping is first to establish for what purpose the map is required, so that an appropriate scale of mapping and hence intensity of observations can be chosen. The more detailed the map, the larger the scale and the more effort required to compile it. Table 5.3 lists typical scales for maps for a variety of purposes and the approximate intensity of observations needed. A detailed map for final production at 1:25 000 such as the one used as the example above would normally need about 100 observations per square kilometre, i.e. one observation per hectare, which, given the variability of soils, might be considered a rather low frequency of observations for a map described as detailed.

It is dishonest and misleading simply to enlarge the scale of a soil map without undertaking the more intensive survey work necessary to substantiate the apparent greater precision. On the other hand it is quite acceptable to reduce the scale of a soil map, if necessary amalgamating or otherwise rationalising the mapping units, but this poses the question as to whether the greater detail was required in the first place. The answer can be yes if an area was first chosen as a sample area prior to a reconnaissance survey of a larger area. On the final map this sample area would, however, have to be simplified to match the rest of the map even though more detail was really known.

A good example of this approach is the 1:250 000 national soil map for England and Wales. Sample areas were mapped in detail (1:25 000) or semi-detail (1:63 360) before the rest of the country was mapped at lesser intensity. Similarly the 1:25 000 national soil map for Scotland is based on more detailed (1:25 000 and 1:63 360) mapping (Figs 5.3 and 5.4).

The great advantage of mapping at a smaller scale is that the final map can cover a relatively large area with relatively few observations per unit area. The penalty is that the map units will have to be broadly defined, they will be relatively impure and the boundaries between them will be fairly imprecise. On such smaller-scale maps the nomenclature of the mapping units can be based on groupings of the units (e.g. soil

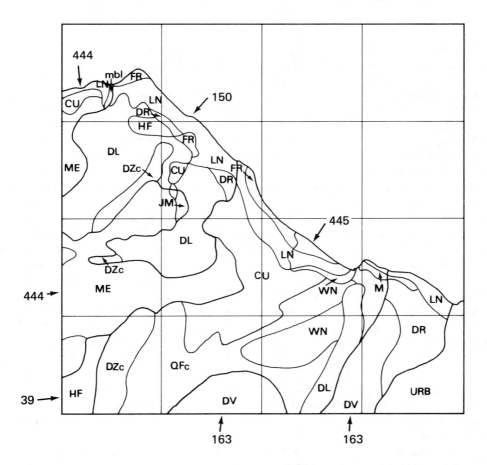

Fig. 5.3 — Part of a soil map produced by the Soil Survey of Scotland, orignally published at 1:25 000. (Source: adapted from Soil Survey of Scotland).

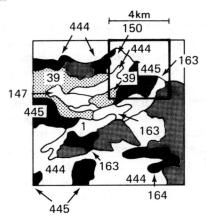

Fig. 5.4 — Part of the national 1:250 000 soil map of Scotland, originally published at 1:250 000, corresponding to Fig. 5.4. (Source: adapted from the Soil Survey of Scotland)

series) used on more detailed maps or can use a higher level within the soil classification system such as soil groups, e.g. podzols and chernozems.

Groupings of units from more detailed mapping (e.g. soil series) are usually called **associations**. These are conceptually different from the soil complexes described above. As the name implies, the soil complex refers to an area in which the soil pattern is too complex to be capable of sensible mapping, whereas the association is a deliberate compilation of geographically related soils undertaken for reasons of scale. Associations can be named after the dominant series present and/or can be given an alphanumeric code.

Thus on the national soil map for England and Wales (Fig. 5.4) an area may be shown as association 712b. The legend and memoir refer to this as the Denchworth Association since the dominant soil belongs to the Denchworth series, but both point out that within areas mapped as 712b subsidiary (or ancillary) series such as the Wickham, Lawford, Evesham, Oxpasture and other series will also be encountered. The problem with using a 'dominant series' name for an association is that a lay user will not appreciate the implication of other soils being present and so will have an erroneous notion of soil uniformity within the map unit.

On the 1:250 000 national soil maps of the Soil Survey of England and Wales the numeric part of the map unit code is based on the soil classification system described in Chapter 4. 712 is the code for the pelo- subgroup of the stagnogley group (71) of the major group of surface-water gley soils (7), i.e. the subgroup to which the dominant soil of the association, the Denchworth series, belongs. The map also uses colours (not shown in Fig. 5.4) so that, for example, all associations whose dominant soils are surface-water gley soils, i.e. which have codes beginning with 7, are in shades of green. Thus the map also shows the general distribution of the main categories of soils within that classification system.

Other small-scale maps follow a similar convention of trying to link the mapping units to the appropriate taxonomic system and using codes and colours to show the broad taxonomic groupings. Examples are the various sheets of the FAO–UNESCO

Soil Map of the World, the European Community map for the members of the EEC, and the soil map of the USA based on the Soil Taxonomy. Both use map units based on higher levels of the appropriate classification rather than associations of more-detailed lower-level units like soil series.

Other groupings can be used, e.g. the catena (literally a chain) of soils, used in surveys of certain tropical areas where there tends to be a recurrent pattern of soils related to position on the slope. The term **soil association** used by the Soil Survey of Scotland is conceptually similar. It denotes a sequence of soils generally similar in respect of parent material and textures but differing in drainage and hence usually related to topographic position.

5.4   PREPARING TO MAKE A SOIL MAP — SCALE AND TYPE OF SURVEY

As has been discussed, soil maps are made by examining the soil at a number of sample locations (or observation points), naming the soils according to the classification system in use and then drawing boundaries between areas of different soils. The surveyor is therefore faced with a number of decisions:

(a)   Where to make the observations;
(b)   How many observations to make;
(c)   What to record at each observation point;
(d)   What nomenclature/classification system to use for the soils;
(e)   Where to draw boundaries between areas of different soils.

To a large extent the answers to these questions depend on the scale of map required, which in turn will be dictated by both the intended use of the map and the amount of time and effort which can be devoted to the exercise or for which the surveyor will be paid. Surveyors who are part of a team must make sure they know what their colleagues are expecting and perhaps break the sad news to them that in the time available a map of the desired precision cannot be produced. Soil surveying is almost always a compromise of making the best possible map within a limited time. Like many surveying operations, however, soil surveying is subject to a law of diminishing returns. A general picture can be obtained with relatively little effort and subsequent more detailed observations will usually just improve the precision rather than fundamentally change the picture. Thus if there is only limited time (or finance) then the surveyor should try to cover all the area with a fairly wide scattering of observation points and use any spare time at the end to refine areas in which he or his colleagues are particularly interested or where the soils seem to be particularly complicated. This is much better than having to mark any of the map 'unsurveyed' because time ran out.

A soil surveyor will initially be unfamiliar with the area and its soils, and progress may be dishearteningly slow. As he or she becomes more familiar with the area, more insight into the soil pattern will be gained and progress thereafter will be much quicker.

All this tends to assume mapping will be by free survey, i.e. the surveyor decides where to make observations as he or she proceeds across the area, where they can be spaced out because the soil pattern is simple and where a greater intensity is needed because the pattern is more complicated. When done by a skilled soil surveyor, free survey can be the most efficient method of soil surveying but it can be difficult to integrate the efforts of two or more surveyors on the same job and to estimate in advance the amount of time needed. Often, too, colleagues (or clients) may be uneasy that some parts of the study area may have a rather sparse cover of observation points.

These problems can be overcome by a grid survey in which an agreed network of observation points is established before work commences. The dimensions of the task can be predetermined and subdivision of the work is easier. Non-skilled labour, if available, can be sent on ahead to clear the way and to make the auger borings or to dig the pits in advance of the professional surveyor. In a grid survey all the area is evenly covered but it can be frustrating to have to make observations where the information is not needed or when grid points are atypical. Also a great deal of time can be spent trying to get to a specific point when equally useful information could be obtained from a more accessible location. Grid surveys are often the most practical method in areas with few landmarks or in dense vegetation where paths have to be cut. Thus grid surveys tend to be used more frequently in tropical areas than in temperate ones.

Perhaps for a beginner a mixture of free and grid survey is best. Start with a widely spaced free survey to get a feel for the area, follow this with a more systematic gridded or similar arrangement of observation points and then finish with a more-detailed free survey at critical points or to fix a soil boundary more closely.

5.5   PREPARING TO MAKE A SOIL MAP — BASE MAP AND BACKGROUND INFORMATION

The production of a soil map typically consists of the following steps:

(a)   collection of as much background information as possible, including base maps, aerial photographs and geological maps which will indicate what soils are likely to be present and where they are likely to change;

(b)   a reconnaissance survey of the different facets of the area to be mapped, on the basis of which the soil classes to be mapped can be determined and a draft mapping legend constructed;

(c)   systematic mapping of the area;

(d)   refining boundaries and final map drawing;

(e)   full descriptions of typical profiles;

(f)   preparation of accompanying report and any interpretative work, e.g. crop suitabilities, land classification and irrigation suitability.

5.5.1   Base maps and aerial photographs

A good base map, or failing that a cover, preferably stereoscopic, of aerial photographs is an indispensable part of a soil survey. It should be at a sufficiently large scale to allow observation points to be marked on easily and to provide enough landmarks for locating their position accurately. On the other hand the scale should not be so large that large unwieldy sheets of paper have to be dealt with in the field.

In Britain a base map at a scale of 1:10 000 is ideal for maps to be produced at a final scale of 1:25 000 or 1:50 000. The 1:10 000 maps show field boundaries, isolated trees and other useful landmarks. 1:2500 maps are easier to annotate since the area being surveyed appears larger but offers an irresistible temptation to overelaboration. It also lacks contour lines which can often assist in locating soil boundaries. With modern photocopiers, however, you can get the best of both by enlarging the 1:10 000 map to a more convenient working scale. In any case you are strongly advised to take only photocopies into the field and always to retain a clean unblemished original. You must, however, make sure you have the necessary permission to photocopy maps. Most map-making bodies guard their copyright jealously and a fee has to be paid or a licence obtained to make copies or publish a soil map using their base map.

An alternative to a base map is to use an aerial photograph. In several countries, e.g. in the USA, soil maps are commonly published using aerial photograph bases. Aerial photographs are, however, more difficult to annotate and you may have to take an original into the field but, again, good modern photocopiers can help to overcome the problems, assuming you have obtained the necessary permissions. Lay users of soil maps can often relate better to aerial photographs on which they can pick out known landmarks. Also aerial photographs can be more up to date, especially in developing countries where tracks, clearings and cropping patterns change frequently.

Even if you have a suitable base map you should study any aerial photographs of your area which are available. Particularly if a soil association map is acceptable (see later) skilled aerial photograph interpreters can produce acceptably accurate soil maps just from studying tonal patterns, etc., with a minimum of field work to check their results. Professional soil surveyors can greatly increase their work rate by combining their field work with a study of aerial photographs, especially in the more accurate location of soil boundaries. Aerial photographs are invaluable in difficult terrain, allowing you to come to acceptable conclusions about areas you cannot easily visit, by extrapolation from more accessible areas.

Beginners cannot hope to make such full use of aerial photographs and should not be too worried if none is available. Nevertheless it can be surprising what even beginners can see, especially after having done some field work in the area.

5.5.2 Geological maps
Geological maps can be valuable aids to soil surveying where the parent material is an important factor in determining soil type, but only if they show drift deposits in addition to the solid geology. Maps showing only the solid geology are of limited use since soils are often formed in superficial drift bearing little or no relationship to the underlying solid rock, notably in areas which have been glaciated or in alluvial floodplains. Even geological maps which claim to show drift deposits may, however, have to be treated with caution as geologists usually map only thick drift deposits while thin coverings of drift are ignored although they may be of great importance in determining the soil pattern. Also geologists are often more concerned with the mode of formation of the drift than with its lithology and composition which are of far more relevance to the character of the soils.

In spite of these limitations, however, geological maps can assist greatly in soil surveying as long as they are sensibly used. At worst they can at least point towards other areas of similar geology which already have soil surveys affording useful guidance.

5.5.3   Vegetation and land-use maps

Contrasting soils often have contrasting vegetation or land-use characteristics. Such differences may be apparent in aerial photographs, and in some cases land-use maps may also show up likely soil boundaries (see for example Figs 7.1 and 7.2). If your interest is in soil–plant relationships then you will probably be compiling a land-use or vegetation map alongside the soil survey. Indeed in many projects a soil surveyor may be one of the few workers, or even the only worker, who will systematically visit all parts of a project area and so may be an invaluable compiler of 'local information' of use to his colleagues.

5.5.4   Other soil surveys

Before starting work a soil surveyor should familiarise himself with the results of other soil surveys in similar landscapes and/or similar geological or ecological settings. This will greatly assist him to avoid or be aware of problems encountered by other surveyors but, even more important, he will be able to use the same mapping units and conventions and so produce a compatible map. Sadly there are many instances of soil maps being produced which, in themselves, are quite acceptable, but which are virtually useless in a wider context because the surveyor has used a non-standard approach.

Before or during the survey, a soil surveyor will usually confer with whoever farms or uses the land (often when obtaining permission to be on the land), and with agricultural advisory officers, land drainage officers and other local specialists.

5.6   EQUIPMENT NEEDED FOR FIELD WORK

Obviously you need to be well clad and shod before starting out. Since you may be working on your own well away from human habitation you should always leave a note of where you are and when you are likely to return, in case of accident, and also leave an address or organisation name on your vehicle. Carrying a whistle to attract attention can be reassuring.

5.6.1   Recording observations

You will need a clipboard or map case for holding your field sheets and notes, and you are well advised to carry spare copies of maps, writing materials, etc. If your notes and maps get wet it is invaluable to have spare dry copies you can bring into use. Many soil survey organisations use standardised data sheets for note taking. These can be rather complicated, especially for a beginner; so, at least to start with, you could use the fairly simple sheet laid out in Fig. 5.5. As you become more experienced you may want to make up your own standardised data sheets.

Opinion varies as to writing materials. Some surveyors prefer to use permanent and waterproof pens, and others to use pencils so that amendments can easily be made. Some surveyors dispense with notebooks altogether and use cassette recorders, but there are tales of an entire day's work being wasted because the surveyor did not realise the machine was malfunctioning.

5.6.2   Soil augers

In most terrain the best tools with which to make rapid soil observations are soil augers (Fig. 5.6). Many surveyors favour the so-called Edelman or Dutch auger.

Various models and sizes are available, but a single combination-type head of about 3–5 cm diameter is probably the most useful for general purposes. Models can be obtained with interchangeable heads and/or extension pieces for deeper borings. These always feel less robust than single-head augers and all the various bits and pieces which have to be carried around make them very inconvenient for general soil surveying.

Soil type		Date	Stop No.	Soil type
Classification	Area			
Location			Elevation	
Natural vegetation (or crop)	Climate			
Parent material				
Physiography				
Relief	Slope		Erosion	File No.
Drainage	Ground water		Permeability	
Moisture	Salt or alkali			
Stoniness	Root distribution			
Remarks				

(a)

Horizon	Depth	Thickness	Boundary	Colour	Check, D(ry) or M(oist)	Texture	Structure	Consistence	Reaction	Special features
				D M						
				D M						
				D M						
				D M						
				D M						
				D M						
				D M						
				D M						
				D M						

(b)

Fig. 5.5 — Pro forma sheet for recording field notes: (a) front side of sheet; (b) reverse side of sheet. Compare with full profile description pro-forma (Fig. 3.3)

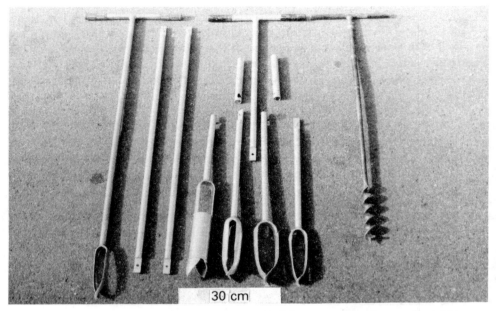

Fig. 5.6 — Soil augers: (left to right) single-head combination-type Dutch auger; extendable
Dutch auger with selection of heads and extension rods; screw auger.

Whenever possible you will want to record soil properties to at least 1 m and the
auger should be at least this long. Most surveyors use a 1.2 m auger but if you are of
short stature you may find it impossible to impart sufficient downward force to get the
auger boring started. Beware also of large-diameter augers which require much
strength to pull out of the ground as well as leaving very conspicuous evidence of your
activities.

You can make a simple screw-type auger of your own by buying a shipwright's or
Scotch auger from an ironmonger and welding it onto a T-bar of suitable length.
These augers are most useful in collecting surface samples but can be used to make
deeper borings. They tend to be more affected by stones, however, and if the soil is
dry and sandy it often falls off the auger and cannot be sampled. Both Dutch and
home-made screw augers benefit from the shaft being permanently marked with
distances from the tip.

The technique of augering is to start by screwing the auger (clockwise) into the
ground till the top of the bit or head just begins to disappear. Then pull it out (a slight
anti-clockwise twist can help) and examine the soil you have obtained. Some
surveyors like to place the samples on trays or along the ground so that their
sequence can be maintained. Then put the empty auger back into the hole and drill
deeper for the next sample. You will quickly learn how far you need to go before
withdrawing the auger with the next sample fully filling the bit. If you try to drill too
deeply each time you will find it very difficult to pull the auger out and you will lose
some of the soil in the process.

Before you pull the auger out you should note where the ground surface cuts the
shaft so that you can relate any horizon changes to the depth from the surface. For
accurate work you need a tape measure firmly attached to your clothing or clipboard

so that you do not lose it. Carry on in this way until you have completed the boring to your satisfaction. Tidy soil surveyors backfill the hole with the loose soil when they are finished or at least make it safe at the surface by treading it closed.

5.6.3 Soil exposures
You should take advantage of any natural soil exposures, roadside cuttings, trenches, etc., but beware that the soils are often disturbed or truncated at such locations. You will probably need a spade to clean up the profiles; so you would probably treat these as extra observations to be examined separately at some convenient time in your survey.

From time to time you may want to collect samples of soil either to check on some feature more closely back at base or perhaps to refer to from time to time during your subsequent surveying to ensure you are being consistent in, for example, soil texturing. Polythene bags and indelible markers are best. Paper labels inside bags often disintegrate before you can refer back to the sample.

5.7 THE FIELD WORK
Your first task in any new area is to familiarise yourself with the sorts of soils you will subsequently be dealing with in more detail. You should therefore plan a route across the area which covers as many of the different landscape facets, vegetation types and geological substrates as possible. At this stage your aim ought to be to cover the ground quickly and not to waste too much time making elaborate soil descriptions. You are looking for fairly major differences in the soil and trying to work out whether there is any recognisable pattern, e.g. are consistent soil differences associated with certain geological deposits, different types of vegetation or different topographic positions?

Each new area will present its own challenge and there is no substitute for experience. You might gain some insight into how a soil surveyor's mind works by looking again at Fig. 5.2. Usually there will be no actual notes, and the surveyor will just build up a picture in his mind as he goes along.

When you have gained some insight into the soils of the area you are mapping you need to take the area more systematically, if not on a formal grid at least ensuring there are no huge gaps in your sampling pattern. As we have previously recommended (see Fig. 5.2 for example) you will probably want to make extra observations at critical points especially where you are at or near a soil boundary and this may involve some backtracking.

Correct location on the map of your observation points is of course vital. You will often have to measure distances by pacing. An average pace is about 0.8 m but it is best to calibrate your pace with a known distance on the ground and hence length on the map. Directions can conveniently be determined by, for example, walking from one landmark such as a field corner towards another. Many crops are grown in regular rows and/or their cultivation produces parallel tracks (tramlines) parallel to one of the field boundaries and pacing along one such tramline helps you to keep track of where you are as well as making access easier and reducing crop damage.

Grassland or similar open vegetation can be traversed more randomly but it is easier to become confused as to where you are exactly. In critical cases you may have to resort to elementary triangulation or to use surveying equipment such as a tacheometer. In dense vegetation including woodland you may find the easiest course of action is to make small 'excursions' away from a known track always returning to a known point so that any location fixing errors are not compounded. Remember, however, that the accuracy of knowing your location depends on map scale and at surveys using 1:10 000 field sheets an error not exceeding 20 m can be quite acceptable.

Now assume you are the surveyor beginning work in the area shown in Figs 5.1 and 5.2. For clarity the first few observation points are shown separately in Fig. 5.7.

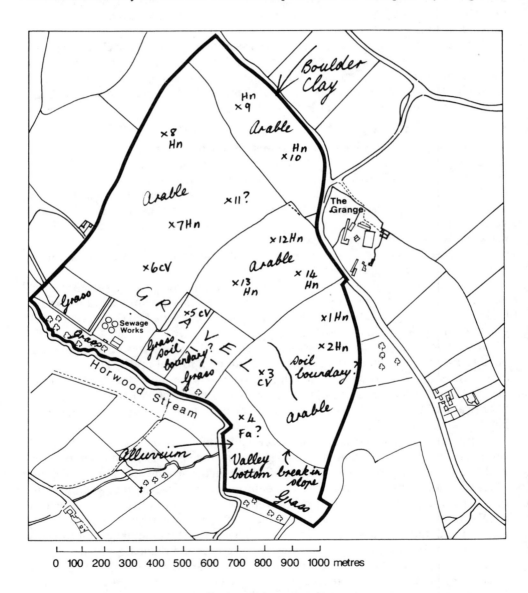

Fig. 5.7 — Field sheet to show the first few observations made in the soil survey which produced Fig. 5.2. Original at 1:10 000 but reduced in scale in this reproduction

Previous study of geological and topographic maps shows that the survey area is on a boulder clay plateau in the north, falling away to a valley bottom, floored by alluvium in the south, and with exposures of gravels on the valley sides. You would therefore plan your first foray into the site at least so as to cross all these landscape and geological facets.

Assume you are starting near The Grange. Observations around a gateway are undesirable; so pace a known distance in a known direction out into the field and make boring No. 1. The record you make at this stage may be like this:

No. 1 0–24 cm DB cl, calc.
       24–43 cm YB c, calc.
       43–50 cm YB c, v. calc., + ochreous mottles and occasional small lumps of chalk
       50+ cm chalky boulder clay (cbc) (YB,SB and G mottled c) with abundant lumps of chalk, v.calc.
               Hanslope series, gentle slope to S (about 2°), wheat

Now (in your imagination) walk about 100 m south and make boring No. 2. You should really make a record as for No. 1, but assume the soil is very similar and at this stage you want to save time so you simply note:

No. 2 As No. 1 but 26 cm topsoil, 45 cm to mottles and 60 cm to cbc

The dangers inherent in this abbreviated note taking have already been pointed out, but all soil surveyors use such short-cuts.

The ground between borings 2 and 3 begins to fall away and your earlier inspection of the geological map showed that, while borings 1 and 2 were on till (boulder clay), No. 3 was likely to be on gravels. As you make your way to boring 3, then, you should look out for signs of a corresponding change in the soils. In a case like this you would probably notice the soils becoming stonier and, if you had sensitive feet and the ground was not too dry and hard, you might also notice the ground felt different to your tread. By counting your paces you could mark a tentative soil boundary as shown in Fig. 5.7. Since boring 3 is a new kind of soil you would need to make a fuller description such as:

No. 3 0–28 cm DB scl, slightly stony (about 10% by vol.) non-calc.
       28–57 cm YB scl with reddish patches, v.stony and difficult to auger, non-calc.
       57+ cm Too stony to auger
               Chelmer series, mod.slope (about 5°), wheat, not growing as well as at borings 1 and 2

The land you are surveying has a stream running through it, with a flat valley bottom, floored (according to the geological map) by alluvium, and there is a marked land-use change from arable on the surrounding higher land to indifferent grassland on the valley bottom. Obviously you will expect a different soil in the valley bottom, with the soil boundary at the field boundary along the break in slope. Anxious to expand your experience of different soil series you temporarily leave the stony valley sides and head for the valley bottom. Auger boring No. 4 will not disappoint you:

No. 4   0-10 cm   Black humose c, prominent ochreous mottles, wet
        10–90 cm   G soft c with reddish brown mottles. V. wet, boring filled up with
                   water
        90+ cm   Black peat (apparently buried by later alluvium) Fladbury series,
                   valley bottom, rush infested permanent pasture. NB Check that
                   presence of peat at depth does not make it another series or might
                   have to have a phase of the Fladbury to cover it in due course

Even with only four borings you are hopefully beginning to see the likely soil
pattern which will help you to plan the rest of your survey. There are three basic
landscape elements: plateau tops (boulder clay, Hanslope series), valley sides
(gravel, Chelmer series) and valley bottom (alluvium, Fladbury? series). Borings
5–10 inclusive confirm to you that this is basically correct. Boring 11 is a surprise,
however:

No. 11   0–28 cm   DB cl non-calc.
        28–60 cm   SB c non-calc with large reddish brown mottles. Seems to be
                   large flints which can be pushed aside by the auger
                   Ditto but with greyish mottles in addition. Unknown series,
                   same topography and land use as Hanslope soils. Can not see
                   any crop evidence or change in topography which would help
                   locate a boundary

At this stage you might consider backtracking towards boring 10 making shallow
borings as you go and testing with acid to try to discover where the soil changes from
being the calcareous Hanslope series to what appears to be a non-calcareous
'relative'. On the other hand you may consider that this is a problem you are going to
have to come back to and you will defer any more detailed work till then. A short
linear transect in the vicinity with closely spaced observations, e.g. 10 m apart or so,
would give you some indication of the degree of soil variability.

Borings 12–14 take you back to your starting point with no major surprises en
route, but you notice that, conveniently, a drainage ditch is being dug along the edge
of one of the fields and you make a mental note to go back there for a closer look and
perhaps make a full detailed profile description if the exposed soil seems typical of
what you are finding elsewhere.

Before you go back out into the field you should make clean copies of your notes
and map, and check up on the queries raised by your reconnaissance. You find, for
example, that the peat below the alluvium makes the soil the Midelney rather than
the Fladbury series and you make a note that when you come back to survey the area
systematically you will have to see whether this is the dominant soil on the valley
floor or whether you have just been unlucky in encountering an atypical Midelney
soil in an area otherwise of Fladbury series. The problem of the calcareous Hanslope
soil and its non-calcareous relative, which you have discovered is the Faulkbourne
series, looks as if you will have to do a systematic grid-type survey in this part of the
site to enable you to draw any boundaries by interpolation between auger borings.
You resolve also to have a closer look at the aerial photographs, perhaps marking
your auger boring observation points onto them, to see if they show any likely soil
boundaries, including any you had already noted in the field.

The next step, that of systematically covering the area, is the most time consuming, and, as already discussed, can be a combination of a semi-grid survey with addition inspection points as necessary. This will produce the complete auger boring pattern already shown in Fig. 5.2. During this stage of the work you should be looking particularly for soil boundaries which, as discussed above, you will have to locate either by interpolation between auger borings (hence the need for additional borings in key places) or by noting some feature in the field which suggests that there is a likely soil boundary. In this latter case you will have to make some auger borings on either side of your suspected boundary to confirm your theories.

Also at the systematic survey stage you should be choosing possible locations for digging and describing the type examples of the soils you are mapping. These must be really typical of the soil which they represent, avoiding convenient (but highly disturbed) existing sections or profiles which have a feature which has particularly interested you but which is entirely atypical.

5.8 THE ACCOMPANYING REPORT

During the systematic survey stage you will be able to refine your legend to give the final version, e.g. Table 5.1. When you are satisfied with your map, e.g. Fig. 5.1 and legend, and arranged for the final cartography you will have to turn your attention to the accompanying report. In fact, if the area you are mapping is large, you might have already started some preliminary writing-up, checking the sense of what you had written next time you went out into the field. If you are a photographer you could also be building up a collection of photographs from which to illustrate your report.

The accompanying report (for a large project often called a memoir, bulletin or record) should consist of at least the following:

(1) a general description of the location and extent of the area;
(2) a description of the main landscape features;
(3) a description of the geology (solid and drift);
(4) some climatic information;
(5) a general account of the land use;
(6) a description of the method of survey (e.g. free, grid, combination, or density of observations);
(7) the soil classification being used and the kinds of soils encountered, i.e. an extended legend;
(8) an account, in some detail, of each of the mapping units (see below);
(9) an interpretation of the soil map for potential users, e.g. crop suitabilities, drainage requirements or ecological significance (see Chapter 7);
(10) a bibliography or list of references including any which would guide the reader to accounts of similar soils or landscapes where he or she might find additional information.

Many of the memoirs, bulletins, etc., of the various national soil survey organisations provide excellent models on which to base your own, perhaps more modest, report. The temptation in writing reports to accompany soil maps can be to include too much and to overwhelm the reader. Try to present a balanced picture, not concentrating too much on any aspect which you personally might have found extremely fascinating. Also keep asking whether the information will help a user of the map to understand it any better. If not, leave it out. A case in point would be an extensive treatment of the solid geology of the area (perhaps because you are a geologist and there is much information you can draw on) where virtually all the soils are formed in overlying drift.

Probably the most useful parts of a soil report are the descriptions of the mapping units. A published example for a map unit similar to one of those on the example map is set out in Table 5.4. It should include at least one full profile description of the dominant soil, and more if there are other important soils not described elsewhere in the report or if there are significant variants. The way of describing and classifying 'master' profiles has already been described in Chapters 3 and 4. Sometimes analytical results are included but they are not an obligatory or essential part of a soil report. Soil analysis is a highly complex subject requiring a well-equipped laboratory and trained personnel.

Table 5.4 — Typical description of a soil mapping unit

Hanslope series

Classification and reference Typical calcareous pelosol (Hodge and Seale, 1966; Sturdy, 1971)

Lithology and geology Clayey; chalky till. Locally called the Springfield Till 10YR or chalky boulder clay. A clayey glacial deposit rich in chalk stones, containing flint erractics with some quartz and quartzite pebbles.

Standard profile characteristics

Horizon sequence Ap or Ah, BW or Bw(g), Bg or BCgk

Particle size class Clay loam Ap over clay

Stones Stoneless or very slightly stony, often more stony in Ap

Colour Brown or dark greyish brown Ap; light olive brown or yellowish brown but often with grey mottling in Bw(g), light olive brown or yellowish brown with increasing grey mottling in Bg or BCg

Structure Fine or medium subangular blocky structure in Ap, medium or coarse angular blocky in Bw or Bw(g) becoming very coarse angular blocky in BCg

Consistency Moderately weak or moderately firm in Ap; moderately or very firm below, moderately to very sticky

CaCO₃ Usually calcareous in Ap and very calcareous with abundant chalk pieces by 40 cm.

Soil moisture regime Moderate or strong subsoil structure coupled with large content of porous chalk gives these soils the capacity to absorb much surface water after rain. Moderately to slowly permeable subsoil horizons cause wetness in autumn, winter and early spring, but deep surface cracking in late summer restores soil structure.

Table 5.4 (*Contd.*)

Hanslope series

Principal variations
(i)   Wholly clayey profiles occur on upper slope sites where loamy A horizons have been eroded
(ii) Profiles with silty topsoils adjoin Hamble and Hook soils on deeper spreads of loess
(iii) Partially leached profiles occur where the upper 40 cm lack chalk stones but retain more than 1% calcium carbonate

Profile description
Profile no. TL 71/1585; Hanslope series
Locality Leighs Lodge, Great and Little Leighs; 500 m north of Lavender Bridge (grid reference TL715185)
Elevation: 52 m (170 ft) OD
Slope 3°
Aspect SE
Land use Arable
Horizons

0–24 cm Ap	Brown (10YR 4/3) firm clay loam with light olive brown (2.5Y 5/5) material from below; moderate medium subangular blocky; slightly stony with common fine macropores and common roots; sharp smooth boundary
24–48 cm Bw	Light olive brown to yellowish brown (2.5Y–10YR 5/5) very firm clay with few fine distinct strong brown (7.5YR 5/8) mottles; slightly stony with small medium and large rounded angular and nodular flint stones; pockets of chalk stones; weak coarse subangular blocky; calcareous; fine discrete ferrimanganiferous segregations; few roots; narrow undulating boundary
48–102 cm Bg	Yellowish brown to light olive brown (10YR–2.5Y 5/4) very firm clay with common medium yellowish brown (10YR 5/8) and common medium and large light brownish grey (10YR 6/2) mottles; ped faces grey and yellowish brown; weak to moderate coarse prismatic breaking to fine angular blocky; slightly stony with small and medium rounded quartzite and angular to subangular flints; calcareous and chalky; common fine macropores; few roots; fine discrete ferrimanganiferous segregations; diffuse boundary
102–120 cm 2BCgk	Brown (7.5YR 4/3) firm slightly stony clay with common fine to medium yellowish red (5YR 5/8) and common medium and large grey (10YR 6/1) mottles; weak medium and coarse angular blocky; abundant very fine macropores; calcareous and chalky with secondary calcium carbonate; roots absent
120–170 cm	On auger: similar brown calcareous clay
170+	London Clay *in situ*

Table 5.4 (*Contd.*)

Hanslope series

Analyses

Horizon	Ap	Bw	Bg
Depth (cm)	0–24	24–48	48–102
Sand, 100 μm–2 mm (%)	3	4	4
Sand, 200–600 μm (%)	18	12	11
Sand, 60–200 μm (%)	14	11	12
Silt, 2–60 μm (%)	38	33	37
Clay, <2 μm (%)	27	40	36
Organic carbon (%)	1.5		
CaCO$_3$ equivalent (%)	1.2	7.2	31.9
pH in water (1:2.5)	8.2	8.4	8.1
pH in 0.0 M CaCl$_2$ (1:2.5)	7.3	7.3	7.6

Notes: Large calcium carbonate and alkaline pH values typical of these relatively weakly leached soils on chalky till

Identification   Typical calcereous pelosol in clayey chalky till (chalky boulder clay or Springfield Till); clayey within, or at the base of, the plough layer (about 25 cm), and below.

Distinguished from:

Faulkbourne: a typical argillic pelosol, a similarly clayey soil but not calcareous within 40 cm, chalky clay usually reached by 80 cm;

Hornbeam: a stagnoglcyic palaeo-argillic brown earth; the clayey variant of Hornbeam has strong brown or reddish colours at depth and seldom has chalky clay within 80 cm;

Windsor: a pelo-stagnogley soil developed in non-calcareous London Clay which is completely stoneless at depth; secondary carbonate may occur below 70 cm but this is brown, and there are no chalk stones

Hanslope map unit

Extent	2100 ha (5200 acres); 23% of mapped area
Relief	Hanslope soils occur on the flat plateaux and interfluves and upper valley-side slopes
Homogeneity	85%, Hanslope
Included profile classes	Faulkborne (10%); Bengeo and Hook (5%)
Commentary	Hanslope soils characteristically occur on upper valley-side slopes probably by erosion of the leached mantle on the plateau. On steeper breaks of slope more extreme erosion exposes chalky clay at the surface. Hanslope soils are most widespread in White and Black Notley and are extensive in Fairstead, Faulkbourne, Terling and Little Waltham. Silty topsoils occur where Hanslope adjoins Hook and Hamble

Table 5.4 (*Contd.*)

Hanslope series	

	soils. The high base status of these soils is reflected in the rich woodland flora including dog's mercury, primrose and cowslip; wood anemone, violets, spotted orchids and honeysuckle also occur
Land use	Mainly cereals and sugar beet. Woodland on these soils is mainly coppiced oak, hornbeam or sweet chestnut. Shallow excavations are numerous indicating the use of chalky till as a source of agricultural marl
Land capability	2sw

Source: Burton and Seale (1981)

The final part of a report should be primarily for the benefit of potential users who will almost certainly not be soil scientists. The interpretation of soil maps for such users has become more sophisticated in recent years and forms the subject of Chapter 7 with some preliminary consideration of soil, climate and plant interactions in Chapter 6.

5.9 VERY DETAILED MAPS (ABOUT 1:2500)

The basic procedures for making detailed soil maps are the same as those already discussed but there are a few differences. Firstly the intensity of auger borings will need to be much greater and this will favour the grid survey rather than the free survey approach. The soil differences you will be looking for will be more subtle than those for less detailed maps and even soil series and phases may not provide enough discrimination.

There maybe a specific objective, e.g. for a set of fertiliser trials. The temptation to record only information relevant to that purpose should be resisted. Later use of the same land for other trials would require a repeat survey. The answer to both these problems is to make full auger boring descriptions and to collect samples for analysis as required. These results could then be included verbatim in the accompanying report and all the auger boring locations shown on the map. Such information would not be included on a less detailed map and in its accompanying report but for a very detailed map it would allow production of many different but compatible single factor maps which could also help to interpret the map for the user.

5.10 RECONNAISSANCE MAPS (1:100 000 AND SMALLER SCALES)

These maps rely much more on indirect information, including aerial photograph interpretation and much less on field observations than the sort of detailed map described so far in this chapter. Field work is usually limited to selected small areas and transects to check on the composition of the map units already chosen and to confirm boundaries between them. The whole exercise requires a degree of skill and

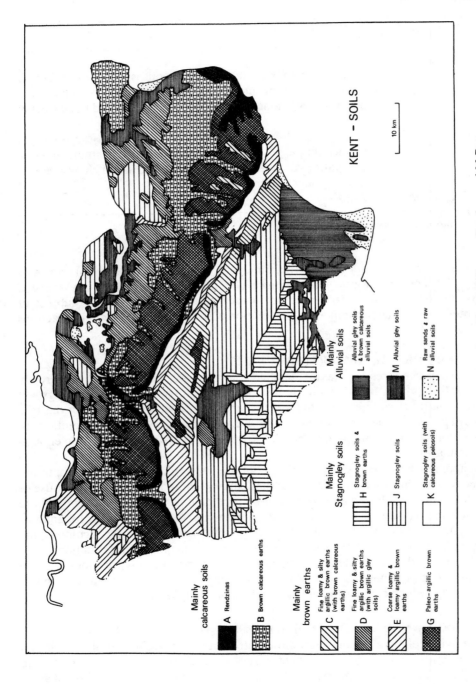

Fig. 5.8— A reconnaissance soil map of Kent, England. (Source: Burnham and McRae (1978)).

experience beyond the capabilities of a beginner, unless he or she is prepared to settle for a very simple map with a few obvious map units, each of which is likely to contain a variety of soils.

An example of such a map, based largely on geological maps, obvious landscape features and agricultural regions is shown in Fig. 5.8. It took the author and a colleague about 1 day to draw a draft map and legend from their knowledge of the area and a further 9 or 10 days to refine it by sample mapping in key areas. The map units are soil associations (see above).

Small-scale maps, especially in developing countries, often rely heavily on aerial photographs, and the concept of land facets has proved useful. A land facet is defined as an area with a recurring pattern of topography, soils and vegetation but in practice it means an area which, so far as can be ascertained on an aerial photograph, has uniform environmental conditions. The textbooks recommended in Chapter 9 provide further information on this subject.

6

Climate, soil and plant interactions

6.1 INTRODUCTION

So far soil has been examined as an entity in itself, but this chapter explores interactions with other environmental factors. It deals in particular with some of the soil properties which have a bearing on plant growth (especially of crops and trees) and their interaction with the other main determinant of plant growth, the climate. We are dealing with **land** as opposed to **soil** *per se,* an important distinction. The concept of **land** embraces all the attributes of the biosphere of which the soil is only one. In practice these attributes are usually taken to include the climate, topography, soil, water, underlying geology, plant and animal populations, and man's activities.

A distinction is sometimes made between properties which are **land characteristics** as distinct from **land qualities.** The former are the sort of properties that can be measured or assessed without excessive effort and include virtually all the soil properties such as texture, structure and stoniness so far described. Simple climatic data, e.g. rainfall, discussed further below, would also be regarded as land characteristics. More complex attributes which are determined by a set of interacting land characteristics are called **land qualities,** the derivation of some of which will be dealt with below. Examples are soil water availability (derived essentially from the soil characteristics of texture, stoniness and horizon depths) and evapotranspiration (derived from a number of climatic characteristics such as temperature, wind speed and net radiation). Estimates of many of the more complex land qualities are available already calculated, while others are not difficult to work out, merely a little tortuous on occasions. At the end of each section a reminder will be given of the main properties just dealt with, the availability of information concerning them and/or the raw data needed to work them out. Some of the properties discussed will be used again when Chapter 7 explains how to interpret a soil map for practical purposes.

The main properties are those which relate to water, both too much of it, expressed as the drainage class or wetness class of a soil profile, or too little of it, i.e. the likely droughtiness of a soil–climate combination. The relevant climatic parameters also relate mainly to water, e.g. mean annual rainfall, but also to temperature and wind speeds. These climatic factors are amongst those which should ideally be included in a report to accompany a soil map (see Chapter 5).

As with virtually all soil or soil-related properties there are no guidelines in this subject which are universally accepted and different procedures and methods apply in different countries. You should therefore find out what are the local conventions for the area in which you are working (or a closely comparable area) and use those. The examples given below are mainly from the extensive work done by the Soil Survey of England and Wales, which has also been used by the Soil Survey of Scotland in their system of land capability classification for agriculture (see Chapter 7). Some examples from the USDA Soil Taxonomy and FAO work are also given.

6.2   CLIMATIC PROPERTIES

6.2.1   General

Most counties have a network of meteorological stations recording daily weather observations from which the long-term climatic properties (in effect the average weather) can be determined. The national Meteorological Office will then compile the data into maps and tables which are readily available. Ideally, however, data from a meteorological station in or close to the study area should be used if available, together with the means of correcting any of the data, e.g. by making allowance for altitude, if necessary.

The advent of computers has meant that much of the information in the more advanced countries is present in a database or databank, often produced in the interests of agriculture. There is for example an agroclimatic databank for England and Wales giving information for 970 meteorological stations and on a 5 or 10 km square grid, as part of the soil information system of the Soil Survey of England and Wales. These are in a form compatible with the methods used for the study of soil, climate and crop interrelationships of which examples appear elsewhere in this chapter.

6.2.2   Temperature and related properties

Daily **mean, maximum and minimum temperatures** are usually recorded for all meteorological stations (e.g. Table 6.1) but in themselves are not really much use. It

Table 6.1 — Typical mean monthly and annual air temperatures for a site in northern England

	Jan	Feb	March	April	May	June	July	August	Sept	Oct	Nov	Dec	Year
					Mean air temperature (°C)								
York (17 m (57 ft) OD): 1931–60													
Maximum	5.9	6.8	9.6	12.8	16.3	19.4	21.0	20.5	18.0	18.7	9.5	7.1	13.4
Minimum	0.8	1.1	2.4	4.4	6.9	10.0	12.2	11.8	9.8	6.6	4.0	2.2	6.0
Mean	3.3	4.0	6.0	8.6	11.6	14.7	16.6	16.2	13.9	10.2	6.8	4.7	9.7
Askham Bryan (3.3 m (110 ft) OD): 1961–9													
Maximum	5.5	5.6	8.7	11.7	15.0	18.9	19.4	19.2	17.5	13.8	8.4	5.5	12.4
Minimum	0.3	0.4	1.2	3.7	6.1	9.1	10.6	10.2	9.2	6.5	2.6	−0.3	5.0
Mean	2.9	3.0	5.1	7.7	10.6	14.0	15.0	14.7	13.2	10.1	5.5	2.6	8.7

Source: Matthews (1971)

is better to use them to derive the periods over which temperatures are above or below certain threshold values, e.g. for working out the number of frost days (e.g. Table 6.2).

Table 6.2 — Average number of days of occurrence of specified phenomena at St. Andrews, Scotland.

	Jan	Feb	March	April	May	June	July	August	Sept	Oct	Nov	Dec
Hail (39–41 years)	0.5	0.5	0.8	0.9	0.9	2.0	0.1	0.1	0.1	0.2	0.5	0.4
Thunder (40–41 years)	0.1	0	0.1	0.1	1.0	0.9	1.4	0.9	0.3	0.2	0.1	0
Fog at 0900 hours (49–52 years)	0.9	0.6	0.9	0.5	0.9	0.5	0.6	0.9	0.7	0.9	0.7	0.7
Air frost (9–11 years)	13.2	12.2	7.2	3.2	0.5	0.1	0	0	0	0.7	9.8	13.6
Ground frost (50–53 years)	16.9	15.0	13.7	9.0	3.4	0.5	0	0	1.3	4.9	11.7	15.4
Gale (36–38 years)	0.9	0.4	0.4	0.6	0.2	0.2	0.1	0.2	0.4	0.5	0.5	1.1

Source: adapted from Laing (1976)

A good measure of the heat energy available for plant growth in Britain is the **accumulated temperature above 0°C** for the first 6 months of the year and maps of median accumulated temperature above 0°C for this period are available (e.g. Fig. 6.1). The unit of measurement is the day °C and the total is obtained from daily measurements of mean air temperature. Values of accumulated temperature above 0°C for January to June range from more than 1650 in southwest England to less than 850 in the north Pennines, with values in the Midlands around 1400.

More commonly, accumulated temperature is summed above a plant growth threshold (e.g. 5.6°C) and values for this are on the agroclimatic databank as well as appearing on separate maps for England and Wales and for Scotland. Crop suitability classifications (see Chapter 7) are based mainly on accumulated temperature values above 0°C, except sugar beet which is based on accumulated temperature values above 5.6°C, while maize should ideally be based on accumulated temperature values above 10°C.

It has been found in Western Europe that the best response to fertiliser application in the spring is when 200 day °C has accumulated. The farming press now routinely monitor the situation each spring as the 200 day °C point approaches.

Soil temperatures are generally more important for crops than are air temperatures (especially the screen temperatures normally measured) and some meteorological stations accordingly measure soil temperatures (e.g. Table 6.3). It is now considered that soil temperature data are a better guide to the **length of the growing season**. This is now defined in Britain as the average period during which the soil temperature at 30 cm depth remains above 6 °C. Again, maps for this property are

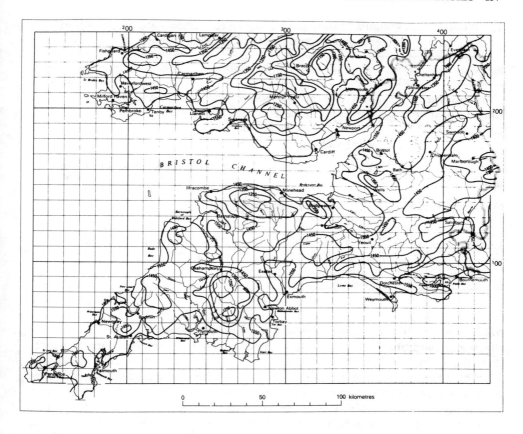

Fig. 6.1 — Median accumulated temperature (in day °C) above 0°C for southwest England: January–June 1959–1978. (Source: Findlay *et al.* (1984)).

Table 6.3 — Typical mean monthly and annual soil temperatures for a site in northern England (York): 1921–1950

						Mean temperature (°C)							
	Jan	Feb	March	April	May	June	July	August	Sept	Oct	Nov	Dec	Year
30 cm (1 ft)	3.9	3.9	4.9	7.6	10.8	14.0	15.8	15.8	14.0	10.8	7.3	5.0	9.5
120 cm (4 ft)	6.1	5.5	5.6	7.1	9.1	11.5	13.4	14.2	13.9	12.2	9.7	7.5	9.6

Source: Matthews (1971)

also available for England and Wales, and data are held in the agroclimatic databank.

As a reminder, Table 6.4 shows the availability of data for the properties discussed above.

Table 6.4 — Availability of data for temperature, accumulated temperature, soil temperature and length of growing season

Property	Whether directly available	Raw data for calculation
Temperature (mean, maximum and minimum)	Yes, national Meteorological Office, local meteorological stations, agroclimatic databank, some soil survey publications	Not available
Accumulated temperature	Yes, as above	Daily mean temperatures
Soil temperature	Yes, selected meteorological stations	
Length of growing season	As above, agroclimatic data bank, some soil survey publications	Soil temperatures

6.2.3   Rainfall, evapotranspiration and soil moisture deficit

Mean annual rainfall is the commonest climatic property quoted, and maps of mean annual rainfall, averaged over specified periods, are usually readily obtainable. Monthly or even daily rainfall figures are best, for a meteorological station in or close to the study area and with an indication of how the results could be corrected, e.g. by taking altitude into account. If possible some indication of typical, abnormally wet or abnormally dry years should be sought. More specialist information can sometimes be provided, e.g. rainfall intensity (for assessment of erosion hazards) such as in Table 6.5, or how much precipitation fell as snow rather than rain. Some typical rainfall data are presented for an area in England in Table 6.6.

Table 6.5 also gives data for **potential transpiration** as well as for rainfall. This is also measured in millimetres (or inches) but represents losses of water from the soil surface rather than additions as rainfall. Potential transpiration is formally defined as the amount of water transpired per unit area by a vigorously growing short green crop which completely covers the ground and is amply supplied with water from soil reserves or irrigation. Potential transpiration is calculated from standard meteorological data and these calculations can also cover the direct evaporation from bare soils in the winter. Thus the general term **evapotranspiration** is often used.

The balance between the rainfall and the evapotranspiration has proved to be a useful measure of the dryness of a particular climate. This is the concept of the **potential soil moisture deficit** (PSMD) which is the calculated difference between the rainfall and the potential evapotranspiration over the period when the latter exceeds the former. It represents the quantity of water required by the crop in addition to that supplied by the rainfall over the summer period. Soils which can supply this amount of water from the reserves held in the profile prevent the onset of drought but, the less water the soil can supply (its available water capacity), the more the crop will suffer from drought, unless artificially irrigated.

Table 6.5 — Maximum rainfall intensity for various locations in Indonesia
(Source: Greenland and Lal, 1977)

Duration (min)	Maximum rainfall intensity (mm/h)						
	Jakarta	Bogor	Pasuruan	Padeng	Pontianak	Ambon	Mean
5	192	192	192	192	228	216	204
15	140	156	140	172	160	156	156
30	118	130	128	152	146	96	128
60	88	110	86	100	80	63	88

SMD's are usually calculated on a monthly basis from the rainfall and evapotranspiration figures as in Table 6.6, and like the two properties from which it is derived is measured in millimetres (or inches). The example in Table 6.6 shows that in the first few months of the year evapotranspiration is less than rainfall and so no moisture deficit builds up in the soil. Indeed it shows quite a substantial surplus rainfall, assuming no drainage impediment, will leach through the soil to the water table or to any artificial drainage system. In April, however, transpiration begins to exceed rainfall in our example and a soil moisture deficit begins to accumulate reaching a maximum PSMD of 112 mm at the end of August. Thereafter rainfall exceeds transpiration on a monthly basis and, as soil water reserves are replenished, the accumulated moisture deficit declines reaching zero some time in December.

At this stage the soil, assuming it is free draining, will have reached profile field capacity and the date on which this occurs can be predicted for normal, wet or dry years. The soil profile remains at or near field capacity, with surplus rainfall draining away until the following April and again the date can be predicted at which the soil becomes drier than field capacity, i.e. when the moisture deficit situation begins. It should be noted that the duration of the field capacity period is calculated solely from climatic data although it concerns the likely water status of the soils. It is used to plan land drainage schemes, to assess the workability and trafficability of land and to estimate the potential grazing season. Similar soil water balance considerations linked with temperature data are used to define moisture regimes in the USDA Soil Taxonomy (Fig. 6.2).

The data in Table 6.6 give the maximum PSMD, and maps showing this are now available for the whole of England and Wales. The maximum PSMD is appropriate for grass or other perennial crop which covers the ground completely. Most arable crops, however, do not fully cover the ground until partly through the growing season and also stop growing before the theoretical maximum PSMD has developed. Methods to allow for the different growth patterns of common crops have been devised and crop-adjusted PSMDs can be calculated. These adjusted figures are available from the agroclimatic databank or in map form. The adjusted PSMD for winter wheat in Mid July, at which time it has ceased to draw on the soil water reserves is less than the maximum (grass) value. Hence winter wheat is less likely to suffer from moisture stress than is grass in the same soil type.

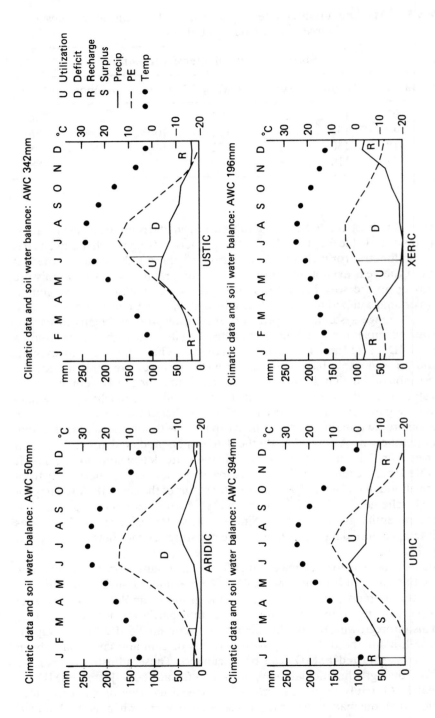

Fig. 6.2 — Climatic data and soil water balances for aridic, ustic, udic and xeric moisture regimes as recognised in Soil Taxonomy. (Source: USDA (1975)).

Table 6.6 — Average rainfall, potential evapotranspiration and soil moisture balance (all values in mm) for a soil whose profile available water capacity (AP) is 124 mm

Month	Rainfall	Potiential evapo-transpiration	Monthly rainfall deficit	Monthly rainfall surplus	Available soil moisture at end of month[c]	Drainage water[d]
	(R)	(PT)	(PT−R)[a]	(R−PT)[b]		
Jan	64	4		60	124	60
Feb	48	12		36	124	36
Mar	41	32		9	124	9
April	43	56	13		111	—
May	55	79	24		87	—
June	53	86	33		54	—
July	58	87	29		25	—
Aug	60	73	13		12	—
Sept	52	40		12	24	—
Oct	55	20		35	59	—
Nov	64	3		61	120	—
Dec	55	1		54	124	50
Total	648	493	112 (by end of Aug)	267		155

[a]For the months where $PT>R$.
[b]For the months where $R>PT$.
[c]Calculated from figure for previous month minus any monthly rainfall deficit or plus any monthly rainfall surplus during recharge period, with a maximum of 124 mm (i.e. assumes the soil returns to field capacity and
[d]all rainfall in excess of that requirement drains away freely).

Maximum (i.e. grass) PSMD values are typically above 200 mm in much of East Anglia (where the adjusted values for winter wheat are about 125 mm), are commonly 150–175 mm in the Midlands and southeast England (100–125 mm for winter wheat) but fall to below 25 mm in the uplands of Wales and Cumbria.

Three kinds of information can then be obtained from these rainfall–evapotranspiration analyses. Firstly they can be used for irrigation scheduling. For example irrigation with 2.5 cm irrigation water is recommended for potatoes in England and Wales when the accumulated moisture deficit reaches 50 mm.

Secondly they give the accumulated maximum PSMD (appropriate for grass) and various crop-adjusted values. These can be combined with data for the water-holding capacity of the soil (see below) to assess the droughtiness of a particular soil–climate regime. This is an important consideration in the assessment of the suitability of land for growing crops (see Chapter 7).

Thirdly the number of days the soil is at or above field capacity over the winter can be calculated. In turn this climatic property can be used to assess the trafficability of soils and hence the number of days likely to be available for machinery to work on the land (see machinery work days below), an important property in assessing crop suitability (see Chapter 7). Similarly the **duration of the field capacity period** is one of the factors used to assess the ability of land to withstand poaching by stock and thence in the evaluation of the suitability of land for grassland (see also Chapter 7).

Table 6.7 provides a reminder of the availability of the data discussed in this section.

Table 6.7 — Availability of data for rainfall, potential evapotranspiration, PSMD, crop-adjusted PSMD and duration of field capacity period

Property	Whether directly available	Raw data for calculation
Rainfall	Yes, National Meteorological Office, local meteorological stations, agroclimatic data bank, some soil survey publications	Not available
Potential evapo-transpiration	Yes, as above	Not available
PSMD	Yes, as above	Sum of monthly rainfall and potential evapotranspiration figures
PSMD (crop adjusted)	Yes, as above	More complicated manipulation of monthly rainfall and evapotranspiration figures
Duration of field capacity period	Yes, as above	As PSMD but using daily figures as appropriate

6.3   SOIL PROPERTIES

6.3.1   Available water capacity

The **available water capacity** (AWC) of a soil is the amount of water held by a soil which a plant can use. It is virtually the same as the water held by capillary action. As explained in Chapter 1, if a soil is saturated with water and allowed to drain some of the water is so loosely held in the larger pores that the soil cannot retain it (the so-called gravitational water). The water the soil then holds at this point (often called the field capacity) is its **retained water capacity** (see below). This retained water includes both the water held in the pores mainly by capillary action and which can be used by plants (the available or capillary water), and the tightly held hygroscopic water which is unavailable to plants. Thus the AWC of a soil is always less than its retained water capacity, the difference being the tightly held hygroscopic water and a small portion of the capillary water.

Soil water contents can be expressed in several ways, as a gravimetric percentage, a volumetric percentage or, when it is to be used with meteorological data, as an amount per unit depth of soil. Conventionally it is expressed in this last form in terms of millimetres per centimetre (or inches per foot). A moisture content of P mm/cm is equivalent to $1.2 \times P$ inches per foot or a volumetric percentage of $P/10$. Conversion of volumetric to gravimetric percentages and vice versa requires knowledge of the bulk density of the soil (its weight per unit volume). Assuming the bulk density (in grams per cubic centimetre) is known, then %(volumetric) = %(gravimetric) × bulk density.

The AWC depends mainly on soil texture, and to a lesser extent on organic matter content and bulk density. Average AWCs have been worked out from a study of several hundreds of samples and are given in Table 6.8. For simplicity it can be assumed that the main determining factor is texture, that organic matter can be accounted for by differentiating between topsoils and subsoils and that the soils have an average bulk density for that texture.

Soils hold water with greater force the drier they become and, within the available water range, plant roots experience greater difficulty in extracting the drier the soil. As explained in Chapter 1, soil physicists relate the degree of availability of water to the suction (measured in bars) required to remove it. In practice, however, only two categories of available water need to be distinguished; these are shown in

Table 6.8 — Available water (0.05–15 bar) and easily available water (0.05–2 bar) for topsoils and subsoils in relation to texture

(Source: adapted from Hall *et al.* (1977) and MAFF, (1984). The data from Hall *et al.* assume medium packing density for all the soils, and the sand fraction to be mainly in the medium range. The MAFF data, in brackets, do not specify either packing density or nature of sand fraction. The 'easily available water' data are for subsoils only. The data are given as mm moisture per cm depth of soil to facilitate calculations of available moisture for a soil profile (see text) and comparisons with moisture deficit data

Soil texture	Available water (0.05–15 bar)				Easily available water (0.05–2 bar)
	Topsoils		Subsoils		Subsoils
Clay	1.8	(1.8)	1.5	(1.5)	0.9
Sandy clay		(1.7)		(1.5)	
Silty clay	1.7	(1.8)	1.6	(1.5)	0.9
Sandy clay loam	1.7	(1.7)	1.7	(1.5)	1.1
Clay loam	2.0	(1.8)	1.5	(1.5)	0.9
Silty clay loam	2.0	(1.8)	1.7	(1.5)	1.0
Silt loam	2.5	(2.2)	2.2	(2.1)	1.8
Sandy silt loam	2.1	(1.9)	1.8	(1.7)	1.1
Sandy loam	1.6	(1.7)	1.5	(1.5)	1.2
Loamy sand	1.4	(1.2)	1.2	(0.9)	0.9
Sand		(0.8)	0.9	(0.5)	0.7
Peat		(3.5)		(3.5)	

Table 6.9 — Adjustments to profile available water for particular crops

	Depth (cm)	Suction (bar)
Wheat		
Barley	0–50	0.05–15
Temporary grass	50–120	0.05–2
Potatoes	0–70	0.05–15
Sugar beet	0–80	0.05–15
	80–130	0.05–2
Permanent grass	0–70	0.05–15
	70–100	0.05–2

Source: Soil Survey of England and Wales

Table 6.8. Total available water is that removed from soils at suctions between 0.05 and 15 bar. The portion of it easily available, when the soil is relatively moist, is defined as that which can be removed with less suction, 0.05–2 bar.

The AWC of the entire profile can be calculated by summing the contributions made by individual layers of different textures, with correction for stoniness as necessary. In its simplest form the calculation takes the following form. Consider a soil profile of total rooting depth 1 m, consisting of 25 cm sandy silt loam, over 50 cm sandy loam, both of negligible stone content, with the final 25 cm of the profile a sand with 30% stones. The total AWC is then:

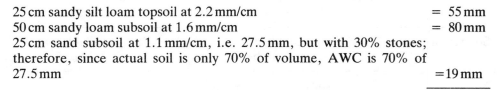

25 cm sandy silt loam topsoil at 2.2 mm/cm   = 55 mm
50 cm sandy loam subsoil at 1.6 mm/cm   = 80 mm
25 cm sand subsoil at 1.1 mm/cm, i.e. 27.5 mm, but with 30% stones; therefore, since actual soil is only 70% of volume, AWC is 70% of 27.5 mm   =19 mm

Total Profile AWC =154 mm

A more sophisticated method is now preferred which takes the rooting pattern of the crop into account as well as the two kinds of soil available water, the total and the easily available (see Table 6.10) The final result is called the **crop-adjusted profile available water capacity** (crop-adjusted AP). Separate calculations have to be carried out for different crops, usually grass, winter wheat, spring barley, potatoes and sugar beet which have contrasting rooting patterns.

For example, the profile available water (AP) for wheat (and temporary grass and other cereals) is calculated using the 0.05–15 bar values for the top 50 cm of the profile while the rest of the profile down to 120 cm, the assumed maximum rooting depth of cereals or less if the rooting zone is shallower, uses the 0.05–2 bar easily available values (see Table 6.9).

For the above example the calculation of AP (winter wheat) is as follows:

25 cm sandy silt loam topsoil at 2.2 mm/cm	= 55 mm
25 cm sandy loam subsoil at 1.6 mm/cm	= 40 mm
25 cm sandy loam subsoil at 1.2 mm/cm	= 30 mm

25 cm sand subsoil at 0.7 mm/cm, i.e. 17.5 mm, but with 30% stones;
therefore since actual soil is only 70% of volume, AP is 70% of 17.5 mm = 12 mm

AP (winter wheat) 137 mm

Table 6.10 shows the availability of data for the AWC, the AP and the crop-adjusted AP.

Table 6.10 — Availability of data for the AWC, the AP and the crop-adjusted AP

Property	Whether directly available	Raw data for calculation
AWC	Yes, in tabular form for top-soils and subsoils according to textures in soil survey publications	Basic laboratory data
AP	Only for some type examples of selected soil series	AWC values as above plus depth, texture and stoniness of soil horizons. Sum AWC contribution of each horizon for depth of rooting
Crop-adjusted AP	As above	As above but using total and easily available water capacities with calculations adjusted for growth pattern of particular crop

6.3.2 Droughtiness

The two components of droughtiness are the climatic moisture deficit (MD) discussed earlier and the ability of the soil to satisfy it as represented by AP. The value of AP−MD can be calculated for individual crops from the crop-adjusted AP and MD figures and rated according to Table 6.11. Some typical results for contrasting soils in contrasting climates are given in Table 6.12.

As a reminder, Table 6.13 gives the availability of data for droughtiness class.

6.3.3 Retained water capacity

The retained water capacity of a soil was explained in Chapter 1 but basically is the amount of water left in a soil after all the water which can drain out solely under the influence of gravity has done so. It depends mainly on soil texture, the packing

Table 6.11 — Droughtiness classification

AP−MD (mm)	Droughtiness class
	a Non-droughty
+50	
	b Slightly droughty
0	
	c Moderately droughty
−50	
	d Very droughty

Source: Soil Survey of England and Wales

Table 6.12 — Typical droughtiness assessments for contrasting soils and locations in England and Wales

Site	Winter wheat	Spring barley	Maincrop potatoes	Sugar beet	Permanent grass
Hanslope series at three locations					
AP (mm)	118	118	75	120	128
Melton Mowbray					
AP−MD (mm)	+9	+16	−16	+29	−24
Dryness class	b	b	c	b	c
Cambridge					
AP−MD (mm)	+8	+14	−31	+14	−60
Dryness class	b	b	c	b	d
Lowestoft					
AP−MD (mm)	−3	+4	−48	−2	−80
Dryness class	c	b	c	c	d
Sandy soils at four locations					
Newport or Freckenham series (sandy phase)					
AP (mm)	99	99	68	113	95
Newport					
AP−MD (mm)	+9	+17	−17	+28	−51
Dryness class	b	b	c	b	d
Gleadthorpe					
AP−MD (mm)	−4	+1	−22	+23	−57
Dryness class	c	b	c	b	d
Melton Mowbray					
AP−MD (mm)	−10	−3	−23	+22	−57
Dryness class	c	c	c	b	d

Table 6.12 (*Contd.*)

Site	Winter wheat	Spring barley	Maincrop potatoes	Sugar beet	Permanent grass
Lowestoft					
AP−MD (mm)	−22	−15	−54	−9	−113
Dryness class	c	c	d	c	d
Newport or Freckenham series (sandy loam topsoil)					
AP (mm)	106	106	75	120	102
Lowestoft					
AP−MD (mm)	−15	−8	−47	−2	−106
Dryness class	c	c	c	c	d
Gleadthorpe					
AP−MD (mm)	+3	+8	−15	+30	−50
Dryness class	b	b	c	b	d

Source: Thomasson (1979)

Table 6.13 — Availability of data for droughtiness class

Property	Whether directly available	Raw data for calculation
Droughtiness class (AP−MD)	Only for some type examples of selected series	Crop-adjusted AP minus crop-adjusted MD

density which normally is assumed to be medium (though proving that it is this and not high or low packing involves yet another complication) and organic matter content. Table 6.14 gives some typical values of the retained water capacity for topsoils of various textures. These values are required in the assessment of the workability and trafficability of soils which, in turn are used in crop suitability assessments (see Chapter 7).

Table 6.15 provides a reminder of the availability of data for retained water capacity.

6.3.4 Drainage and wetness classes

For many years the drainage status of a soil profile has been assessed by the profile morphology especially signs of gleying and their proximity to the surface of the soil. Thus particular attention is paid to the brightness or dullness of soil colours, the incidence of mottling and greyish colours usually caused by waterlogging and attendant anaerobism, and in very badly drained soils the surface build-up of peat and peaty layers. Five **drainage classes** are normally recognised: well drained, moderately well drained, imperfectly drained, poorly drained, and very poorly

Table 6.14 — Retained water capacity for topsoils and subsoils in relation to texture (Source: adapted from Hall *et al.*, 1977.) The data are given as mm moisture per cm depth of soil. In the soil assessment for workability (Table 6.20) the classes of retained water capacity are High >4.5 mm/cm, Medium 3.5–4.5 mm/cm and Low <3.5 mm/cm

Soil texture	Retained water capacity (mm/cm soil)	
	Topsoils	Subsoils
Clay	4.80	4.35
Silty clay	4.87	4.01
Sandy clay loam	3.89	3.37
Silty clay loam	4.51	3.78
Silt loam	4.00	3.42
Sandy silt loam	3.50	3.33
Sandy loam	3.10	2.72
Loamy sand	2.00	2.16
Sand	—	1.38

Table 6.15 — Availability of data for the retained water capacity

Property	Whether directly available	Raw data for calculation
Retained water capacity	Yes, in tabular form for top-soils according to textures in soil survey publications	Basic laboratory data

drained, which are obviously in the order of worsening drainage as shown in Fig. 6.3 (ignore the duration of wet states for the moment). Sometimes a category of excessively well drained is included but this is more a reflection of low retained water capacity or low AWC due to coarse textures and stoniness than the actual drainage status.

Drainage classes are based on indirect evidence such as colour mottling which is assumed to be a direct indication of waterlogging. Profile morphology can, however, be an unreliable guide to soil waterlogging. Some reddish parent materials, e.g. notably those derived from Permo-Triassic rocks, resist gleying and remain reddish and unmottled even if badly drained while conversely some parent materials have greyish colours which can look like gley features even in well-drained soils. Colour mottling can occur in soils for reasons unrelated to drainage, perhaps inherited from the parent material or due to an earlier phase of intensive soil weathering. Soils with low contents of iron (whose compounds produce the characteristic gleying colours) exhibit little or no gleying even if badly drained particularly highly calcareous soils

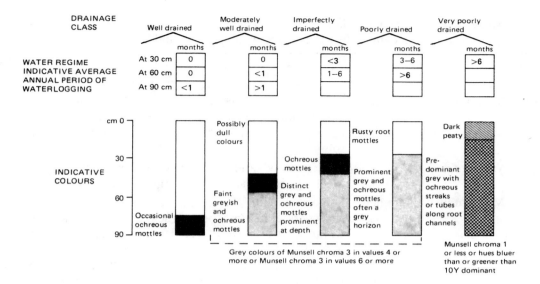

Fig. 6.3 — Drainage class and water regime related to profile morphology. (Source: Soil Survey of England and Wales)

or, conversely, highly leached or podzolised soils. Finally gley features remain as relict features long after drainage improvements have been carried out and so are no guide whatsoever to current drainage status. For this last reason the drainage class is sometimes referred to as the 'natural' drainage class implying that, while the profile morphology is thought to be a reliable guide to the drainage regime under which the soil formed, this is now substantially different (and probably unknown).

Thus direct definition of drainage classes on the basis of profile morphology is unwise, though in practical terms the easiest kind of definition to apply to soils. The problem can be circumvented by making the formal definitions of the drainage classes on the basis of the average periods during which the soil is saturated with water and the depths at which saturation occurs. These definitions are then accompanied by descriptions that commonly, though not necessarily, occur in soils of each class, and hence the two parts of Fig. 6.3. These are defensible definitions, though they are virtually impossible to apply directly. The full definitions are set out in Table 6.16.

The Soil Survey of England and Wales have now moved completely to the definition of soil drainage status on observed periods of waterlogging and to differentiate these from the drainage classes with their profile morphology connotation have called them **wetness classes**. The definitions and approximate correspondence with the earlier drainage classes, assuming no drainage improvements, are given in Table 6.17. One of the advantages of wetness classes, however, is that the drainage status of a soil can be expressed not only in its natural state but also what it is (or would be) following drainage improvements.

Table 6.16 — Drainage class, water regime and probable soil morphology as recognised by the Soil Survey of England and Wales

Class	Definition
Well drained (excessive)	Coarse-textured soils with small AWC and only saturated during and just after heavy rain. Surplus water is removed very rapidly. Any water table is well below the solum
Well drained	Soil is rarely saturated in any horizon within 90 cm. Mottling is usually absent throughout the profile
Moderately well drained	Some part of the soil in the upper 90 cm is saturated for short periods in winter or after heavy rain but no horizon within 50 cm remains saturated for more than one month in the year. Colours typical of well-drained soils on similar materials are usually dominant but may be slightly lower in chroma, especially on ped faces and faint to distinct ochreous or grey mottling may occur below 50 cm
Imperfectly drained	Some part of the soil in the upper 50 cm is saturated for several months but not for most of the year Subsurface horizon colours are commonly lower in chroma and/or yellower in hue than those of well-drained soils on similar materials. Greyish or ochreous mottling is usually distinct by 50 cm and may be prominent below this depth. There is rarely any gleying in the upper 25 cm
Poorly drained	The soil is saturated for at least half the year in the upper 50 cm but the upper 25 cm is unsaturated during most of the growing season The profiles normally show strong gleying. A horizons are usually darker and/or greyer than those of well-drained soils on similar materials and contain rusty mottles. Grey colours are prominent on ped faces in fissured clayey soils or in the matrix of weakly structured soils
Very poorly drained	Some part of the soil is saturated at less than 25 cm for at least half the year. Some part of the soil within the upper 60 cm is permanently saturated The profiles usually have peaty or humose surface horizons and the subsurface horizon colours have low (near neutral) chroma and yellowish to bluish hues

Source: Soil Survey of England and Wales

Table 6.17 — Categories of soil wetness (wetness classes) used by the Soil Survey of England and Wales and corresponding drainage classes based on soil profile morphology

Wetness class	Duration of wet states	Drainage class[a]
I	The soil profile is not wet within 70 cm depth for more than 30 days[b] in most years[c]	Well drained
II	The soil profile is wet within 70 cm cepth for 30–90 days in most years	Moderately well drained
III	The soil profile is wet within 70 cm depth for 90–180 days in most years	Imperfectly drained
IV	The soil profile is wet within 70 cm depth for more than 180 days, but not wet within 40 cm depth for more than 180 days in most years	Poorly drained
V	The soil profile is wet within 40 cm depth for more than 180 days and usually wet within 70 cm for more than 335 days in most years	Very poorly drained
VI	The soil profile is wet within 40 cm depth for more than 335 days in most years	Very poorly drained

[a]The drainage classes only correspond approximately to wetness classes.
[b]The number of days specified is not necessarily a continuous period.
[c]'In most years' is defined as more than 10 out of 20 years.
Source: Jarvis and Mackney (1973)

Ideally wetness class should be measured by dipwells installed for several years, but of course this is rarely feasible except for key benchmark sites. A soil profile can be allocated to a wetness class according not just to the intensity of and the depth to gleying (as with drainage classes), but also to the depth to any slowly permeable horizon and the average field capacity days (see above). Table 6.18 sets out the criteria.

Slowly permeable horizons are those with textures which are clayey (clay, sandy clay and silty clay), fine loamy (clay loam or sandy clay loam) or fine silty (silty clay loam). In a relatively dry climate (less than 175 field capacity days) it is assumed that soils can be loosened and made permeable to at least 40 cm, and hence the entries marked with a superscript [a] in Table 6.18.

You might like to try out your ability to use this table for the following simple profile descriptions before reading the answers at the end of the paragraph.

Profile 1   0–25 cm   Dark brown clay loam
            25–44 cm Brown silty clay loam with ochreous mottles
            44 cm+   Grey and brown mottled clay
            190 field capacity days

Table 6.18 — Relationship of wetness class to field capacity days and depth to slowly permeable horizon

Average field capacity days	Gleyed within 70 cm depth for the following depths to slowly permeable horizon				Ungleyed within 70 cm depth; depth to slowly permeable horizon,
	<40 cm	40–80 cm	>80 cm		>80 cm
			Drainage outfalls limiting	Drainage outfalls not limiting	
<100 [a]		II	II–VI	I	I
100–125 [a]		II–III[1]	III–VI	I	I
125–150 [a]		II–III[1]	III–VI	I	I
150–175 [a]		II–IV[1]	III–VI	I	I
175–200	IV	III–IV[1]	IV–VI	I	I
200–225	V	III–IV[1]	V–VI	I–II	I
225–250	V	IV–V[1]	V–VI	II	I
250–300	V–VI	V	V–VI	III	I
>300	VI	VI	VI	IV	I

[1]The drier of the two wetness classes indicated is likely to occur either on slopes or in soils where the slowly permeable horizon is between 60 and 80 cm depth. Soils in these circumstances are normally not gleyed within 40 cm depth.

[a]In climates with less than 175 field capacity days, subsoiling or other soil-loosening techniques are usually effective to 40 cm depth. In this table it is assumed that permeability has been improved to at least that depth.
Source: Soil Survey of England and Wales
[a]See Table 6.14. Source: Soil Survey of England and Wales

Source: Soil Survey of England and Wales

Profile 2   Similar, with 170 field capacity days

Profile 3   0-27 cm   Dark brown silt loam
             27–58 cm   Brown silt loam
             58–77 cm   Brown silt loam with ochreous mottles
             77 cm+   Greyish brown silty clay loam with ochreous and grey mottles
             145 field capacity days

Profile 4   0-30 cm   Dark brown sandy silt loam
             30–50 cm   Brown sandy silt loam
             50 cm+   Greyish brown sandy silt loam with ochreous mottles
             160 field capacity days, drainage outfalls not limiting

Profile 1 in a relatively wet climate, with heavy textures and gleying close to the surface is an example of wetness class V. In a drier climate a similar profile, Profile 2, could be loosened to at least 40 cm so that the classes in the second column apply. Given the heavy textures and prominent gleying of the profile the wetter of the two suggested classes, i.e. wetness class IV is the more likely. Both Profile 1 and Profile 2 would be classed as poorly drained in the drainage class system.

The slowly permeable horizon in Profile 3 is well down the profile but has caused waterlogging and gleying higher in the profile. The table indicates a choice between wetness classes II and III of which the former is the correct one, given the depth of the slowly permeable horizon and the absence of mottling within 40 cm of the surface. The drainage class would be moderately well drained but very close to imperfectly drained.

Profile 4 has no slowly permeable horizons and so it is likely that this is a groundwater gley situation. Given that drainage outfalls are not limiting such a soil would be placed in wetness class I, at least potentially. In an unimproved state and/or where drainage outfalls were limiting the table indicates a range between wetness classes III and VI. You would now have to resort to experience, helped greatly by seeing the soil during the winter, to decide where within this range you would place the soil. The absence of grey colours and the absence of mottling close to the surface would favour allocation to wetness class III rather than to VI. Profile morphology alone would require the soil to be placed in the imperfectly drained category but would give no indication of the possibilities afforded by drainage which would effectively transform the soil to well drained.

Table 6.19 indicates the availability of data for drainage and wetness classes.

Table 6.19 — Availability of data for drainage and wetness classes

Property	Whether directly available?	Raw data for calculation
Drainage class	Allocation of series to drainage classes routinely reported in soil map lengends, bulletins, etc.	Profile morphology
Wetness class (ideally)		Dipwell observations for several years
Wetness class (in practice)	As above	Profile morphology (depths to gleying and to slowly permeable horizons), duration of field capacity period, and, in some cases, information on drainage outfalls

6.3.5   Workability and trafficability

The ability to 'get onto the land' (i.e. its **trafficability**) and to carry out cultivations and other operations without structural damage to the soil (its **workability**) depends both on climatic and on soil characteristics. A first approximation would be to say that land could not or should not be worked during the field capacity period (see above). This is the period, mainly in late autumn, winter and early spring, when there is zero soil moisture deficit, as calculated from meteorological data.

However, as any farmer or gardener will tell you, there are times when one kind of soil can safely be worked or trafficked even within the field capacity period while another cannot. Thus soil physical properties, especially those affecting soil water, have to be incorporated in any assessment based on the field capacity period. This has led to the concept of **machinery work days** when the land can safely be worked during the main autumn and spring activities of harvesting tillage and drilling. They are calculated for the periods between 1 September and 31 December (autumn) and between 1 March and 30 April (spring) as described below. The relevant soil properties are wetness class, depth to slowly permeable horizon, nature of topsoil and, if a mineral topsoil, its retained water capacity (Table 6.20). The derivation of these has been explained above.

Table 6.20 — Soil assessment for workability

Wetness class	Depth to slowly permeable horizon	Mineral topsoils Retained water capacity[a]			Humose or peaty topsoils
	(cm)	Low	Medium	High	
I	>80 (sandy)	aa	—	—	—
	>80	a	a	a	a
II	>80	a	ab	b	a
	40–80	b	b	bc	b
III	>80	b	c	c	b
	40–80	c	c	cd	c
	<40	c	cd	d	d
IV	>80	c	d	d	d
	40–80	c	d	de	e
	<40	d	de	e	f
V	All depths	e	f	f	f
VI	All depths	f	f	f	f

[a] See Table 6.14.

Assume two soils, for which, applying the methods described in Chapter 6, the information given in Table 6.21 has been obtained. Table 6.20 shows that the soil assessments for workability are de for the Denchworth soil and a for the Hamble. These assessments are then used to weight the field capacity data as shown in Table 6.22. The weightings are expressed as the number of additional days where landwork is likely to be possible because of relatively free drainage and light textures, or further likely restrictions to landwork on heavier wetter soils.

Table 6.21 — Relevant information for the two soil examples considered

Soil series	Denchworth	Hamble
Texture	Clayey	Silty
Wetness class	IV	I
Depth (cm) to slowly permeable horizon	40	Not present
Topsoil (mineral or humose/peaty)	Mineral	Mineral
Retained water capacity	High	Medium

Table 6.22 — Soil weightings applied to field capacity days for estimating machinery work days

Soil assessment	Soil weighting (days)		
	Autumn (1 Sept–31 Dec)	Spring (1 march–30 April)	Total
aa	+30	+20	+50
a	+20	+10	+30
ab	+10	+5	+15
b	0	0	0
bc	−10	−3	−13
c	−20	−5	−25
cd	−25	−8	−33
d	−30	−10	−40
de	−35	−13	−48
e	−40	−15	−55
f	−50	−20	−70

Consultation with the Meteorological Office (giving them the 10 km grid square for which the data is required) reveals that the median date of return to field capacity is 16 November, and that this lasts until the following 28 March.

The calculation of machinery work days is then given in Table 6.23. Such calculations can be presented diagramatically as in Fig. 6.4 which show clearly the differences in machinery work days not only between soil types in the same general location, but also the differences where the same soil occurs in different climatic areas or between normal and particularly wet years. The average period of machinery work days is not a continuous period ending suddenly, for example, in the typical Denchworth soil above, on 12 October exactly 42 days after 1 September. The true situation is that as the soil profile wets up in autumn some of the days in September after a heavy rainfall will not be available for landwork while conversely

Table 6.23 — Calculation of machinery work days

	Denchworth	Hamble
Autumn		
Median date of return to field capacity	16 November	16 November
1 September–16 November (days)	77	77
Soil assessment (Table 6.20)	de	a
Soil weighting (days) (Table 6.22)	−35	+30
Average number of autumn machinery work days	42	107
Spring		
Median date of end of field capacity	22 March	22 March
22 March–30 April (days)	39	39
Soil assessment (Table 6.20)	de	a
Soil weighting (days) (Table 6.22)	−13	+20
Average number of autumn machinery work days	26	59

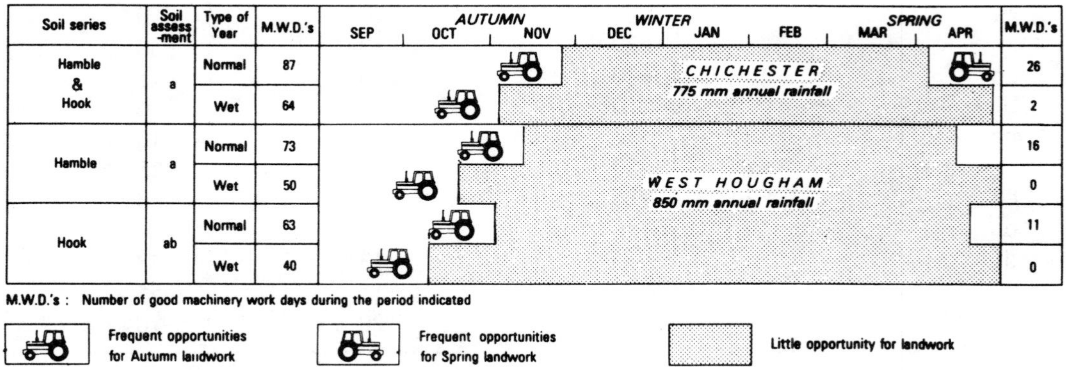

Soil series	Soil assessment	Type of Year	M.W.D.'s	AUTUMN SEP OCT NOV	WINTER DEC JAN FEB	SPRING MAR APR	M.W.D.'s
Hamble & Hook	a	Normal	87		CHICHESTER 775 mm annual rainfall		26
		Wet	64				2
Hamble	a	Normal	73				16
		Wet	50		WEST HOUGHAM 850 mm annual rainfall		0
Hook	ab	Normal	63				11
		Wet	40				0

M.W.D.'s : Number of good machinery work days during the period indicated

Frequent opportunities for Autumn landwork

Frequent opportunities for Spring landwork

Little opportunity for landwork

Fig. 6.4 — The effects of soil and climate on landwork for a typical soil association (Fyfield 4) in England and Wales.

after the calculated end of the machinery work day period there are still likely to be occasional days when some work can be carried out. A similar situation will prevail in the spring. The vagaries of the British climate simply do not allow any more precision than that. The concept of machinery work days is, however, very useful in assessing the suitability of land for crops will be discussed in Chapter 7.

6.4   SOIL TEMPERATURE REGIMES IN THE SOIL TAXONOMY
One of the main differentiating features at the family level of the USDA Soil Taxonomy (see Chapter 4) is the kind of soil temperature regime. The temperature

class limits are set out in Table 6.24 based on soil temperatures at 50 cm depth or at the interface with soft or hard rock; the terms pergelic and cryic are used at higher levels within the classification. They have rather complicated definitions but in essence both refer to very cold soils either with permafrost at depth and mean annual soil temperature below 0°C (pergelic), or no permafrost and mean annual soil temperature between 0 and 8°C.

Table 6.24 — Temperature class limits used in the USDA Soil Taxonomy

Name	Mean annual soil temperature (°C)	Difference between mean summer and mean winter temperatures (°C)
Frigid	Below 8	5 or more
Mesic	8–15	5 or more
Thermic	15–22	5 or more
Hyperthermic	Above 22	5 or more
Isofrigid	Below 8	Less than 5
Isomesic	8–15	Less than 5
Isothermic	15–22	Less than 5
Isohyperthermic	Above 22	Less than 5

Source: Adapted from USDA (1975).

6.5   FAO AGRO-ECOLOGICAL ZONES

An agro-ecological zone approach to the determination of land potential is being developed by FAO, based on the 1:5 000 000 FAO–UNESCO *Soil map of the world* (see Chapter 4). A specially created climatic inventory, matched to the climatic requirements of crops, is superimposed on the soil map units to provide a land inventory which can be used to improve land suitability classification by the FAO framework (see Chapter 7). Studies of this methodology for Africa, southeast Asia and southwest Asia have already been carried out.

Potential crops are first classified into climatic adaptability groups according to their photosynthesis and climatically related characteristics (Table 6.25) and their moisture requirements are compared with the period when water is available for growth. The start of the growing period is taken as the time when precipitation equals half the potential evapotranspiration, followed by a humid period when rainfall exceeds precipitation. The end of the growing season is when precipitation is again less than half the potential evapotranspiration, taking account of an assumed utilisation of 100 mm stored moisture in the soil. The model, therefore, is not so sophisticated as that used in England and Wales (see above). Three other types of water growing period have also been recognised, i.e. all year round humid, intermediate and all year round dry, and restrictions to the growing period due also to temperature are also considered in the model. All this leads to the recognition of a

Table 6.25 — Crop groups of the FAO agro-ecological zones project

Crop group	Examples	Photosynthetic pathway	Optimum temperature for maximum photosynthesis (°C)	General conditions	Mean daily temperature (°C)
I	Wheat, barley	C3	15–20	Moderately cool and cool	5–20
II	Cotton, cassava, groundnut, paddy rice	C3	25–30	Warm	>20
III	Millet, lowland sorghum and maize, sugar cane	C4	30–35	Warm	>20
IV	Highland sorghum and maize	C4	20–30	Moderately cool	15–20

Source: Adapted from Higgins and Kassam (1981).

Table 6.26 — Major climates recognised in the FAO agro-ecological zones project

Climate	Major climates during growing period		24-h mean temperature (°C) regime during the growing period	Suitable for consideration (during the growing period) for crop group
	Number	Descriptive name		
Tropics: All months with monthly mean temperatures, corrected to sea level, above 18°C	1	Warm tropics	More than 20	II and III
	2	Moderately cool tropics	15–20	I and IV
	3	Cool tropics	5/10–15	I
	4	Cold tropics	Less than 5	Not suitable
Subtropics: 1 or more months with monthly mean temperatures, corrected to sea level, below 18°C but all months above 5°C	5	Warm or moderately cool subtropics (summer rainfall)	More than 20	II and III
	6	Warm or moderately cool subtropics (summer rainfall)	15–20	I and IV
	7	Warm subtropics (summer rainfall)	More than 20	II and III
	8	Moderately cool subtropics (summer rainfall)	15–20	I and IV
	9	Cool subtropics (summer rainfall)	5/10–15	I
	10	Cold subtropics (summer rainfall)	Less than 5	Not suitable
	11	Cool subtropics (winter rainfall)	5/10–20	I
	12	Cold subtropics (winter rainfall)	Less than 5	Not suitable
Temperate: 1 or more months with monthly mean temperatures, corrected to sea level, below 5°C	13	Cool temperate	5/10–20	I
	14	Cold temperate	Less than 5	Not suitable

Source: Higgins and Kassam (1981).

total of 14 major climates (Table 6.26) and 21 zones of length of growing period, characterising time available when water supplies and temperature permit crop growth. The soil requirements of the various crops have also been compiled.

Computer analysis of overlays of the climatic inventory over the soil inventory has resulted in unique climate and soil units. These provide quantification of each soil unit (subdivided by slope, texture and other characteristics important to the management of the land) as it occurs in each major climate and growing period zone. Calculations are also made of the biomass and constraint-free individual crop yields by growing period zones, and lead, by comparison with the constraints recognised in the climate and soil units, to a modified land suitability classification. Four land suitability classes (see Chapter 7, section 7.6.2) are recognised. If the yield of a crop from a particular zone is 80% or more of the maximum attainable then that zone is rated as agroclimatically very suitable. Suitable is used for 40–80% yields, marginally suitable for 20–40% and not suitable for below 20%. Soil limitations are then superimposed to give the final ratings.

This kind of computerised modelling approach will undoubtedly become more sophisticated in the future but at the moment it is somewhat 'broad brush' and does not lend itself to the sort of soil map interpretations which a practising soil surveyor has to make (see Chapter 7).

7

Interpreting a soil map for practical purposes

7.1 INTRODUCTION

For the purposes of this chapter we shall assume either you have just finished making a soil map of your own (see Chapter 5) or you have obtained a soil map of an area you are interested in. The question then is: what should you do with it? This chapter discusses the use you can make of soil maps and, in particular, how they can be interpreted to give information in a format directly relevant to the needs of the user. First, however, we shall remind you of some of the limitations of soil maps which were covered more fully in Chapter 5 (which you should read, even if you have no real intention of making a soil map yourself).

The main points made were as follows.

(1) The items being described, named and mapped are soil profiles, usually with a genetic connotation.
(2) The map units are rarely, if ever, pure.
(3) Boundaries between units are rarely discrete and often mark just the approximate centre line of a transition zone.
(4) Soil surveying is based on a sampling procedure; the greater the intensity of sampling, the more detailed the map can be. The sample points are rarely shown on the finished map.
(5) The precision of a soil map depends on the scale. As scale increases, the maps are likely to be more detailed, the purity of the map units improves, but the number of different units increases, always assuming the intensity of observations is commensurate with the scale at which the map is presented.
(6) The value of a soil map for a given purpose depends on the relationship between the minimum size of each mapping unit and the minimum size of 'areas of interest', e.g. fields or discrete vegetation types. Ideally the two minima should be nearly the same. If the soil map is more detailed and has a higher resolution than is needed then simplification by combining appropriate map units is valid (though a waste of the effort put into making such a detailed map in the first

place). A soil map which has a lower resolution has to be treated with caution and cannot validly be enlarged without further field work to substantiate the implied greater precision.

(7) Maps using a standard nomenclature compatible with that used on maps of similar areas elsewhere are much more useful than where the map units have been recognised on an *ad hoc* basis.

(8) The map should have a comprehensive legend and accompanying report.

7.2 KINDS OF SOIL MAP INTERPRETATION

Three main kinds of interpretation can be recognised.

(1) Simple soil map units can be correlated with other features of the area such as vegetation.

(2) Single-factor maps, e.g. a map of all the soils with a particular topsoil texture, can be derived.

(3) The soil information can be combined with other information including climate and topography to derive a land classification. In turn, several kinds of land classification can be recognised:

   (a) suitability of land for particular agricultural operations, e.g. drainage or irrigation;
   (b) suitability of land for a particular crop;
   (c) evaluation of land for non-agricultural purposes, e.g. wildlife conservation or urban development;
   (d) general land capability for agricultural use.

Land classification is a massive subject in itself and only a brief coverage can be given here. There is a wide range of formal land classification systems, some international and, others of only local significance. Most have quite detailed and explicit manuals or tables which permit any reasonably intelligent person to apply them, given that they have the required information in the correct format. The required information is often of the type discussed in Chapter 6, i.e. dealing with soil–climate interactions, such as soil wetness class, droughtiness assessments, duration of field capacity period and accumulated temperatures.

As described in Chapter 6, information on many of these is directly available or can be worked out from basic soil and climate information fairly readily. It would be unwise, however, to embark on any land classification or similar soil map interpretation before ensuring that all the necessary information could be obtained.

7.3 SIMPLE CORRELATIONS

The simplest way of using a soil map is the 'eyeball' method of directly comparing the soil map with a map of the supposedly related feature you are interested in. Converting one of the maps to a transparent overlay helps the process. Statisticians may throw up their hands in horror at such a simplistic approach but, at least as a first step, it is surprising what relationships can be spotted just by looking and thinking rather than a headlong dash into computerised multiple correlations, kriging and the like.

Statistical work could, of course be carried out, such as the chi-squared test which compares observed frequencies with expected frequencies based on some assumed hypothesis. If you are interested in such statistical manipulations of soil survey data some of the references in the bibliography will help you to pursue it further, though it is not a subject for the faint hearted or the mathematical novice.

Manipulation of the data can be facilitated by a computer-based information system which of course needs access to the requisite hardware, software and a friendly computer operator, preferably one who has already worked with spatially organised data.

7.4   DERIVED SINGLE-FACTOR MAPS

A large amount of information about soils is embodied in the name given to it and used for mapping. Any property implicit in the name of the soil can be picked out and a derived map produced to show the incidence of that property. Figs 7.1 and 7.2, for example, show a soil map and derived single-factor map showing water table clases. Agronomists have found that there can often be a better correlation between crop performance and such simple properties as topsoil texture, organic matter content or depth of free drainage than with the genetic soil profiles themselves.

7.5   SUITABILITY OF LAND FOR SPECIFIC AGRICULTURAL PURPOSES

7.5.1   Drainage improvements

Since drainage status is one of the commonest features used to name and classify soils it is not surprising that one of the commonest, and easiest, soil map interpretations is of the drainage status of the soils. From this it is only a short step to recommending the sort of drainage treatments required, and many soil reports include sections on this topic, usually with tables such as Table 7.1. The information can then be presented cartographically, e.g. Figs 7.3 and 7.4, parts of the basic soil map for an area in England and the derived map of predicted underdrainage treatment for arable land use.

These examples are taken from work by the Soil Survey of England and Wales and were derived more or less on an *ad hoc* basis by the surveyor gathering information on drainage practices as he made his map, asking farmers and drainage officers, and applying his basic knowledge of soil behaviour. It shows the benefit of using a standardised nomenclature system since the results of drainage trials are based, in this case, on the soil series of the Soil Survey of England and Wales and so can be directly applied where similar soil series are mapped elsewhere.

7.5.2   Irrigation

The only truly international system for interpreting a soil map for a practical agricultural purpose is the Irrigation Suitability Classification system of the United States Bureau of Reclamation (USBR). This is a complex system involving not only soil information, but other environmental and economic data. Standard texts on land evaluation (see bibliography in Chapter 9) provide a gentler introduction than the USBR's own manual. It is, however, most definitely not a system for beginners.

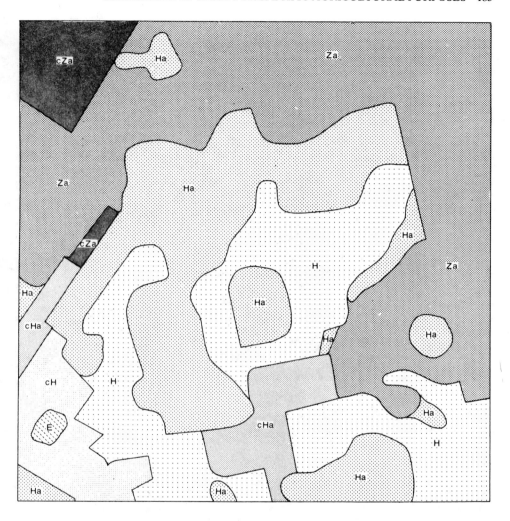

LEGEND

Sandy soils

			mean highest water table in cm below surface
Humic podzols (Humods) A1 < 30 ╎ 30 - 50 cm			
H	oH	high and medium high	> 40
Ha	cHa	low and very low	< 40
Sandy humic gley soils (Aquepts) A1 < 30 ╎ 30 - 50 cm			
Za	cZa	low and very low	< 40
Plaggen soils (Plaggepts) A1 > 50 cm			
E		high and medium high	> 40

Fig. 7.1 — Part of a Dutch soil map (1:10 000) — see also Fig. 7.2 (Source: van Heesen (1971)).

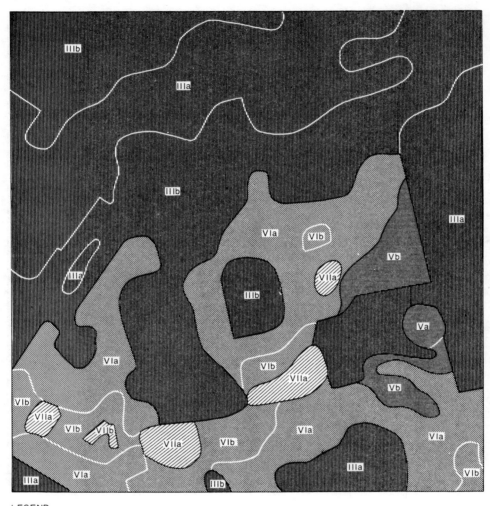

LEGEND

Water-table classes

	I	II	III $\begin{smallmatrix}a\\b\end{smallmatrix}$	IV	V $\begin{smallmatrix}a\\b\end{smallmatrix}$	VI $\begin{smallmatrix}a\\b\end{smallmatrix}$	VIIa	VIIb		
	cm below surface								a	wetter variant of MHW
MHW			< 40		< 40	40 - 80	80 - 120	> 120	b	drier variant of MHW
MLW	1)	1)	80 - 120	1)	> 120	> 120	> 200	> 200	1)	not occurring in the mapped area
									MHW	mean highest water table
									MLW	mean lowest water table

Fig. 7.2 — A map of water table classes derived from the soil map in Fig. 7.1 (Source: van Heesen (1971)).

Table 7.1 — Soil series and drainage design

Soil series	Suitability for moling	Need for subsoiling	Pipe depth	Pipe spacing (cm)	Permeable backfill (m)	Wetness class		Remarks	Soil associations
						Drained land	Undrained land		
Adventurers'	4	C	100–120	20–40	Unnecessary	I and II	V and VI	Pipes are placed as deeply as ditches allow. Close spacing used where peat is shallow. Subsoiling needed to disrupt drummy layer. Risk of ochre accumulation	Adventurers' 1 and 2, Altcar 1 and 2, Clayhythe, Downholland 1 and 3, Frome, Hanworth, Isleham 2, Mendham, Peacock, Willingham
Agney	4	B	100–120	20	Unnecessary	I and II	V	Filter wrap may be necessary to prevent silting of pipes	Agney, Dowels, Normoor
Altcar	4	B	100–120	20–40	Unnecessary	I	V and VI	Pipes are placed as deeply as ditches allow. Risk of ochre accumulation	Adventurers' 1 and 2, Altcar 1 and 2
Ashley	2–3	B	75–90	20	Desirable	I and II	II and III	In some locations, wetness results from surface compaction. If mole drainage is used, permeable backfill is essential	Ashley, Beccles 3, Burlingham 3, Cannamore, Hornbeam 3
Batcombe						II	II and III	Natural drainage is usually adequate for general arable use	Batcombe, Oak 2

Source: Hodge *et al.* (1984).

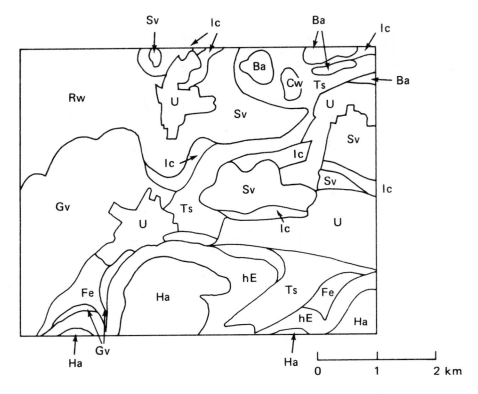

Fig. 7.3 — A portion of a soil map for an area in Berkshire, England (see also Fig. 7.4). Source: adapted from Soil Survey of England and Wales.

7.5.3   Other examples

Soil survey reports from all over the world abound with *ad hoc* soil map interpretations for specific agricultural and related topics sometimes as derived maps but more often in tabular form. Some examples are given in Tables 7.2 and 7.3. In spite of that fact that they are usually compiled on an *ad hoc* basis, these simple interpretations can be amongst the most useful part of any soil map and report.

You should always try to include something along these lines in any report accompanying a soil map you have made (Chapter 4). Look on yourself as a disseminator of the experiences and opinions you have collected during your survey. It is surprising how little some users know about how other people deal with similar soil problems even a short distance away.

7.6   CROP SUITABILITIES

Assessing land for its suitability to grow crops depends on a knowledge of the requirements for the particular crop(s) and how well each of the soil map units can fulfil these requirements. The task may be to find which of the soils in the area is best suited to a particular crop, or alternatively to find the most suitable crop to grow on a particular soil type.

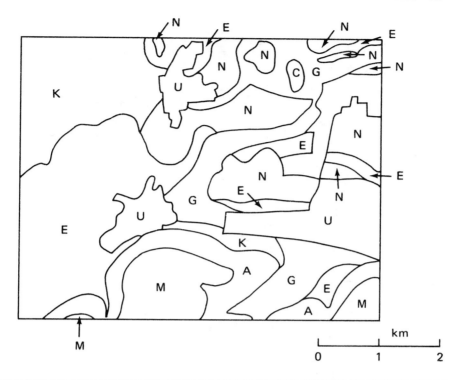

Symbol	Type of system	Tile interval (m)	Depth (cm)
A	Pipe drains without	20–40	>90
C	permeable fill	30–40	<100
E	Pipe drains with	20–30	90–120
F	permeable fill	30–50	90–120
G			
J	Pipe drains with permeable	Variable	Variable
K	fill plus moling	20–40	75–90
N	Drainage not required	20–40	>90

Fig. 7.4 — A derived map showing the predicted underdrainage treatment for the soils of the area in Fig. 7.3. (Source: adapted from Soil Survey of England and Wales).

For finding the soils most suited to a particular crop, the simplest approach, most applicable to developing countries, is to see whether wild varieties of the potential crop prefer some of the map units to others. An example is oil palm in The Gambia where it is reasonable to assume that the most suitable map units would be those where wild oil palms are commonest (Table 7.4). When the map units are rated according to those properties of drainage, soil depth, soil fertility, etc., thought to affect oil palm growth a generally similar picture of the relative suitability of the map units emerges (Table 7.4).

Table 7.2 — Typical *ad hoc* interpretation of soil map. (Class — the soils are rated for orchard suitability as first- (1), second- (2), or third- (3) class orchard soils or as unsuitable (U))

Soil	Topography	Suitability for irrigation	Suitability for fruit-growing	Class	Remarks
Conroy hill soils (CH)	Moderately steep and some rolling slopes, many rock outcrops	Mostly unsuitable but some contour ditching possible on easier slopes	Mostly unsuitable but some small patches up to 5 acres of deep rock-free soil may be suitable	U	Bare rock and shallow stony soils on ridges and slopes. Deeper soils at foot of slopes and in gullies.
Waenga loamy sand (W3)	Slope 2° to 5° on middle part of fan. Surface mainly smooth	Too steep for border dykes. Contour ditching	Suitable for stone fruit orchards	2	Soils porous and droughty. Steeper slopes liable to erode under irrigation.
Waenga sandy loam (W4)	Gentle slopes on middle part of fan. Surface mainly smooth	Border dykes or contour ditching	Suitable for all types of fruit trees	1	This is possibly the most suitable soil for orchards.
Omeo mottled silt loam (O5)	Surface mosaic of slightly raised gravel ridges and waterlogged depressions	Irrigation unnecessary	Unsuitable for orchards	U	Poorly drained hollows tend to hold irrigation water. The waterlogging is caused by irrigation of adjacent soils.
Cromwell sands (CR1)	Surface irregular. Mainly small dunes	Mainly Spray	Generally unsuitable for orchards	3	Infertile, extremely porous. Requires levelling and abundant water. Supports pasture.

Source: from McCraw (1964).

Table 7.3 — An interpretation of the irrigation potential of some soils in New South Wales, Australia

Soil series	Intrinsic properties	Surface drainage	Slope	Commandability[a]	Associated microrelief
Burganbigil	Good	Good	Long; moderate gradient	Good	Smooth
Purdanima	Good; highly permeable	Excellent	Short and steep; variable gradient	Doubtful	Uneven but no gilgais
Thulabin sandy loam	Very good	Very good	Short and steep; variable gradient	Doubtful in many cases	Uneven but no gilgais
Thulabin loam	Very good	Very good	Long; moderate gradient	Usually possible	Smooth
Tuppal	Fair	Poor; sometimes occluded	Very low gradient	Good	Usually with gilgais
Wandook	Poor	Occluded	Very low gradient	Good	Usually with gilgais
Billabong	Poor	Fair	Long; low gradient	Good	Usually smooth
Riverina	Poor	Poor	Very low gradient	Good	Occasionally with gilgais
Mundiwa	Fair to poor	Poor; sometimes occluded	Long; very low gradient	Good	Occasionally with gilgais
Willbriggie	Fair	Fair	Long; low gradient	Good	Usually with gilgais
Coree	Fair	Poor; sometimes occluded	Long; very low gradient	Good	Usually with gilgais
Yooroobla	Very good	Fair	Long; low gradient	Good	Highly gilgaied
Wunnammurra	Very good	Fair to poor	Very low	Good gradient	Highly gilgaied

[a]Commandibility is the ease with which irrigation water can be brought to the side.
Source: Churchward and Flint (1956).

Table 7.4 — The suitability of various map units for oil palm in the Gambia

Map unit		Topographic position	Estimated depth to water table		Soil fertility	Rooting	Presence of wild palms	Present land use	Suitability for oil palm
			Rainy season	Dry season					
40	Tubakuta	Upland	>20 ft	>20 ft	Low	No barrier	Few	Cultivation	Not recommended
41	Jambanjeli	Upland	>20 ft	>20 ft	Low	No barrier	Few or common	Cultivation	Not recommended
43	Mayo	Margin of interfluve	>20 ft	>20 ft	Low	No barrier	Few	Cultivation	Not recommended
33	Kalaji	Depression on broad interfluve	Possibly perched <6 ft	>20 ft	Low	Fossil cuirasse at 3 ft	None	Woodland	Not suitable
34	Bwiam	Depression	Possibly perched <6 ft	>20 ft	Low	Concretionary layer at 6 ft	None or few	Woodland	Not suitable
30	Nyambai	Depression	Possibly perched <6 ft	>15 ft	Low	Concretionary layer at 6 ft	Common to many	Woodland and shifting cultivation of upland rice	Possible
32	Sifoe	Swamp margins	<6 ft	<20 ft	Low	No barrier	Common to many	Woodland and rough grazing	Least unsuitable
22	Jabang	Valley bottom	Surface	<20 ft	Low	Water table during rains	Common	Rice	Too wet

Source: Hill (1969).

Soil survey reports frequently discuss, for each of the mapping units, the sorts of crops likely to be suitable and those to be avoided, e.g. Table 7.5. In the USA, yield predictions are also supplied (e.g. Table 7.6), enabling a farmer to work out which of the crops might be the most profitable in the prevailing market circumstances.

Table 7.5 — Typical description of and cropping advice for a soil mapping unit in an USDA soil survey report

---

Dunbar loamy sand, 2–5% slopes (DvB) — This somewhat poorly drained soil is in small areas on uplands. Included with it in mapping were small areas of Wicksburg and Duplin soils. Also included were some areas where sandstone crops out or is within 10 in of the surface.

This soil commonly is not cultivated, because the subsoil is clayey. It is suited to corn, small grain, millet, coastal Bermuda grass, Bahia grass and white clover. It is poorly suited to tobacco. This soil responds to feriliser but is slow to warm up in spring. Planting is delayed in years when rainfall is heavy in spring.

Because erosion is the chief hazard, a good use of the soil is for gowing perennial grass or trees. The soil can be used for two crops, however, if erosion control measures are applied. Among these are the use of suitable cropping systems, contour cultivation, terraces, grassed waterways, stripcropping, and grass-based rotations. An example of a suitable cropping system is 2 years of Coastal Bermuda grass and 1 year of corn that is planted and cultivated so that the Bermuda grass is not destroyed.

Most of the acreage is in natural vegetation consisting of scattered pines and a few oaks.

Source: Rigdon (1975)

Again, as with assessments for agricultural practices there are a multitude of examples of such *ad hoc* assessments of crop suitabilities to be found in soil survey memoirs and bulletins (see Table 7.7 for example), but most are applicable only to the particular area being described.

More formalised systems are available, usually produced by national soil surveys or aid agencies, with more general application. The methodologies are clearly, if sometimes rather tortuously, laid out and simply require comparison of the values of each of the properties for the various map units with the declared class limits. The difficulty is often that the properties used in the suitability classification are not those directly used in classifying the soils and so some conversion work has to be done, as described in Chapter 6 for England and Wales. Also data from other sources, notably climatic data, have to be obtained and applied.

Two examples which show the sorts of difficulties involved are given below. Of course the best choice would usually be a system already derived for the particular area. Each system will have its own idiosyncrasies but will probably involve much the same sort of thought processes as the following examples.

Table 7.6 — Part of a typical table of yield predictions in an USDA soil survey report

Yields are those which can be expected under a high level of management. Absence of a yield indicates that the soil is not suited to the crop or the crop generally is not grown on the soil. Yields are per acre, Bu — bushel, AUM — Animal-unit-month, the amount of forage or feed required to feed one animal unit (one cow, one horse, one mule, five sheep, or five goats) for 30 days

Soil name and map symbol	Corn	Corn silage	Oats	Wheat	Alfalfa hay	Grass-legume hay	Pasture
	Bu	Ton	Bu	Bu	Ton	Ton	AUM
AaA . . . . Alvira	95	19	60	—	—	3.0	6.0
AaB . . . . Alvira	95	19	60	—	-	3.0	6.0
AaC . . . . Alvira	90	18	55	—	—	3.0	6.0
AbC . . . . Alvira	—	—	—	—	—	—	—
AgB . . . . Armagh	80	16	60	—	—	2.5	5.0
AhB . . . . Armagh	—	—	—	—	—	—	—
At . . . . Atkins	100	20	60	—	—	3.0	5.5
BcB . . . . Braceville	105	21	80	40	4.5	3.5	8.5

Source: Cerutti (1985).

Table 7.7 — *Ad hoc* suitability assessment. The primary topographic positions are the valley bottom, the lower slope and the upper slope. The secondary topographic positions are I (central valley bottom), IV (side of valley bottom), VI (lower part of lower slope), VIII (upper part of lower slope) and X (upper slope). The management units are a, b, k, l, o, p, s, u, v, w, x and y

	Valley bottom				Lower slope				Upper slope			
	Central I		Side IV		Lower part VI		Upper part VIII		X			
	a	b	k	l	o	p	s	u	v	w	x	y
Early first season												
Highly suited crops	—	—	—	—	—	—	—	—	—	—	Cassava	—
Moderately suited crops	—	—	—	—	Cassava	Cassava	Cassava, pigeon pea	Cassava, pigeon pea	Cassava	Cassava, pigeon pea	Cassava	Pigeon pea
Major first season												
Highly suited crops	Cocoyam	—	—	—	—	Rice, cocoyam	—	—	—	—	Maize, yam, cassava, sweet potato, cowpea, soybean	—
Moderately suited crops	Rice, soybean	Rice	Rice, maize, sweet potato, cocoyam, cowpea, soybean	Rice	Maize, yam, cassava, sweet potato, cowpea, soybean	Rice, maize, yam, cassava, sweet potato, cocoyam, cowpea, soybean	Cassava, sweet potato, cowpea, soybean, pigeon pea	Cassava, pigeon pea	Cassava	Maize, yam, sweet potato, cowpea, soybean, pigeon pea	Pigeon pea	Pigeon pea
Second season												
Highly suited crops	Rice, cocoyam	—	—	—	Cocoyam	Rice	—	—	—	Cowpea	Lam, cassava, cowpea, soybean	—

(continued overleaf)

Table 7.7 (*Contd.*)

	Valley bottom				Lower slope				Upper slope			
	Central I		Side IV		Lower part VI		Upper part VIII		X			
	a	b	k	l	o	p	s	u	v	w	x	y
Moderately suited crops	—	Rice	Rice, cocoyam	Rice	Rice, yam, cassava, sweet potato, soybean	Yam, cassava, sweet potato, cocoyam	Cassava, cowpea, soybean, pigeon pea,	Cassava, cowpea, soybean, pigeon pea	Cassava,	Cassava, Yam, cassava, sweet potato, soybean, pigeon pea	Maize, sweet potato, pigeon pea	Pigeon pea
Dry season												
Highly suited crops	—	—	—	—	—	—	—	—	—	—	Cassava	—
Moderately suited crops	—	—	—	—	Cassava	Cassava	Cassava, pigeon pea	Cassava, pigeon pea	Cassava	Cassava, pigeon pea	Pigeon pea	Pigeon pea

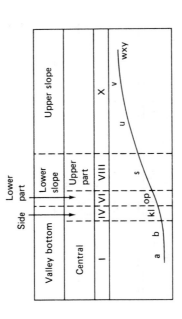

Source: Bridges and Davidson (1982) after Veldkamp (1979).

Table 7.8 — Allocation of suitability classes for winter cereals in England and Wales

Machinery work days after 1 September	Suitability for following AP–MD values				
	Over 40 mm	>20 to 40 mm	>0 to 20 mm	0 to −19 mm	−20 mm and lower
Over 80	Well suited	Well suited	Well suited	Moderately suited	Marginally suited
>50 to 80	Well suited	Well suited	Moderately suited	Marginally suited	
>20 to 50	Moderately suited	Moderately suited	Moderately suited	Marginally suited	
20 and less	Marginally suited	Marginally suited	Marginally suited		

Increasingly restricted workability

Increasing droughtiness

Source: Soil Survey of England and Wales.

7.6.1 Crop suitability classifications of the Soil Survey of England and Wales

The first example is the crop suitability classification used by the Soil Survey of England and Wales, or, more specifically, the part which assesses the suitability for winter cereals. The classification system is set out in Table 7.8, and similar tables are available for other common British crops. They are all based on the interactions between soils and climate which were discussed in Chapter 6 and some of the data manipulations described in that chapter are a necessary prerequisite to applying these crop suitability classifications.

The classification is based on the workability of the land and on its droughtiness. The former reflects the requirement that there should be an adequate number of days when weed control, tillage and crop establishment can be undertaken during September and October. This is the concept of machinery work days described in Chapter 6. In turn this is based on the climatic property of the field capacity period and on soil properties including wetness class, depth to any slowly permeable horizons and nature of the topsoil, especially its texture.

The second major factor used in assessing crop suitability classes is the droughtiness which in turn depends on the available water-holding capacity of the profile (AP) and the climatic moisture deficit (MD), a measure of the dryness of the climate, both adjusted for the crop in question as described in Chapter 6.

The regional bulletins of the Soil Survey of England and Wales give estimated machinery work days for a number of soils and a range of climates (see Chapter 6, particularly Fig. 6.8). Deriving these from first principles is rather tedious.

The first of the two droughtiness parameters, the AP, can be calculated from soil textures, stoniness and horizon depths as explained in Chapter 6 or is given for typical profiles of common soil series in various soil survey publications. The moisture deficit parameter can be obtained, suitably modified for the crop under consideration, from the meteorological office or the agroclimatic databank or can be derived from maps given in the soil survey regional bulletins.

Assume you have obtained the information in Table 7.9 for the two contrasting soils for which machinery work days were calculated in Chapter 6. From Table 7.9 it can be seen that the Denchworth soil should be rated as moderately suited for growing winter wheat, whereas the Hamble would be well suited.

Table 7.9 — Information for the two soils for which machinery work days were calculated in Chapter 6

	Denchworth	Hamble
Machinery work days after 1 September	26	59
AP (adjusted for winter wheat) for typical profile	135	155
MD (adjusted for winter wheat) from meteorological office	110	110
Therefore AP-MD	25	45

7.6.2 The FAO framework

The second example is the FAO framework for land suitability classification which is not in itself a rigid classification system but rather a standard set of principles and concepts on which local classifications can be based. Separate classifications are constructed for each of the main land utilisation types being considered, e.g. smallholder rain-fed annual cropping, oil palm estates and even non-agricultural uses such as forestry or tourism. Suitability is normally assessed under current circumstances as well as the potential suitability after major improvements (as in a development programme) have been carried out.

The structure of the FAO framework is set out in Table 7.10. There are two orders, suitable (S) and non-suitable (N) with a conditional phase (Sc) of the suitable order for use when certain additional conditions have to be met. It is not intended to be an uncertain classification or an intergrade between suitable and non-suitable. The orders can be subdivided into as many classes as are deemed necessary, but there are normally three suitable classes (S1, S2 and S3) and two non-suitable classes (N1 and N2). Each Class (except S1) is divided into subclasses depending on the kind of limitation, denoted by one or at most two limitation symbols, such as e for erosion, d for drainage and y for soil fertility. Units are recognised on the basis of specific management requirements or production characteristics, but many applications of the FAO framework do not go to this degree of detail. The criteria whereby each of the classes and subclasses are defined are a matter for local determination and so considerable experience is needed before an FAO-based system can be constructed from first principles. The classifier will, in effect, be formalising his or her own impressions of the suitability of the land for its various uses, perhaps guided by similar classifications elsewhere, and will adapt and modify the criteria as necessary so as to produce sensible results compatible with the definitions in Table 7.11. This is not to denigrate the system, but merely to emphasise that it is a framework for local adaptation and not a single universally applicable system.

Examples of land suitability class limits for typical applications of the FAO framework are given in Table 7.12 for sugar cane in Mauritius and for an area in India in Table 7.13 (see also Fig. 7.5).

7.7 LAND SUITABILITY FOR NON-AGRICULTURAL PURPOSES

Some of the non-agricultural purposes for which soil map interpretations have been derived are suitability classifications for:

(1) use of soils as constructional materials;
(2) building site development;
(3) waste disposal;
(4) recreational and amenity uses;
(5) wildlife habitats.

Many of these interpretations originated in the USA and have been modified for use in other countries, e.g. the UK. The classification systems are usually laid out as tables giving the soil and site limitations which render the land well suited,

Table 7.10 — Structure of the FAO framework for land evaluation

		Category		
	Order[^a] Kind of suitability	Class[^a] Degree(s) of (un) suitability characteristics	Subclass[^b] Kind of limitation	Unit[^c] Management requirements or production
S	Suitable			
	S1	Highly suitable		
	S2	Moderately suitable	S2 m / S2 e	S2 e 1 / S2 e 2 / S2 e 3 / etc.
	S3	Marginally suitable	S2 m / etc.	
	etc.			
Sc	Conditionally suitable[^d]			
	Sc2		Sc2 m	
	N1	Currently not suitable	N1 m / N1 e	
N	Not suitable[^e]			
	N 2	Permanently not suitable		
	etc.			

[^a]: The class names shown here are those recommended for a three-class system. Up to five suitable classes are permitted.
[^b]: The number of subclasses should be kept to a minimum necessary to distinguish land with significantly different management requirements or production potential. As few limitation symbols as possible should be used for each subclass. Note that S1 land is not divided into subclasses.
[^c]: Units are normally for use at the farm planning level and are often definable by differences in detail of their limitation(s).
[^d]: For small areas of land where certain conditions additional to those specified for the 'suitable' classes must be fulfilled for successful land use; once these conditions are met, the land is included in the class or subclass indicated by the code following the Sc designation. NB 'conditionally suitable' does *not* imply that the interpretation is uncertain, either because the land is only marginally suitable or because the relevant factors are not understood.
[^e]: The additional symbol NR (not relevant) is used for areas not being considered.
Source: Adapted from FAO (1976).

Table 7.11 — The recommended definitions of classes in the FAO framework for land evaluation

Class	Designation	Definition
S1	Highly suitable	Land having no significant limitations to sustained application of a given use, or only minor limitations that will not significantly reduce productivity or benefits and will not raise inputs above an acceptable level
S2	Moderately suitable	Land having limitations which, in aggregate, are moderately severe for sustained application of a given use; the limitations will reduce productivity or benefits and increase required inputs to the extent that the overall advantage to be gained from the use, although still attractive, will be appreciably inferior to that expected on class S1 land
S3	Marginally suitable	Land having limitations which, in aggregate, are severe for sustained application of a given use and will so reduce productivity or benefits, or increase required inputs, that this expenditure will be only marginally justified
N1	Currently not suitable	Land having limitations which may be surmountable in time, but which cannot be corrected with existing knowledge at currently acceptable cost; the limitations are so severe as to preclude successful sustained use of the land in the given manner
N2	Permanently not suitable	Land having limitations which appear so severe as to preclude any possibilities of successful use of the land in the given manner

In quantitative classificaitons, both inputs and benefits must be expressed in common measurable terms, normally economic.

Where additional refinement is needed, this should be done by adding classes (S4, S5) rather than by subdividing classes, since the latter procedure is reserved for subclass designation.

Class S1 may sometimes not appear on a map of a given area, although it may be included in the classification, if such land occurs — or is believed to occur — in other areas relevant to the study.

Boundaries between suitability classes wil be subject to revision with time in the light of technical developments and economic and social changes. However, the boundary of class N2 is normally physical and permanent.

Source: Adapted from FAO (1976).

Table 7.12 — The criteria for land suitability classes in the FAO framework for land evaluation used for sugar cane in Mauritius

Land suitability class	Land suitability subclass	Land qualities				
		Availability of water	Limiting superhumid climate	Availability of plant nutrients	Land cultivability	Erosion susceptibility
S1		High	Non-limiting	High	Easy to fairly easy	None to slight
S2		Moderate	Moderately limiting	Moderate	Moderately difficult	None to slight
S3		Low	Highly limiting	Low	Difficult	Moderate
	CS1 Et		as for suitability class S1			Moderate
	CS2 Et		as for suitability class S2			Moderate
	CS3 Et		as for suitability class S3			Moderate to Strong
N1		Low	Highly limiting	Low	Very difficult	Strong
N2		Low	Highly limiting	Very low	Very difficult	Very strong

Source: Arlidge and Wong (1975).

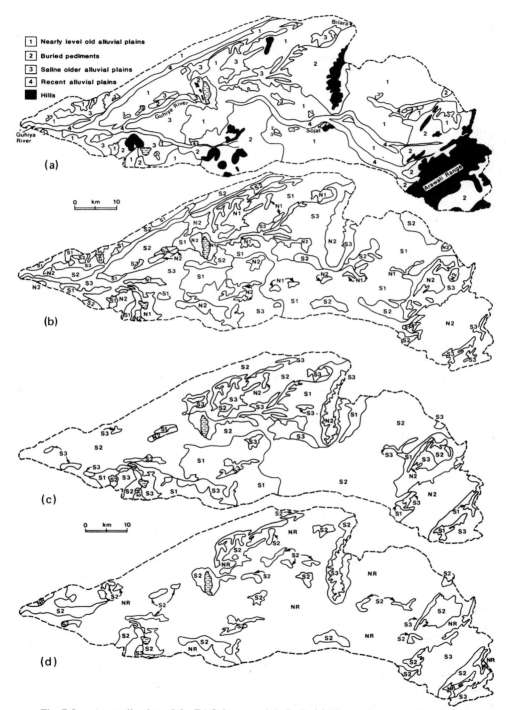

Fig. 7.5 — An application of the FAO framework in India (a) Major physiographic units; (b) land suitability for arable farming; (c) land suitability for grazing and livestock production; (d) land suitability for woodland forestry. See also Table 7.13. (Source: Shankarnarayon *et al.* (1983)).

Table 7.13 — Land quality criteria used to produce the map of land suitability for arable farming of an area in India (see Fig. 7.5) according to the FAO Framework (Source: adapted from Shankarnarayan *et al.*, 1983)

Land quality	S1 Excellent	S2 Medium	S3 Marginal
Topography	Plain flat land		
Rooting depth (cm)	>90	45–90	35–45
Subsoil texture	Medium to moderately fine	Coarse to medium	Course
Soil salinity (1:2 soil:water ratio) (mS/cm)	<1	1–2.5	>2.5
Soil erosion	None to slight	Slight to moderate	

Land failing to meet the requirements for Class S3 would be rated N, not suitable.

moderately well suited, poorly suited or unsuited to that particular use as in Table 7.14, a suitability classification for winter playing fields. Assuming the necessary information about the relevant properties is to hand, these tables are fairly easy to use. To be in a particular category land must fulfil all the requirements. Failure in even one relegates the land to a lower category. Thus the logical way to use the table is to start with the column of requirements of the best class, testing the soil and site values until (unless the land is well suited) one is arrived at which cannot be met. Then go to the next column for that property and test again. There is no need to retest the properties which were already satisfied for the better class since the requirements concerning these for the lower classes will be the same as or less demanding than those already met. You should, however, continue to test down to the end of the column in case some other property is even more limiting.

The use of Table 7.14 can be demonstrated by considering a piece of level land (not in a floodplain) which has a sandy silt loam soil with a retained water capacity of 35%, an air capacity of about 15% and hydraulic conductivity K of 0.5 m/day. It has 10% stones and is only 60 cm deep over rock which, however, ensures free drainage (wetness class I). You should find firstly that the air capacity (and hydraulic conductivity) relegates it from well suited to moderately well suited, and then that its depth renders it only poorly suited, its final and correct classification.

The bibliography in Chapter 9 gives details of publications dealing with this and other, generally similar non-agricultural interpretations.

One major group of non-agricultural interpretations, those relating to forestry, cannot be adequately covered in a book such as this. There are many ways of evaluating land for forestry, including site indices, yield classes, production classes, capability classes and subclasses, yield predictions using equations and economic measures of forest productivity. References to these are given in the bibliography

Table 7.14 — Suitability of land for winter playing fields in Great Britain

Property	Well suited	Moderately well suited[b]	Poorly suited	Unsuited[a]
Soil wetness class	I	I–III in drier areas	I–IV	V and VI
Air capacity (%)	>20 to 80 cm; depth	>10 to 50 cm; >5 below 50 cm	>10 in topsoil can be <10 below	<10 in topsoil
Hydraulic conductivity K (m/day)	>1	>0.1	>0.01	<0.01
Depth to rock[c] (cm)	>100	>75	>50	<50
Retained water capacity in topsoil (%)	<30	<45	<55	>55
Topsoil texture	Sandy loam; with >70% sand); fine and medium loamy sand and sand	As well suited plus coarse loamy sand and sand; sandy loam (with <70% sand); loam	As moderately well suited plus silty clay loam; sandy clay silty clay and clay (each with <45% clay); all humose soils	Clays with >45% peat
Volume of stones (%)	<1	<6	<16	>16
Rock outcrops (%)	None	<2	<10	>10
Flood hazard	None	Once in 2 years or less; 3 days on each occasion	Not more than twice per year; 3 days on each occasion	More than twice per year
Slope (%)	0–1.8 (0–1°)	0–2.5 (0–1.5°)	0–5.2 (0–3°)	>5.2 (>3°)

[a]Land with any property whose value exceeds the limits of the poorly suited class should be unsuited.
[b]Wetness class IV soils in areas with less than 700 mm mean annual rainfall, if subsoil permeability is moderate or rapid.
[c]Depending on rock type; soft rocks at depth impose fewer limitations.
Source: McRae and Burnham (1981); adapted from Palmer and Jarvis (1979).

Table 7.15 — Forest productivity of soil series in an area mapped by the Manitoba soil survey
(Source: Smith *et al.*, 1967)

Parent material	Moisture class	Soil name	Coniferous species					Hardwood species						
			jP	wS	bS	bF	tL	tA	bPo	wB	As	wE	bO	mM
Very highly calcareous loamy till	fresh	Aneda	—	5	—	—	—	5	5	5	5	5	5	5
	fresh	Carrick	—	5	—	—	—	4	5	4	5	5	—	—
	moist	Lundar	—	5	—	—	—	4	4	5	4	4	5	5
	moist	Piney	—	3	—	—	—	4	4	4	4	4	—	—
	wet	Meleb	—	4	5	—	4	—	4	—	—	—	—	—
Weakly calcareous loamy till	fresh	McArthur	—	3	—	4	—	3	—	3	—	—	—	—
Highly to moderately calcareous lacustrine clay	fresh	St Norbert	—	5	—	—	—	4	—	—	5	5	5	5
	fresh	Lettonia	—	4	—	5	—	3	—	—	—	—	—	—
	moist	Morris	—	5	—	—	—	4	4	—	5	5	5	5
	moist	Peguis	—	3	—	4	—	3	4	—	4	4	5	5
	moist	Pine Valley	—	3	—	4	—	3	4	—	4	4	—	—
	moist	Red River	—	5	—	—	—	5	4	—	5	5	5	5
	moist	Thalberg	—	3	3	4	—	3	4	—	4	4	—	—
	wet	Fyala	—	—	6	—	4	5	5	—	—	—	—	—
	wet	Lee River	—	—	5	—	4	5	4	—	—	—	—	—
	wet	Osborne	—	—	5	—	4	5	5	—	—	—	—	—

Productivity in gross mean annual increment of merchantable volume

1	over 110 cu.ft./acre	5	31–50 cu. ft/acre
2	91–110 cu. ft./acre	6	11–30 cu. ft./acre
3	71–90 cu. ft./acre	7	less than 10 cu. ft./acre
4	51–70 cu. ft./acre		

Species abbreviation

Aspen, trembling	tA	Elm, white	wE	Maple, Manitoba	mM	Poplar, balsam	bPo
Ash, red	As	Fir, balsam	bF	Oak, bur	bO	Spruce, black	bS
Birch, white	wB	Larch, tamarack	tL	Pine, jack	jP	SPruce, white	wS

but, as with all other interpretations, the best advice is to find out the local convention, to acquire the manual or other paperwork on the system and to use it (adapted if necessary) for the situation under investigation. Table 7.15. gives one example of an evaluation for forestry.

7.8 LAND CAPABILITY CLASSIFICATIONS

The previous two sections have looked at ways of classifying the suitability of land for specific and fairly tightly defined purposes. These include suitability classifications for a specific crop, a specific agricultural operation, e.g. drainage, or for a particular non-agricultural land use, e.g. winter playing fields. Land-use planners, however, would need separate suitability classifications for all the different and probably conflicting land-use options they are called upon to consider. It would seem much easier if there was a general overall classification of how 'good' land was for broader land-use categories such as agriculture in general (as opposed to specific crops) or forestry in general (as opposed to particular tree species).

Fortunately (or unfortunately) such classifications are available and are referred to as land capability classifications. You should always bear in mind, however, that they are generalised classifications, and not necessarily applicable to particular enterprises; they are empirical and have inbuilt value judgements which may be flawed, and the answers they give can only be as reliable as the information used to apply them. This last point is frequently overlooked. Anyone who has had anything to do with soils knows how frustratingly variable they can be; yet this is often obscured in subsequent interpretations, the results of which sometimes seem to take on the aspect of holy writ. It is for these reasons, often overlooked especially by planners and legislators, that one has sometimes cause to deplore the existence of such land capability classifications.

Such classifications are, however, often used by governments to apply land-use policies aimed at protecting the 'best' land against irreversible development for another use. For example in England and Wales the Agricultural Land Classification system has, for many years been a powerful tool in town and country planning. In other countries taxation and land values are related to their ranking according to a type of land capability classification.

Basically there are two methods: the so-called category systems and the so-called parametric systems. Both involve the identification of the important soil and site properties which affect the success of an enterprise. The systems are then constructed so that the values of these properties either define categories (categoric systems) or are combined mathematically to give an index on a sliding scale (parametric systems).

The best example of a category system is the USDA Land Capability Classification. Derivatives are common in many parts of the world including Canada (the various classifications which are used in the Canada Land Inventory), the UK (the Agricultural Land Classification and a separate Land-Use Capability Classification used for a time by the two national Soil Surveys) and extensively in *ad hoc* surveys in developing countries. In this last mentioned situation the classifications based on the USDA Land Capability Classification are giving way to the suitability classifications embodied in the FAO Framework.

The original Land Capability Classification system allocates land to one of up to about eight categories (I–VIII) depending on the severity of its long-term limitations for agricultural and other uses (Table 7.16). Subclasses are based on the nature of the limitations and are denoted by up to two subscripts, e.g. s for soil based limitation, and e for erosion limitation.

Derivatives of the systems have different numbers of classes (sometimes called grades), recognise different kinds of limitations and of course set different class values according to local circumstances. Some, notably the Agricultural Land Classification of England and Wales and the Land Capability Classification for Agriculture used in Scotland, have subclasses which reflect ranked order within a category, e.g. subgrades 3a, 3b and 3c of the Agricultural Land Classification of England and Wales, and not the kind of limitation.

Parametric systems use the numerical values of certain properties, e.g. soil depth in centimetres, or give a ranked value, e.g. 100 for a well-drained soil ranging to 10

Table 7.16 — The definitions of Classes in the USDA Land Capability Classification
(Source: Klingebiel and Montgomery, 1961)

Class I	– Soils in Class I have few limitations that restrict their use
Class II	– Soils in Class II have some limitations that reduce the choice of plants or require moderate conservation practices
Class III	– Soils in Class III have severe limitations that reduce the choice of plants or require special conservation practices, or both
Class IV	– Soils in Class IV have very severe limitations that restrict the choice of plants, require very special management, or both
Class V	– Soils in Class V have little or no erosion hazards but have other limitations, impracticable to remove, that limit their use largely to pasture, range, woodland, or wildlife food and cover
Class VI	– Soils in Class VI have severe limitations that make them generally unsuited to cultivation and limit their use largely to pasture or range, woodland, or wildlife food and cover
Class VII	– Soils in Class VII have very severe limitations that make them unsuited to cultivation and that restrict their use largely to grazing, woodland or wildlife
Class VIII	– Soils and landforms in Class VIII have limitations that preclude their use for commercial plant production and restrict their use to recreation, wildlife, or water supply, or to aesthetic purposes

for a poorly drained soil, and then combine these values mathematically to give a final score or index. The mathematical manipulations can be additive as in systems used in Germany and Eastern Europe, multiplicative as in the Storie Index of California, or more complex as in some methods proposed by FAO. Examples of these systems which are generally of only localised importance can be found in the textbooks and manuals listed in Chapter 9.

Very many categoric and parametric systems have been tried out in various parts of the world over the years. The best advice is, therefore, to find out what system is favoured in the locality you are working in and apply that, however imperfect you may find it to be. What the world does not need are yet more new systems, especially ones dreamed up by beginners. If all else fails then acquire the original handbook for the land capability classification or some well-established derivative (such as developed by a national soil survey or Ministry of Agriculture, Fisheries and Food) and modify it to meet local needs.

An example of a categoric system, distantly related to the Land Capability Classification is set out in detail below. One obvious candidate to serve as the example would be the Agricultural Land Classification of England and Wales, but this has been rejected for a number of reasons. Firstly the categories are very poorly defined and, in practice, resort has to be made to 'case law' to operate the system. Secondly, even the definitions which are published for some of the categories have been widely criticised as incomplete, not mutually exclusive, ambiguous and theo-retically unsound. Thirdly the system is about to be superseded by a new national agricultural land classification. Unfortunately this new system was not available in time for inclusion in this book. It will, however, be somewhat similar to the Land Capability Classification for Agriculture system used in Scotland and so this has been taken as the example. It includes concepts which should now be familiar, like PSMD, droughtiness assessments based on crop-adjusted MD and AP, wetness classes and other properties explained in Chapter 6.

The system ranks land on the basis of its potential productivity and cropping flexibility as determined by the extent to which its physical characteristics (soil, climate and relief) impose long-term restrictions on its agricultural use. Seven classes are recognised ranging from the best class, class 1, which is land capable of producing a very wide range of crops to class 7, land of no agricultural value. Classes 3 and 4 each have two divisions, and classes 5 and 6 have three, giving 13 categories overall. The brief definitions of each category are given in Table 7.17.

Table 7.17 — The definitions of Classes in the Land Capability Classification for Agriculture of the Soil Survey of Scotland
(Source: Bibby *et al.*, 1982)

Land suited to arable cropping
Class 1 — Land capable of producing a very wide range of crops
Class 2 — Land capable of producing a wide range of crops
Class 3 — Land capable of producing a moderate range of crops
        (there are two Divisions)
Class 4 — Land capable of producing a narrow range of crops
        (there are two Divisions)
Land suited only to improved grassland and rough grazing
Class 5 — Land capable of use as improved grassland
        Division 1 — Land well suited to reclamation and to use as improved grassland
        Division 2 — Land moderately suited to reclamation and to use as improved grassland
        Division 3 — Land marginally suited to reclamation and to use as improved grassland
Class 6 — Land capable of use only as rough grazing
        Division 1 — High grazing value
        Division 2 — Moderate grazing value
        Division 3 — Low grazing value
Class 7 — Land of very limited agricultural value

There are a number of assumptions underlying the classification. In particular the system does not group land according to its most profitable use and, by assuming a satisfactory level of land management, does not take the present farming circumstances into account. However, if it is considered that a given limitation could and should be removed or reduced under such a standard level of management (a good example is drainage installation), the land is classified as if such improvements had been undertaken.

The manual describing the system sets it out in more detail than is possible here and you should of course refer to it directly as necessary. The derivation of the various limiting factors is discussed at length in the manual, and in particular some of the vegetation analysis when considering the quality of hill land (classes 5, 6 and 7) has to be read in the original form.

Guidelines are given for the allocation of land to the various categories. These can be converted to a sort of land judging form as set out below which will assist a beginner to derive the correct classification for a particular piece of land (Table 7.18). To use this form you should first record the actual value of (or assessment of) each factor being considered. Many of the factors are self-explanatory and either come from basic soil and site descriptions or are derived according to the procedures explained in Chapter 6. For some, however, you do need the original manual, notably for the climatic zones used at the start of the form.

Having done this for each factor, then derive the best possible class to which the land could belong if that factor were the sole limitation. You will find that for many of the factors the land might receive a fairly high ranking but that there will be some which downgrade the quality of the land. The correct land classification is then the *lowest* category indicated with this limitation responsible irrespective of how good the land might be in other respects. Sometimes two or more limitations cause the same extent of downgrading but you are not allowed to 'add them together' and downgrade the land still further. Class 1 land of course will show no significant limitations and the final column of the form will be full of 1's.

The guidelines are fairly explicit and mutually exclusive for the higher categories (classes 1–4) but in classes 5 and 6 there are some rather tortuous requirements set, which are really intended to subdivide these classes once you have already allocated land to them. These considerations have been omitted from the main form to avoid overcomplicating it. If the indicated class is 5 or 6 you should refer to a supplementary table (Table 7.19). Finally, having derived the appropriate classification for your land you should read the full definition and guidelines in the original monograph to make sure your answer is sensible.

To allow you some practice, two typical Scottish situations are given below and you are invited to see whether you arrive at the same answers as are given at the end of the section.

Example A —
Foudland series, a deep (more than 60 cm) freely drained podzol on extremely stony fluvioglacial gravels at a height of about 100 m on a gently sloping site (less than 3°) at Craibstone, Aberdeenshire.

Climatic information: climatic Zone 3.1; median PSMD, 108 mm; accumulated temperature, 1070 day °C; hourly median wind speed, between 5 and 5.5 m/s.

Details of soil: gravelly coarse sand throughout with a stone content of about 40% small stones, but capable of cultivation with no major workability or structural limitations. Very droughty for all crops including grass.

Other details: no flood risk, no erosion risk.

Table 7.18 — Land judging form to apply the Scottish system of land capability for agriculture

Property and value	Interpretation of value	Best possible class
Climate		
Climatic zone		
	Zone 1 1	
	Zone 2 2	
	Zone 3.1 . . . . 3.1	
	Zone 3.2 . . . . 3.2	
	Zone 4.1 . . . . 4.1	
	Zone 4.2 . . . . 4.2	
	Zone 5 . . . . 5.1	
	Zone 6 . . . . 6.1	. . . .
PSMD . . . . (mm)		
	More than 130 mm 1	
	95–129 mm 2	
	80–94 mm 3.1	
	70–79 mm 3.2	
	60–69 mm 4.1	
	50–59 mm 4.2	
	30–49 mm 5.1	
	Less than 30 mm 6.1	. . . .
Accumulated temperature . . . . . . (day °C)		
	More than 1150 day °C 1	
	1050–1149 day °C 2	
	975–1049 day °C 3.1	
	925–974 day °C 3.2	
	875–924 day °C 4.1	
	850–874 day °C 4.2	
	750–849 day °C 5.1	
	625–749 day °C 6.1	
	Less than 625 day °C 7	. . . .
Hourly median wind speed . . . . (m/s)		
	Less than 5 m/s 1	
	5–5.5 m/s 3.2	. . . . . .

Table 7.18 (*Contd.*)

Property and value	Interpretation of value	Best possible class
Gradient Slope angle . . . . (°)		
	Less than 3° 1	
	3–7° 2	
	7–11° 3.2	
	11–15° 4.2/5.2	
	15–25° 5.3	
	More than 25° 7	
Soil Stoniness . . . . (%)		
	Up to 5% 1	
	6–15% (if small) 2	
	16–35% (if small) 3.1	
	36–70% (if small) 4.1	
	More than 70% 5	
	If stones are larger, unspecified lower acceptable percentages are set	
Stoniness or depth to prevent ploughing		
	No 1	
	Yes 5.1	
Stones or boulders to prevent sward improvement		
	No 1	
	Yes 6	

Droughtiness
(follow the order given)
    Potatoes . . . .
    Winter wheat . . . .
    Spring barley . . . .
Better of the
two cereals		

	If very droughty for better of the two cereals 4.1	

Table 7.18 (*Contd.*)

Property and value	Interpretation of value	Best possible class
	If moderately droughty for better of the two cereals, then: if very droughty for potatoes . . . . 4.1 if moderately droughty for potatoes 3.2	
	If slightly droughty for better of the two cereals, then: if very droughty for potatoes . . . . 3.2 if moderately droughty for potatoes . . . . 3.1 if slightly droughty for potatoes . . . . 2 if non-droughty for potatoes 2	
	If non-droughty for winter wheat, then: if moderately droughty for potatoes . . . . 2 if slightly droughty for potatoes . . . . 2 if non-droughty for potatoes 1	. . . .
Structural problems	None or minor . . . . 1 Moderate 3.1	. . . .
Soil depth . . . . (cm)	60 cm or more . . . . 1 45–59 cm . . . . 2 20–44 cm . . . . 3.2 less than 20 cm, ploughable . . . 4.2 less than 20 cm, non- ploughable 5	. . . .
Wetness Wetness class (after any necessary drainage)		

Table 7.18 (*Contd.*)

Property and value	Interpretation of value	Best possible class
	Wetness class I or II	1
	Wetness class III	2
	Wetness class IV	
	if waterlogging within 40 cm is 140 days or less.	3.2
	if waterlogging within 40 cm is 141 days or more	4.1
	Wetness class V.	5.2
	Wetness class VI	5.3
Workability limitations		
	Negligible	1
	Slight	2
	Moderate.	3.1
	Moderately severe	4.2
Flood risk		
	Negligible	1
	Non-damaging winter floods and/or very rare summer floods	3.1
	Damaging (winter) floods:	
	less than 1 year in 5	3.1
	1 year in 5 to 1 year in 4	4.1
	1 year in 3 or more often . . .	5.1
	most years.	6.1
	Damaging summer flooding . . .	4.2
Erosion Erosion risk		
	Very slight	1
	Slight	2
	Moderate.	4.1
	Severe.	6.1

Final classification . . . .
(worst of the 'best possible classes')

*Main reasons for the allocation of
the land to this class* . . . .

Table 7.19 — Supplement to the land judging form to apply the Scottish system of Land Capability Classification for Agriculture (Table 7.18)

Reminder   PSMD . . . . mm

Wetness class . . . .

Test your classification against the following requirements in a sieving operation, starting with the requirements for the initial class indicated from the main form. If the requirements are met then the initial classification is correct; if not then retest against the requirements for the next lowest class until you arrive at a class whose requirements can be met.

Class 5.1
    Must be wetness class I
        or wetness class II
        or wetness class III if mineral soil and PSMD >80 mm
        or wetness class IV if deep peat and PSMD >100 mm
  If none of these requirements met, go to class 5.2 and retest

Class 5.2
    Must be wetness class I, II, III or IV
        or wetness class V where PSMD >100 mm
  If none of these requirements met, go to class 5.3 and retest

Class 5.3
    Must be a mineral soil (any wetness class)
        or peat where PSMD >100 mm
  If none of these requirements met, go to class 6 and retest

Class 6

Mineral soil	Class 6.1
Flushed organomineral soils and peats	Class 6.2
Unflushed organomineral soils and peats	Class 6.3

Example B —
Winton series, an imperfectly drained brown earth, (wetness class 2 after drainage), in clay loam glacial till, at an altitude of about 20 m on a gently sloping site (less than 3°) near Leuchars, Fife.

Climatic information: climatic zone 2; median PSMD, 148 mm; accumulated temperature, 1175 day °C; hourly median wind speed, less than 5 m/s.

Soil details: clay loam textures becoming clay at depths below 70 cm, slightly stony (about 5%). Slightly droughty for potatoes and winter and spring cereals. Minor structural problems and slight workability problems.

Other details: no flood risk, no erosion risk.

If you have correctly applied the above form you should have found that Example A was in class 4, division 1, due essentially to the extreme stoniness and that Example B was in class 2 because of climatic zone, droughtiness considerations and slight workability limitations.

8

Simple soil physical and chemical analyses

8.1 INTRODUCTION

The pedological novice is faced with a bewildering array of possible physical and chemical analyses he or she might be tempted to perform. They are described at length in various textbooks on the subject, such as those listed in Chapter 9, with one major text (Page *et al.*, 1986), for example, devoting 779 pages to chemical analyses alone. Thus the main problem is deciding which analyses are worth carrying out and which can be ignored. Your choice may be dictated by your personal interests and you should consult the textbooks for appropriate methods. If you wish specifically to compare your results with those of other workers you should use exactly the same methods as they have used, and which ought to be specified in their reports.

Some analyses, however, are commonly carried out on a routine or semi-routine basis and these are discussed below. Methods are set out for performing those which do not require special equipment or particularly tricky analytical techniques. Note, however, that these are by no means definitive methods, simply acceptable ways of carrying out the determinations. Other workers will almost certainly prefer their own, slightly different procedures.

8.1.1 Sampling

Most of the laboratory analyses are carried out on samples brought in from field work and it is vital to ensure that these samples are truly representative of the soil for which the results are required. Errors caused by faulty sampling are far greater than any which are likely to result in the subsequent analyses. In pedological studies the sample units are normally the various horizons of the typical soil profiles you wish to study. Then, assuming the profile you wish to sample is truly representative of that soil type (see Chapter 6), it is necessary merely to ensure that the bulk sample is taken from the entire horizon and is not biased towards the top, middle or bottom of the particular horizon. Samples of 2–3 kg are usually taken.

In some studies particularly for available nutrients or soil pH the sample unit is the topsoil of an entire field. In this case a composite bulk sample is taken of several subsamples from many parts of the field. A common procedure is to walk in a zig-zag pattern across the field taking a subsample about every 20 m, making sure the sample is to the full depth of the topsoil. You should, of course avoid any areas which are likely to be atypical, e.g. the edges of fields or near gateways, and take separate bulk samples for parts of fields where there may have been a difference in cropping history and/or there is a change in the soil type. It is normally recommended that at least five subsamples per hectare are taken.

8.1.2   Sample pre-treatment

The soil samples from the field should be clearly and indelibly labelled before being taken to the laboratory. Normal convention is for the soils to be air dried and gently ground to pass a 2 mm sieve, discarding the stones, with or without measuring the actual stone content. Subsequent analyses are carried out on the <2 mm 'fine earth' with a determination of the moisture content carried out at the same time so that all results can be reported on an oven dry basis (see section 8.2). You should not, however, oven-dry the soil being used in the actual determination. You can assume that all soil analytical results are expressed on a gravimetric oven-dry <2 mm soil basis unless otherwise specified. One notable exception is stone content (see section 8.4) which is normally reported as a percentage of the total soil volume including stones.

8.1.3   Practical points

Some kinds of soils pose particular analytical problems and the methods given below may not be applicable. In particular you may require special methods, at least for some of the determinations, for peaty soils, highly calcareous soils, highly saline soils, very anaerobic soils (e.g. paddy soils) and for tropical soils high in iron and aluminium oxides. You should consult soil analytical textbooks for the appropriate methods in these cases.

It is assumed that you have access to normal laboratory equipment (the methods set out below tell you what you need for each determination), including a balance capable of weighing in grams to at least two decimal places, though for making some standard solutions you may need a more accurate one. In all cases it is assumed you will use distilled water and the appropriate grade of reagent.

Note that in the procedures given below the following terms are used with precise meanings:

(a) Weigh, measure or add *exactly* means that the amount specified is critical and must be precisely indicated;
(b) Weigh, measure or add *accurately* with or without the word *about* means that the amount need not be exactly that specified but should be known precisely;
(c) Weigh, measure, or add *approximately* means that the amount to be used is not critical and the exact amount does not need to be known but should be close to the amount specified.

An instruction specifying that a reagent should be added by pipette implies an *exact* addition. It is assumed that unless otherwise stated masses are recorded in grams (g) and volumes in millilitres (ml).

Finally and most importantly, remember that many laboratory reagents are extremely corrosive and/or poisonous and should be treated with great respect, especially if the procedures involve heating or a reaction evolves heat (e.g. adding strong acid to water).

8.2 SOIL MOISTURE

Principle
The standard gravimetric method (used to calibrate other methods) measures the loss in mass when a moist soil is dried in an oven at 105°C overnight.

Equipment
Oven (set at 105°C), weighing machine, desiccator and, for each soil analysed, a porcelain basin (or similar vessel).

Procedure
(1) Weigh accurately a porcelain basin and record its mass M_a.
(2) Add approximately 10 g of sample and reweigh accurately to give M_b.
(3) Place overnight in the oven, cool in a desiccator and weigh accurately to give M_c.

Calculation

$$\text{Moisture content} = \frac{M_b - M_c}{M_c - M_a} \times 100\%$$

Notes
The moisture content is always expressed as a percentage of the oven-dried soil. Most analytical determinations are carried out on moist or air-dry soils but the results should be expressed on an oven-dry basis by carrying out a simultaneous soil moisture determination. If, say, the mass of air-dry soil used in a determination was 10.46 g, and its moisture content was determined as 6.82% then the mass M_0 of equivalent oven-dry soil is $[10.46/(100 + 6.82)] \times 100$, i.e. 9.79 g.

Other methods for soil moisture determinations
Soil moisture content can be monitored in the field by installing either suitably calibrated tensiometers, or devices based on electrical conductivity, e.g. gypsum blocks or soil moisture blocks. An expensive soil moisture neutron probe can also be used, with the probe inserted into previously installed semi-permanent access tubes. These methods are beyond the scope of this book, though may be of great importance in, for example, investigations of land for irrigation purposes, and you should refer to appropriate textbooks. A device called a 'speedy moisture meter' is available which is based on the evolution of acetylene when moist soil comes into contact with calcium carbide. It allows soil moisture determinations to be carried out more or less immediately in the field.

Other investigations of soil moisture
The determination of soil moisture contents under specific conditions, e.g. at permanent wilting point, or held against a specific suction, e.g. 0.05 bar and hence calculation of the available water capacity are beyond the scope of this book. They require special equipment such as a pressure plate apparatus or tension tables and are best left to experienced soil scientists. Descriptions of the methods can be found in standard texts. Similarly measurements of soil permeability and infiltration using single- or double-ring infiltrometers are specialist techniques described more fully elsewhere.

8.3   BULK DENSITY AND POROSITY

Principle
Bulk density and porosity are calculated from a measurement of oven-dry mass of a known volume of soil. A known volume of soil can be collected simply by pushing or hammering a sufficiently robust open-ended tin into the soil but it is better to use a special core sampler which has brass ring liners inside a sample head with a cutting edge, and capable of being driven into the soil.

Equipment
As for gravimetric moisture determination plus sampling device (see above) of known volume.

Procedure
(1) Collect a sample which fully fills the sample tin or ring, usually by overfilling slightly (do not compact the sample by doing this) and cutting it down to the exact size with a knife.
(2) Determine accurately the oven-dry mass M_0 of the sample net of the container (if you pre-weigh it moist you can determine the moisture content at the same time).
(3) Record the volume V_c of the container.

Calculation

$$\text{Bulk density} = \frac{M_0}{V_c} \quad \text{g/cm}^3$$

$$\text{Porosity} = 100 - (\text{bulk density}/2.65 \times 100)\%$$

(assuming a true particle density of 2.65 g/cm^3).

Notes
The results can be highly variable and several replicate determinations should be made. The method is particularly difficult in stony soils which make the sampling difficult or impossible and the presence of stones in the sample affects the results. If desired you can break up each sample after the final weighing, remove the stones and determine their mass M_s and volume V_s, e.g. by a water displacement technique.

Then:

$$\text{bulk density (stone free)} = \frac{M_0 - M_s}{V_c - V_s} \times 100\,\text{g/cm}^3$$

In soils with more than about 10% stones core sampling is impossible and bulk density has to be calculated from measurements made in the field while determining stone content (see section 8.4).

8.4   STONE CONTENT

Principle
A bulk sample of known volume is collected in the field and the stones sieved out. The method also allows determination of soil bulk density if required.

Equipment
Spade, bucket, large measuring cylinder, sieve or sieves of appropriate mesh size, plastic balls about 2 cm in diameter and, if bulk density is also being determined, a spring balance, small polythene bags and subsequently the equipment needed for moisture determinations.

Procedure
(1) Dig out a sample of soil about 30 cm × 30 cm × 30 cm, in as rectangular a shape as possible (a wooden template can help) and place in the bucket.
(2) If you wish also to determine bulk density record the mass M_m of the moist sample (net of the empty bucket) and also retain separately a portion of the fine earth (i.e. without stones) in a sealed bag for subsequent moisture determination.
(3) Measure the volume V_v of the void by filling with the plastic balls, measuring these out with the measuring cylinder.
(4) Either in the field or back in the laboratory sieve out the stones using a sieve or sieves of appropriate mesh sizes and record their volume V_s. If determining bulk density, record also their mass M_s (see notes).
(5) If determining bulk density, determine also the moisture content U of the fine earth subsample.

Calculations

$$\text{Stone content} = \frac{V_s}{V_v} \times 100\%$$

$$\text{Oven-dry mass of of stone-free soil } M_0 = \frac{M_m - M_s}{100 + U} \times 100\,\text{g}$$

$$\text{Bulk density of stone-free soil} = \frac{M_0}{V_v - V_s}\,\text{g/cm}^3$$

Notes

An approximate value of stone content can be made by simply measuring the volume of the void with a ruler or tape measure, or by filling the bucket to capacity and using that as the volume of soil though this will usually give an underestimate of the volume because of the 'bulking up' of the soil as it is dug out and transferred to the bucket. Such procedures are not accurate enough for bulk density determinations. If you need to know the size distribution of the stones, e.g. using the size limits given in section 2.4.2, then a set of sieves of appropriate mesh sizes will be needed. Stones larger than about 5 mm can usually be dry sieved out directly from the sample as collected, but if you need to measure smaller stones down to 2 mm it is best to sieve out the larger stones, to take a subsample from the material which has passed the sieve and to determine the stones in it by wet sieving. You should express all the results as a percentage of the whole soil including stones.

8.5 PARTICLE SIZE ANALYSIS (PIPETTE METHOD)

Introduction and principles

Particle size analysis involves dispersing the soil in water and measuring the amounts of silt and clay by sedimentation techniques. Sand is determined by wet and/or dry sieving. Two main methods are in common use. In the pipette method (described below) the silt and clay are determined by withdrawing samples by pipette at appropriate times and depths in a suspension within which the particles are settling (their rate of settling is proportional to their diameter). In the hydrometer method the silt and clay are determined using a special hydrometer which measures the density of a soil suspension after a settling period has elapsed. Within both methods there are numerous variations, especially in the pre-treatment of the sample and the order in which the operations are carried out, although basically the same techniques are being used. The procedure described below involves:

(a) the dispersion of the soil in water after destruction of organic matter with peroxide;
(b) the removal of sand by wet sieving;
(c) the determination of silt and clay by pipette sampling.

The sieve sizes specified are 63 and 212 μm being the nearest commercially available to the 60 and 200 μm silt–sand and fine sand–coarse sand divisions.

Equipment — dispersion

Hot-plate (or Bunsen burner and stand), shaking machine (preferably end-over-end or reciprocating) and, for each soil analysed a 600 ml tall-form beaker with a clock glass and a shaking bottle (at least 500 ml, preferably 1 l).

Reagents — dispersion

6% (20 volume) hydrogen peroxide.
Capryl alcohol in dropping bottle.
10% (w/v) sodium hexametaphosphate (Calgon).

Procedure — dispersion
(1) Weigh accurately about 10 g soil into a 600 ml tall-form beaker. Use soil from which the stones greater than 2mm have already been sieved out (and determined if necessary) and carry out a simultaneous determination of soil moisture to give the equivalent mass M_0 of oven-dry soil used.
(2) Add approximately 50 ml hydrogen peroxide, cover with a clock glass and allow to stand overnight.
(3) Next day wash down the clock glass into the beaker, add a further 50 ml hydrogen peroxide and heat the sample gently until the reaction subsides. Do not allow the sample to boil. Use a few drops of capryl alcohol to quell overvigorous frothing.
(4) Finally boil for a least 1 h, adding water if necessary to prevent drying out, to destroy excess peroxide.
(5) Cool and transfer the entire contents of the beaker to the shaking bottle using a jet of water from a wash bottle to ensure all the sand particles are transferred. Rub down any soil adhering to the beaker walls and ensure this is also transferred.
(6) Make up the volume of the shaking bottle to about half full.
(7) Add exactly 5 ml of 10% sodium hexametaphosphate solution and shake for at least 12 h.

Notes — dispersion
Soils low in organic matter may not require the additional 50 ml hydroxide after overnight standing. The peroxide treatment does not destroy twigs, etc. Sometimes a treatment to destroy carbonates is included in the dispersion procedure.

Equipment — separation of sand
63 μm sieve with clock glass, and, for each soil analysed, a 1 l cylinder and glass funnel.

Reagents — separation of sand
None.

Procedure — separation of sand
(8) Dry the sieve and its clock glass in an oven and record the total mass M_{sv}.
(9) Pour the entire suspension from the shaking bottle through the sieve (held on a suitably sized funnel) into the 1 l cylinder. Do this in small increments and use a jet of water near the end of the operation to ensure that all the sand grains are transferred.
(10) Wash the material on the sieve thoroughly with a jet of water but do not attempt to rub any material through the mesh. Do not exceed 1 l of suspension in the cylinder.
(11) Transfer the sieve to its clock glass and dry overnight in an oven at 105°C.
(12) Record the mass M_s of sieve and clock glass plus sand.
(13) Retain the sand for further size separation if required (see notes).

Calculation — sand

$$\text{Sand } (>63\,\mu\text{m}) = \frac{M_s - M_{sv}}{M_0} \times 100\%$$

Notes — separation of sand

Ideally you need a separate sieve for each soil analysed, but they are expensive and so it is often necessary to carry out the sand separation for a batch of samples sequentially using only one or two sieves. You may frequently find that some additional material passes through the sieve during the oven-drying process especially if the sieve is shaken gently. This $<63\,\mu\text{m}$ material either can be returned to the suspension in the cylinder prior to the pipette analysis (see below) or can be weighed separately and the result added to the value for the silt from the pipette analysis. The sand $>63\,\mu\text{m}$ can be further subdivided by dry sieving (preferably using a sieve shaker) on a nest of sieves of appropriate size (see section 2.3.1 for discussion of common size separations). The $63\,\mu\text{m}$ mesh sieve is not very robust and the small mesh size makes sieving a slow procedure. Thus some workers prefer to use a $212\,\mu\text{m}$ sieve at this stage and to carry out a decantation operation at the end to recover the $63\text{–}212\,\mu\text{m}$ fraction, but this also necessitates a more specific pipette sampling operation to determine exactly the $<63\,\mu\text{m}$ fraction in the suspension (see soil analysis textbooks for details).

Equipment — pipette analysis

20 ml pipette, preferably held in a special stand allowing it to be lowered into the suspension to a set depth (alternatively an ordinary pipette mounted in a large cork or rubber bung can be used); both kinds of pipette need a piece of tubing with a controlling stopcock attached to the mouthpiece so that a pipette sample can be withdrawn from the suspension; stopwatch and, for each soil analysed, two small vessels (small beakers or disposable aluminium baking cases) to collect and oven dry the pipette samples.

Reagents — pipette analysis

None.

Procedure — pipette analysis

(14) Make up the volume of the suspension in the cylinder to exactly 1 l and allow to reach ambient temperature. Record the temperature of the suspension.

(15) Mix the suspension thoroughly using a paddle or by inversion (sealing the flask with a bung or the palm of the hand). Make sure all the sediment on the bottom becomes resuspended.

(16) Place the cylinder on a bench and immediately take a 20 ml sample of the suspension at about 15–20 cm depth (the depth is not critical), to represent the $<63\,\mu\text{m}$ fraction.

(17) Transfer the pipette sample to a pre-weighed beaker (or baking case). Rinse the pipette and add the rinsings to the beaker.

(18) Evaporate the sample to dryness by placing overnight in an oven at 105°C and, in due course, weigh accurately to give the mass M_z of $<63\,\mu$m material sampled.
(19) Mix the contents of the cylinder again as in step (15).
(20) Place the cylinder on a bench away from direct sunshine or a source of heat and start the stopwatch.
(21) Consult Table 8.1 for the length of settling time before the suspension should be sampled for $<2\,\mu$m clay at 10 cm depth.

Table 8.1 — Length of settling time for $<2\,\mu$m clay at 10 cm depth

Temperature (°C)	Time (h:min)	Temperature (°C)	Time (h:min)
14	10:23	20	8:00
15	9:05	21	7:48
16	8:51	22	7:37
17	8:37	23	7:26
18	8:24	24	7:16
19	8:12	25	7:06

(22) Make a mark on the pipette 10 cm from the tip. About 1 min before the end of the settling time insert the pipette, with the stopcock closed, into the suspension with as little disturbance as possible so that the tip is 10 cm below the surface.
(23) At exactly the set time open the stopcock and gently withdraw a 20 ml sample of the suspension to represent the $<2\,\mu$m fraction.
(24) Transfer to a beaker, etc., and dry as in steps (17) and (18) and weigh accurately to give the mass M_c of the sample of $<2\,\mu$m material.
(25) At a convenient stage evaporate a 5 ml aliquot of the hexametaphosphate reagent and weigh accurately to determine the mass M_r of the residue.

Calculation — pipette analysis

$$\text{Silt (2–63 }\mu\text{m)} = \frac{(M_z - M_c) \times 50}{M_0} \times 100\%$$

$$\text{Clay (}{<}2\,\mu\text{m)} = \frac{(M_c - M_r/50) \times 50}{M_0} \times 100\%$$

Notes — pipette analysis
The sample depth and time for the $<2\,\mu$m material can be modified to suit your convenience. For example, at a temperature of 20°C (sample at 10 cm after 8:00 h) the sample could be taken at 5 cm after 4:00 h or 7.5 cm after 6:00 h. It is important to keep the temperature steady during the sedimentation and not to disturb the suspension or to allow convection currents to develop. If the suspension starts to

flocculate (resembling dirty curdled milk) then an extra 5 ml of hexametaphosphate solution should be added, the suspension remixed, and the pipette sampling repeated. The correction factor for the mass of hexametaphosphate has to be modified (M_r becomes $2M_r$ in the above example).

Final calculations

In the above calculations the results are expressed as a percentage of the original mass of (oven-dry) soil, but to take account of the mass of organic matter destroyed in the pre-treatment and any other inadvertent losses and inaccuracies in the procedures it is common practice to convert all the results to percentage of recovered soil, as in the example in Table 8.2.

Table 8.2 — Final calculations for particle size analysis

	Original soil (%)	Recovered soil (%)
Sand ($>63\,\mu$m) (%)	45.2	$(45.2/94.8)\times100 = 47.7$
Silt (2–$63\,\mu$m) (%)	18.3	$(18.3/94.8)\times100 = 19.3$
Clay ($<2\,\mu$m) (%)	31.3	$(31.3/94.8)\times100 = 33.0$
	94.8	$= 100.0$

If this reveals a considerable discrepancy between the recovered fractions and the mass of the original which cannot be explained by the loss of organic matter, then an error has been made somewhere in the various operations and the entire analysis should be repeated. The results can be plotted on a textural triangle (Fig. 2.6) to give the exact textural class.

8.6   CARBONATES

Introduction and principle

The most widely used methods to determine carbonates involve treatment with acid and measuring the CO_2 by various methods, all requiring special equipment. A simpler method, said to be accurate to about 1%, is described below, in which a soil containing carbonates is treated with acid and the excess back titrated with alkali.

Equipment

20 and 100 ml pipettes, burette, and, for each soil analysed, a 250 ml beaker, clock glass and 250 ml conical flask.

Reagents

1 N hydrochloric acid (normality N_a).
1 N sodium hydroxide solution (normality N_k).
Bromothymol blue indicator.

Procedure
(1) Weigh accurately about 5 g of soil into a 250 ml beaker and carry out a simultaneous determination of soil moisture content to give the equivalent mass M_o of oven-dry soil used.
(2) Add 100 ml of acid slowly by pipette (or from a burette) and cover with a clock glass. Add a few drops of indicator to check there is excess acid and add a known extra volume of acid if necessary. Record the total volume V_a of acid used (100 ml plus any additional added).
(3) Allow to stand for 1 h, with occasional stirring, and allow to settle before step (4).
(4) Pipette 20 ml supernatant into a conical flask (or filter and take a 20 ml aliquot), add a few drops of indicator and titrate with alkali to the end point. Record the volume V_k of alkali required.

Calculation
Since 1 ml normal acid is equivalent to 0.05 g of $CaCO_3$, and a 20 ml aliquot is taken,

$$CaCO_3 \text{ equivalent} = \frac{(V_aN_a - V_kN_k)0.25}{M_0} \times 100\%$$

Notes
The results are expressed as $CaCO_3$ equivalent since, although all the carbonate is assumed to be $CaCO_3$, any acid-soluble carbonate will react.

8.7 SOIL ORGANIC MATTER BY WET OXIDATION

Principle
A small sample of soil is digested with an excess of a sulphuric acid–potassium dichromate mixture and the remaining dichromate determined by back titration with ferrous ammonium sulphate in the presence of a suitable indicator. The method is commonly referred to as the Walkley–Black method.

Equipment
5 and 10 ml pipettes, 10 and 20 ml safety pipettes or syringes or dispensers for concentrated acids, 200 ml measuring cylinder, burette and, for each soil analysed, a 500 ml conical flask. See notes for additional equipment if the more accurate refluxing method is used.

Reagents
1 N potassium dichromate standard solution (49.04 g of dry K2Cr2O7 per litre).
Concentrated sulphuric acid. **Great care is required.**
Concentrated phosphoric acid. **Great care is required.**
0.4 N ferrous ammonium sulphate (156.85 g/l) in approximately 1 N sulphuric acid. This reagent should be standardised daily to determine its normality N_f by a blank titration against a flask of reagents produced by carrying out the procedures described below but without soil.
Redox indicator solution. Dissolve 0.3 g of barium diphenylamine *p*-sulphonate (warming if necessary) and 58.7 g of barium chloride in water and make up to 1 l. Keep in a dark place.

Procedure

(1) Weigh accurately into a 500 ml conical flask about 0.1 g of a soil very high in organic matter, about 0.5 g of an agricultural topsoil or about 1.0 g of a subsoil. Carry out a simultaneous determination of soil moisture content to give the equivalent mass M_0 of oven-dry soil used.

(2) Add, by pipette, 10 ml of 1 N potassium dichromate standard solution.

(3) Add carefully, by safety pipette or similar, approximately 20 ml concentrated sulphuric acid. NB This will produce heat and spurting especially in calcareous soils. Treat any spillages of acid with copious amounts of water and seek medical attention if necessary.

(4) Swirl the flask gently and allow to stand on a heat resistant surface for 30 min. If the solution becomes greenish add further dichromate and acid in the ratio 1 to 2 until an overall brownish colour is maintained. Record the total volume V_d of dichromate used, including the initial 10 ml.

(5) After 30 min add approximately 200 ml water to quench the reaction.

(6) Add carefully, by safety pipette or similar, approximately 10 ml of concentrated phosphoric acid.

(7) Titrate with standardised 0.4 N ferrous ammonium sulphate solution, adding 5 ml of the redox indicator when the solution has become greenish. Titrate carefully to the end point when the solution (which, with the indicator, has become steadily more blue during the titration) changes from a purplish blue to turquoise green. Record the total volume V_f of ferrous ammonium sulphate solution used.

Calculation

The volume V_u of 1 N dichromate used in digesting the organic matter during the reaction, assuming the dichromate is exactly 1 N, is given by

$$V_u = V_d - V_f N_f$$

1 ml of 1 N dichromate is equivalent to 0.003 g of organic carbon assuming full oxidation, but on average (see notes) there is only 77% oxidation of the organic matter in this method and so a correction factor of 1.30 has to be applied. Thus

$$\text{organic carbon} = \frac{V_u \times 0.003 \times 1.30}{M_0} \times 100\%$$

Since soil organic matter contains, on average, 58% organic carbon, the above result can be converted to percentage organic matter by multiplying by 1.72.

Notes

Ideally the soil used should be finely ground. It is important that excess dichromate is always present; so when in doubt add more (it simply means a longer titration at the end). The mass of soil and the total volumes of dichromate and ferrous ammonium sulphate need to be known accurately, but the volumes of the acids, water and indicator used need be only approximate. If you miss the end point of the titration you can go back by adding some more dichromate (remember to add the volume to the total you have used) and continuing the titration. Studies have shown that the amount of organic carbon oxidised when relying only on the heat of reaction ranges from 44 to 92% with a mean around 77%. A more accurate method for the digestion step is to reflux the soil under a cold-finger condenser for 2 h with a digestion reagent of 10 ml 0.4 N potassium dichromate dissolved in approximately 40% v/v sulphuric acid and 20% v/v phosphoric acid, cooling, quenching with added water and titrating as above. The calculation has to be modified for the different normality of the dichromate and the correction factor omitted since this procedure oxidises all the organic carbon. Fuller details can be found in standard texts.

8.8   LOSS ON IGNITION

Principle
A rather crude measure of soil organic matter can be obtained from the loss in mass of a sample during high-temperature ignition. The determination can conveniently follow on from a determination of the moisture content by the gravimetric procedure already described (see section 8.2) so long as the vessel containing the soil can withstand high temperature.

Equipment
As for moisture content (see section 8.2) plus muffle furnace (or Mekker burner, see Notes).

Procedure
(1) It is assumed that the moisture content determination has already been carried out and a record kept of the mass M_a of the heat-resistant container, the mass M_b of this plus the moist or air-dry soil and the mass M_c plus the soil after oven drying.
(2) Place the container plus soil in a muffle furnace at 850°C for 30 min, cool and reweigh accurately to give M_d.
(3) If desired, re-ignite, cool and reweigh accurately to check that decomposition has been completed.

Calculation

$$\text{Loss on ignition} = \frac{M_d - M_c}{M_c - M_a} \times 100\%$$

Notes
The ignition can be performed over a Mekker burner rather than in a muffle furnace but the temperature obtained is not so high nor so standardised. Samples containing free calcium carbonate will lose weight by its conversion to CaO and a correction can be applied if the content of calcium carbonate is known either from an accurate determination or by subjective assessment (see section 2.6). The corrected loss on ignition for calcareous soils is loss on ignition minus 0.44 × percentage $CaCO_3$. Other losses of mass on ignition are due to dehydration of amorphous oxides and clay minerals; so the method is only a rough approximation to the organic matter content except in very sandy and/or peaty soils.

8.9   TOTAL SOIL NITROGEN

Principle

The soil is digested by a Kjeldahl procedure which converts the nitrogen to the ammonium form, followed by steam distillation of an aliquot to determine the ammonium.

Equipment

Kjeldahl digestion apparatus including heating elements and fume extraction system, steam distillation apparatus with anti-bumping granules, burette and, for each soil analysed, a Kjeldahl digestion flask and a 250 ml conical flask.

Reagents

Sulphuric acid, concentrated, nitrogen free. **Great care is needed.**
Kjeldahl tablets C (5 g of K2SO4 plus 0.1 g of CuSO4) and S (5 g of K2SO4 plus 0.005 g selenium).
40% sodium hydroxide solution. Great care is needed.
Standard 0.1 N hydrochloric acid (normality Na).
Standard 0.1 N sodium hydroxide solution (normality Nk).
Methyl red indicator solution.

Procedure

(1) Weigh accurately a soil sample of about 5 g into a 500 ml Kjeldahl flask and carry out a simultaneous determination of soil moisture content to give the equivalent mass M_0 of oven-dry soil used.

(2) Wash down the neck of the flask with about 25 ml of water thereby pre-wetting the soil before carefully adding approximately 30 ml concentrated sulphuric acid. If any acid is spilled wash with copious supplies of water and seek medical attention if necessary.

(3) Heat the flask gently on the Kjeldahl apparatus and when the frothing has ceased and the water has boiled off add one of each of the tablets.

(4) Heat more strongly and continue heating for at least 30 min after all the black carbon has disappeared (total heating time is about 3 h). Take great care, since you are dealing with hot concentrated acid.

(5) Allow the flask to cool and carefully add approximately 200 ml water while cooling the flask under a stream of cold tap water.

(6) Transfer the entire contents of the Kjeldahl flask quantitatively to the distillation flask of a distillation apparatus and add a few drops of indicator (see Notes).

(7) Place a 250 ml conical flask containing exactly 25 ml of 0.1 N hydrochloric acid and a few drops of indicator under the delivery tube of the condenser, ensuring the end of the tube is below the level of the acid.

(8) Add a few anti-bumping granules to the distillation flask, followed by enough 40% sodium hydroxide solution to turn the indicator in the distillation flask yellow (about 120 ml is usually sufficient). Take care with the strong alkali. Treat any spillages with copious amounts of water and seek medical attention if necessary. During this stage and subsequently the system must remain leak free so that all the ammonia being liberated is collected in the receiving flask.

(9) Apply heat to the distillation flask and boil gently, ensuring the water supply to the condenser is operative.

(10) Distil for about 30 min or until the distillate is no longer alkaline to litmus paper. During the distillation the indicator in the receiving flask should remain pink, and, if it turns yellow, immediately add a known extra volume of 0.1 N hydrochloric acid. Note the total volume V_a of acid in the receiving flask (the initial 25 ml plus any additional).

(11) Remove the receiving flask and rinse down the delivery tube with distilled water. Switch off the distillation equipment.

(12) Titrate the contents of the receiving flask with 0.1 N sodium hydroxide solution, noting the volume V_k used.

Calculation

Since 1 ml of N acid is equivalent to 0.014 g of nitrogen,

$$\text{content of nitrogen} = \frac{(V_aN_a - V_kN_k)0.014}{M_0} \times 100\%$$

Notes

The distillation procedure given above is an 'all or nothing' determination and you may prefer, instead, to make up the digest to a standard volume and to distil an aliquot, thereby allowing a repeat if anything goes wrong. It is very important to ensure no losses of distilled ammonia and to ensure the receiving flask is always acidic and the distillation vessel alkaline. Major errors can occur if any of the 40% sodium hydroxide solution used to make the distillation vessel alkaline accidentally contaminates the receiving flask. Other distillation procedures are equally acceptable but may require adjustments to the size of digestion aliquot used.

8.10   SOIL REACTION (pH)

Principle

Soil pH, which is a measure of soil acidity, is conventionally measured in a 1 to 2.5 w/v soil to water or soil to 0.01 M $CaCl_2$ solution using a pH meter. An alternative method using indicators is also described.

Equipment

pH meter (suitably calibrated), 2 ml and 25 ml pipettes and, for each soil analysed, a small beaker and stirring rod.

Reagents

Distilled water

0.125 M $CaCl_2$ solution (18.4 g of $CaCl_2.2H_2O$ per litre).

Procedure

(1) Weigh out 10 g of soil (or if the soil is very moist an amount which is equivalent to 10 g of oven-dry soil).

(2) Add 25 ml of distilled water, stir and allow to stand for 10 min.
(3) Record the pH when stable.
(4) Add 2 ml of 0.125 M $CaCl_2$ solution (to produce effectively a 0.01 M solution), stir and allow to stand for 10 min.
(5) Record the pH when stable.

Notes
It is probably better to carry out the determination on field moist samples than on dried soils. Small inaccuracies in the soil-to-solution ratio are acceptable; hence there is no need to weigh exactly 10 g soil or to allow for moisture unless the soil is particularly wet. pH values which are normally quoted refer to the values in water, but values in $CaCl_2$, which are about 0.5–1.0 pH units lower, are preferred in some cases.

Indicator methods
A rough measure of soil pH in the field can be made by mixing the soil with an indicator solution, decanting off the solution and comparing its colour with a test card. A suitable soil indicator solution is marketed by BDH Ltd. The test can be improved by shaking the soil in a special graduated test tube with indicator and solid barium sulphate (which helps the supernatant to clear) and the colours compared with a test card. Indicator methods are recommended only where a pH meter is unobtainable.

Lime requirement
As discussed in section 1.9 the amount of lime which has to be added to a soil to bring its pH to some required level, e.g. pH 6.0 or 6.5, depends not only on its actual pH value but also on its cation exchange capacity (CEC) and hence its buffering ability. Lime requirement can be calculated from the changes in pH when soils are treated with buffer solutions, and several methods are described in standard soil analytical textbooks.

8.11   SOIL SALINITY

Principle
The standard method of determining soil salinity is by measuring the electrical conductivity of either a soil paste or, more usually, a soil extract. Extracts of saturated soil are preferred but in the field extracts of 1-to-2.5 or 1-to-5 soil-to-water are often used. The method below is for a 'saturation extract'.

Equipment
Conductivity bridge and cell, and, for each soil analysed, a 50 ml beaker and a Buchner funnel and flask plus toughened filter paper and a vial or other sample container compatible with the conductivity cell.

Reagents
None.

Procedure
(1) Place approximately 20 g soil in a 50 ml beaker, add just enough water to saturate it, stir gently and allow to stand overnight.
(2) Stir again and add small amounts of soil or water so that:
  (a) the soil glistens as it reflects light;
  (b) the soil flows slightly when the beaker is tipped;
  (c) the soil slides freely and cleanly off a spatula (except if it is a clay);
  (d) but there is no free water on the soil surface.
(3) Suction filter on toughened paper on a Buchner funnel and collect the extract.
(4) Measure the electrical conductivity r of the extract and note the cell constant c. If the reading is not at 25°C record the temperature and apply the correction factor f from Table 8.3.

Table 8.3 — Temperature correction factors for readings of electrical conductivity

Temperature (°C)	Correction factor (f)	Temperature (°C)	Correction factor (f)
12	1.341	21	1.087
13	1.309	21.5	1.075
14	1.277	22	1.064
15	1.247	22.5	1.053
16	1.218	23	1.043
17	1.189	23.5	1.032
18	1.163	24	1.020
18.5	1.150	24.5	1.010
19	1.136	25	1.000
19.5	1.125	25.5	0.995
20	1.112	26	0.979
20.5	1.100	26.5	0.974

Source: adapted from Richards (1954).

Calculation

$$\text{Conductivity} = \frac{cf \times 100}{r} \, \text{mS/cm}$$

Notes
The electrical conductivity (usually abbreviated to EC or ECe) is invariably given in millisiemens (previously millimhos per centimetre, abbreviated to mmho/cm or mmho cm-1) and the significance of the results is discussed in numerous texts (e.g.

Richards, 1954; FAO–UNESCO, 1974). These texts also discuss other tests frequently carried out on saline soils, notably the exchangeable sodium percentage (usually abbreviated to ESP) and on potential irrigation waters, notably electrical conductivity (usually abbreviated to ECw) and sodium adsorption ratio (usually abbreviated to SAR).

8.12   CATION EXCHANGE CAPACITY, EXCHANGEABLE BASES AND EXCHANGE ACIDITY

Principle
A sample of soil is leached with a reagent, normally neutral 1 N ammonium acetate for non-calcareous and non-saline soils, to replace exchangeable bases. Aliquots of the leachate can be taken for determination of exchange acidity (but see Notes), total exchangeable bases or individual cations (by appropriate techniques). Excess ammonium nitrate is removed by washing, and the ammonium held on the exchange sites quantitatively replaced by leaching with 1 N potassium chloride. The displaced ammonium ions are determined by distillation and the CEC of the soil calculated. Separate lists of equipment, reagents and procedures are given for each of the sequential steps, i.e.:

(a) leaching;
(b) exchange acidity and exchangeable bases;
(c) CEC.

Equipment — leaching
For each soil analysed, a leaching tube approximately 15 cm long and 3 cm in diameter with a stopcock at the base plus two 250 ml graduated flasks and a suitable stand to allow these to be set up in a 'chicken-feed' arrangement (Fig. 8.1).

Reagents — leaching
Approximately 1 N ammonium acetate solution prepared by mixing equal volumes of 2 N acetic acid (115 ml of glacial acetic acid per litre) and 2 N ammonium hydroxide (108 ml of 0.880 specific gravity ammonia per litre) and adjusting to pH 7, acid-washed sand (or silica granules) and cotton wool.

Procedure — leaching
(1) Place a plug of cotton wool in the base of the leaching tube.
(2) Weigh out accurately about 15 g of soil and mix with an approximate equal volume of sand (to improve permeability). Carry out a simultaneous determination of soil moisture content to give the equivalent mass M_o of soil used.
(3) Add the soil–sand mixture to the tube and place a plug of cotton wool at the top.
(4) Invert a graduated flask containing 250 ml of the ammonium acetate solution into the leaching tube as shown in Fig. 8.1, collecting the leachate in the second 250 ml graduated flask.

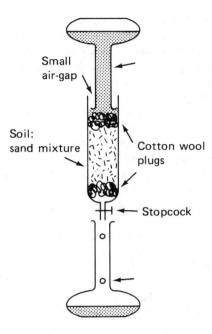

Fig. 8.1 — A chicken-feed system for leaching soils.

(5) Control the rate of leaching with the stopcock so that the leaching takes about 8 h (about one drop every 10 s).

(6) When the leaching is complete make up the leachate to 250 ml with ammonium acetate solution, mix well and retain. Retain the sample in the leaching tube if required for CEC determination and do not allow it to dry out.

Notes — leaching
An alternative to using leaching tubes is to treat the soil with ammonium acetate in a flask overnight, then filter and wash with several more portions of ammonium acetate, collecting all the filtrate and washings for the exchange acidity and exchangeable bases. The subsequent washing with alcohol and replacement of ammonium by potassium chloride are carried out on the sample in the filter paper with several washings of each.

Equipment — exchange acidity and total exchangeable bases
1 ml, 25 ml and 100 ml pipettes, burette, pH meter, hot-plate (or bunsen burner or stand), infrared lamps or other apparatus for evaporation, muffle furnace (or Bunsen burner and stand) and, for each sample analysed, a 250 ml beaker, stirring rod, evaporating basin 10 cm in diameter and clock glass.

Reagents — exchange acidity and total exchangeable bases
Standard 0.1 N hydrochloric acid (normality N_a).
Standard 0.1 N ammonium hydroxide solution (normality N_n).
Bromothymol blue indicator solution.

Procedure — exchange acidity and total exchangeable bases
(1) Pipette 100 ml of leachate into a 250 ml beaker. Steps (2) and (3) may be omitted if determination of exchange acidity is not required.
(2) Insert the electrode of a pH meter and, with stirring, titrate to pH 7 with standard 0.1 N ammonium hydroxide solution.
(3) Record the volume V_{na} of ammonium hydroxide solution used.
(4) Transfer the beaker and contents to a hot plate or bunsen burner and boil to reduce the volume to about 25 ml.
(5) Transfer the solution quantitatively to an evaporating basin and evaporate to dryness, e.g. under infrared lamps.
(6) Ignite the dry residue in a muffle furnace at 450°C or over a Bunsen burner at dull red heat to yield a light-coloured residue.
(7) Cool the basin, cover with a clock glass and add 25 ml of 0.1 N hydrochloric acid by pipette.
(8) Add 1 ml of indicator and warm gently to ensure solution. If the indicator does not show an excess of acid by remaining yellow, add a known extra amount of 0.1 N hydrochloric acid. Record the total volume V_a of acid used (the initial 25 ml plus any extra added).
(9) Rinse the clock glass into the basin and titrate the excess acid with 0.1 N ammonium hydroxide to the blue–green end point. Record the volume V_{nb} of ammonium hydroxide used.

Calculation — exchange acidity and total exchangeable bases
Assuming the suggested aliquots, etc., are as specified above:

$$\text{Exchange acidity} = \frac{V_{na}N_n \times 250}{M_0} \text{ milliequivalents per } 100\,g \text{ of soil}$$

total exchangeable bases =
$$\frac{(V_aN_a - V_{nb}N_n) \times 250}{M_0} \text{ milliequivalents per } 100 \text{ g of soil}$$

Exchange acidity, exchangeable bases and other cations
The sum of exchangeable acidity plus total exchangeable bases should equal the CEC but this is normally determined by continuing with the procedures described below. In many tropical soils, however, the best measure of CEC is the sum of exchangeable bases extracted by ammonium acetate at pH 7 (as described above) plus exchange acidity determined using an unbuffered 1 M potassium chloride solution, which, in general is more satisfactory for determination of exchange acidity than ammonium acetate. The potassium chloride extract can also be used to determine exchangeable aluminium (e.g. colorimetrically with 'aluminon'), which is normally present in significant amounts only in soils below pH 5.

Separate aliquots of the ammonium acetate leachate can be taken for the determination of other individual cations. Potassium and, where necessary, sodium are normally determined by flame photometry, calcium and magnesium by atomic adsorption spectrophotometry or by titration with ethylene diamine tetracetic acid. Full details can be found in analytical textbooks.

Equipment — cation exchange capacity

Leaching apparatus (as already used), 50 ml pipettes, burette, steam distillation apparatus (with anti-bumping granules) and, for each sample, two 250 ml graduated flasks, two 400 ml beakers and a 250 ml conical flask.

Reagents — cation exchange capacity

Ethanol (or rectified spirit).

1 N acidified potassium chloride solution (74.55 g of dried potassium chloride and 1 ml concentrated hydrochloric acid per litre).

Standard 0.1 N hydrochloric acid (normality N_a).

Standard 0.1 N sodium hydroxide solution (normality N_k).

Methyl red indicator solution.

40% sodium hydroxide solution. **Great care needed.**

Procedure — cation exchange capacity

(1) Replace the empty 250 ml graduated flask above the soil–sand mixture in the leaching tube with a fresh 250 ml flask full of ethanol.

(2) Leach the soil–sand mixture with the ethanol, collecting the leachate (which can subsequently be discarded) in a 400 ml beaker.

(3) When the leaching with ethanol is complete, replace the empty 250 ml graduated flask with a fresh 250 ml graduated flask full of acidified 1N potassium chloride solution.

(4) Leach the soil–sand mixture with the potassium chloride solution, collecting the leachate in a fresh 400 ml beaker. Adjust the stopcock so that the leaching takes several hours.

(5) When the leaching is completed, transfer the entire contents of the 400 ml beaker quantitatively to the distillation flask of a distillation apparatus and add a few drops of indicator (see Notes).

(6) Place a 250 ml conical flask containing exactly 50 ml of 0.1 N hydrochloric acid and a few drops of indicator under the delivery tube of the condenser, ensuring the end of the tube is below the level of the acid.

(7) Add a few anti-bumping granules to the distillation flask, followed by enough 40% sodium hydroxide solution to turn the indicator in the distillation flask yellow (about 25 ml is usually sufficient). Take care with the strong alkali. Treat any spillages with copious amounts of water and seek medical attention if necessary. During this stage and subsequently the system must remain leak free so that all the ammonia being liberated is collected in the receiving flask.

(8) Apply heat to the distillation flask and boil gently, ensuring the water supply to the condenser is operative.

(9) Distil for about 30 min or until the distillate is no longer alkaline to litmus paper. During the distillation the indicator in the receiving flask should remain pink, and if it turns yellow immediately add a known extra volume of 0.1 N hydrochloric acid. Note the total volume V_a of acid in the receiving flask (the initial 50 ml plus any additional).

(10) Remove the receiving flask and rinse down the delivery tube with distilled water. Switch off the distillation equipment.

(11) Titrate the contents of the receiving flask with 0.1 N sodium hydroxide solution, noting the volume V_k used.

Calculation — cation exchange capacity

$$\text{CEC} = \frac{V_a N_a - V_k N_k}{M_0} \times 100 \text{ milliequivalents } 100 \text{ g of soil}$$

Notes — cation exchange capacity

The distillation procedure given is an 'all or nothing' determination and you may prefer, instead, to make up the leachate to a standard volume and distil an aliquot, thereby allowing a repeat if anything goes wrong. It is very important to ensure no losses of distilled ammonia and to ensure the receiving flask is always acidic and the distillation vessel alkaline. Major errors can occur if any of the 40% sodium hydroxide solution used to make the distillation vessel alkaline accidentally contaminates the receiving flask. Other distillation procedures, e.g. micro-Kjeldahl distillation apparatus using magnesium hydroxide, are equally acceptable.

8.13 AVAILABLE NUTRIENTS, E.G. AVAILABLE PHOSPHATE

Introduction and principles

The general principle of soil testing for available nutrients is to shake a soil with an extracting solution which will remove a portion of that nutrient which is representative of the amount which is likely to be taken up by a crop over the growing season. The methods are largely empirical and there is wide variation in the extractants used, soil-to-extractant ratios, time and vigour of shaking, method of separating the extractant from the soil and in determining the amount of nutrient extracted. Some methods are specific to only one nutrient and others to several but there is no universal extractant suitable for all nutrients, while equally some extractants are more suitable for some kinds of soils than others and may be totally inappropriate for some situations. Most texts on soil analysis discuss these matters in considerable detail. Your choice of method should be guided by, firstly, local experience and, secondly, the existence of interpretative guidelines for the results. This latter point is vital. Do not undertake or commission any determination of available nutrients unless there is some way of interpreting the results, either as very high, high, medium, etc., or as the amount of fertiliser which should be added for a particular crop. There is a good resume of the more common methods in the *Booker tropical soil manual* together with some general interpretative guidelines.

The method given below as an example is for available phosphate extracted by 0.5 M sodium bicarbonate solution followed by colorimetric determination of phosphate by a molybdenum blue procedure, as used by the Agricultural Development and Advisory Service of the Ministry of Agriculture, Fisheries and Food, with slight modifications. Note that in this method the sample is measured out with a scoop, and not weighed, and so the results are on a volumetric not a gravimetric basis.

Equipment

Shaking machine, colorimeter capable of reading at 880 nm, 5 ml scoop, 5 ml pipettes, 1, 20 and 100 ml pipettes, or syringes or similar dispensers, No. 2 grade filter paper and, for each soil analysed, two 250 ml conical flasks and a 100 ml conical flask, plus a 100 ml conical flask for each of the five standard solutions.

Reagents

0.5 M sodium bicarbonate solution (42 g/l) adjusted to pH 8.5 with sodium hydroxide.

1.5 M sulphuric acid.

0.15% (w/v) ammonium molybdate reagent containing 0.04 g of antimony potassium tartrate and 0.375 g of ascorbic acid per litre, freshly prepared each day. NB **The antimony potassium tartrate is highly poisonous and should be treated with great care.**

Stock solution containing 1 mg of phosphorus per millilitre (4.393 g of dried potassium dihydrogen orthophosphate per litre). Make appropriate dilutions in volumetric flasks with 0.5 M sodium bicarbonate solution to give working standards containing 0, 2, 4, 6 and 8 μg of phosphorus per millilitre.

Procedure

(1) Shake 5 ml of soil (measured out by scoop) with 100 ml of 0.5 M sodium bicarbonate solution for 30 min in a 250 ml flask (or other container which fits the shaking machine).

(2) Filter immediately through a No. 2 filter paper into a 250 ml conical flask.

(3) Pipette into a series of conical flasks 5 ml of extract or 5 ml of each of the working standard solutions, including the blank.

(4) Add, by pipette, 1 ml of 1.5 M sulphuric acid to each flask and swirl to release CO_2.

(5) Add, by pipette, 20 ml of the ammonium molybdate reagent to each flask, swirl to mix, and allow to stand for 30 min. NB Because the reagent is poisonous you should either exercise great care or use a safety pipette.

(6) Measure the colours developed in a colorimeter at 880 nm. The colours are stable for several hours.

Calculations

Construct a calibration curve from the readings of the standards (including the blank) expressing the standards as micrograms of phosphorus per millilitre in the working standards from which the 5 ml was pipetted out in step (3). Read from the curve the concentration c in micrograms of phosphorus per millilitre equivalent to the colorimeter reading given by the solution obtained from the soil extract. Then if the above procedures and dilutions have been followed:

$$\text{phosphorus in soil} = c \times 20 \text{ mg per litre of soil (ppm)}$$

If the colours of the soil extract solution are too intense for the calibration curve repeat steps (3)–(6) but using 1 ml extract and 4 ml of 0.5 M sodium bicarbonate solution. In this case the conversion factor in the above equation is 100 and not 20.

Interpretation of results

The results can be converted to indices using Table 1.9 which also gives a general indication of the significance of the values. The indices are used to make specific fertiliser recommendations as set out in various Ministry of Agriculture, Fisheries and Food Publications.

Notes

The colorimetric procedure is very sensitive to contamination, e.g. from detergent residues on glassware, and should be repeated with fresh uncontaminated glassware if the blank (0 μg P) shows any more than a slight trace of bluish colour. Some extracts are strongly coloured by organic matter and require a rather elaborate pretreatment before colour development. Consult an analytical chemist for advice.

Rapid soil test kits

Several rapid soil test kits are commercially available for determining soil nutrient status and/or pH and lime requirement. The pH and lime requirement procedures are based on indicators as discussed in section 8.10. The available nutrients follow the same principles as above. A sample of soil is shaken with an extractant and the amount of nutrient in the extractant determined usually by colorimetric methods assessed visually. These kits inevitably have drawbacks in that the procedures are not really standardised and many of the measurements have to be approximate. Also the choice of extractants and other procedures is limited because they have to be carried out safely by untrained personnel with minimal facilities. So long as these limitations are borne in mind, however, there is no reason to shun such test kits if you have no access to laboratory facilities which would allow you to carry out the more 'professional' analyses. Remember, too, that the results of any determination, including those with test kits, is very dependent on the initial sampling procedure and that results for which no interpretation is given are useless.

8.14   EXTRACTABLE IRON

Introduction and principles

The study and classification of several kinds of soils, notably those with suspected podzolic features or tropical ferallitic soils requires determination of the amounts of iron, aluminium, and sometimes manganese extractable by various reagents. Common methods involve extraction with a pyrophosphate solution and/or with sodium dithionite solution. The extracting conditions can be critical, especially if the results are to be used in detailed soil classification work and you should refer to the appropriate manuals for the exact procedures. The subsequent determination of iron either colorimetrically or by atomic absorption is fairly routine but determination of aluminium or manganese is more difficult and should not be attempted if you are not an experienced analyst. The following method is given simply as an example of the range of possible methods. It is for the extraction of iron by a pyrophosphate solution and subsequent colorimetric determination. The same extract can also be used, if required, for determination of pyrophosphate extractable aluminium or organic matter.

Equipment

Shaking machine, centrifuge capable of accepting polythene extraction bottles (see below), colorimeter capable of reading at 530 nm, 1, 5 and 100 ml pipettes and, for each soil analysed, two 125 ml (or larger) polythene bottles, and one 50 ml volumetric flask plus further volumetric flasks for standard solutions.

Reagents

0.1 M potassium pyrophosphate solution (38.45 g of $K_4P_2O_7.3H_2O$ per litre).
Approximately 4 N ammonium hydroxide solution (approximately 285 ml 0.880 specific gravity ammonia per litre).
10% thioglycollic acid solution, just neutralised by NH_4OH solution.
Stock solution containing 0.1 mg of iron per millilitre (0.100 g of iron wire dissolved in hydrochloric acid and diluted to 1 l). Make appropriate dilutions in volumetric flasks to give working standards containing 0, 0.02, 0.04, 0.06, 0.08 and 0.10 mg of iron per millilitre (the highest, 0.1 mg/ml, being the undiluted stock solution itself).

Procedure

(1) Weigh accurately about 1 g of soil into a polythene bottle, and carry out a simultaneous determination of soil moisture content to give the equivalent mass M_0 of oven-dry soil used.
(2) Add, by pipette, 100 ml pyrophosphate solution and shake overnight.
(3) Centrifuge to yield a clear supernatant (RCF at least 415).
(4) Pipette into a series of 50 ml volumetric flasks 1 ml of clear supernatant or 1 ml of each of the working standards, including the blank.
(5) Add approximately 1 ml of thioglycollic acid and approximately 5 ml ammonium hydroxide to each of the flasks, and swirl until full oxidation and colour development have taken place.
(6) Make up to the mark with water and mix thoroughly.
(7) Measure the colours developed in a colorimeter at 530 nm.

Calculation

Construct a calibration curve from the readings of the standards (including the blank) expressing the standards as milligrams of iron per millilitre in the working standards from which the 1 ml was pipetted out in step (4). Read from the curve the concentration c in milligrams of iron per millilitre equivalent to the colorimeter reading given by the solution obtained from the soil extract. Then if the above procedures and dilutions have been followed:

$$\text{Pyrophosphate-extractable iron} = \frac{c \times 10}{M_0}\%$$

Notes

Extractable aluminium and organic matter can be determined in aliquots of the same extract by appropriate methods. The remaining soil can be prepared for a subsequent extraction with dithionite by first shaking with water, recentrifuging and discarding the washings.

9

Bibliography

The following is a selected list of recommended books, plus a few articles, for those who wish to develop further their interest in soils. The list also includes the manuals and other publications of various soil surveys which have been drawn on during the writing of the book and which explain some of the subject matter in much greater detail.

The list has been arranged by broad subject area though there is inevitably some overlap. The general list includes standard soil science textbooks such as that by Brady and Russell dealing among other topics with soil formation, classification, etc. Texts more directed towards pedology though usually with good general descriptions of soil properties are those by Bridges, Bridges and Davidson, Courtney and Trudgill, Duchaufour (particularly the French approach) and FitzPatrick. The *Booker tropical soil manual* is a mine of information on all aspects of pedology and related matters, and not only applicable to tropical areas. Books and soil survey reports dealing with specific areas, including the sources of some of the examples in the text are listed separately in section 9.2, entitled 'Soil Formation and Distribution'.

The list of books in section 9.3, 'Soil and profile descriptions', includes manuals from the more important soil survey organisations and texts written by soil surveyors, often for an audience of similarly expert soil surveyors. The definitive manuals of the various classification systems discussed in Chapter 4 are listed in section 9.4, 'Soil classification'. Most of the general textbooks, especially the more pedologically oriented ones give summaries of one or more of the common systems. FitzPatrick gives a particularly good treatment based on the FAO–UNESCO system and Olsen deals similarly with the USDA soil taxonomy.

The largest list is of books dealing with how to make and interpret soil maps. They include the sources of many of the examples quoted in the text, particularly those following the approach developed by the Soil Survey of England and Wales, but also those from USDA, FAO and other sources. A number of the books are from a series of authoritative monographs in soil survey published by the Oxford University Press and the Clarendon Press. Also recommended are the texts by Olson (with many US examples), Dent and Young, Davidson and the *Booker tropical soil manual.*

The list of references in section 9.6 'Methods' gives some of the more commonly quoted texts and soil survey manuals, but the problem with all of these is knowing just what soil analyses are worth carrying out and what the results mean once you have got them. The *Booker tropical soil manual* has, however, useful lists of common methods of soil analyses and their interpretation.

Section 9.7 gives details of other references cited in the text.

9.1 GENERAL

Brady N. C. (1984) *The nature and properties of soils,* 9th Edition. Macmillan, New York.

Bridges E. M. (1978) *World soils,* 2nd edition. Cambridge University Press, Cambridge.

Bridges E. M. and Davidson D. A. (1982) *Principles and applications of soil geography.* Longman, London.

Courtney F. M. and Trudgill S. T. (1976) *The Soil.* Edward Arnold, London.

Duchaufour P. (transl. Paton T. R.) (1982) *Pedology.* George Allen and Unwin, London.

FitzPatrick E. A. (1986) *An introduction to soil science,* 2nd edition. Longman, Harlow, Essex.

Jacks G. V., Tavernier R. and Boalch W. (1960) *Multilingual vocabulary of soil science.* Food and Agriculture Organisation, Rome.

Landon J. R. (ed.) (1984) *Booker tropical soil manual.* Booker International Ltd, London; Longman, Harlow, Essex.

Lutz J. F. (ed.) (1965) Glossary of soil science terms. *Soil Science Society of America Proceedings* **29** 330–351.

Pitty A. F. (1979) *Geography and soil properties.* Methuen, London.

Russell E. W. (1973) *Soil conditions and plant growth,* 10th edition. Longman, London.

Simpson K. (1983) *Soil.* Longman, London.

White R. E. *Introduction to the principles and practie of soil science,* 2nd edition. Blackwell, Oxford.

9.2 SOIL FORMATION AND DISTRIBUTION

Ahn P. M. (1970) *West African soils.* Oxford University Press, Oxford.

Dregne H. (1976) *Soils of arid regions.* Elsevier, Amsterdam.

Knapp B. J. (1979) *Soil processes.* George Allen and Unwin, London.

Lof P. (1987) *Soils of the world.* A wall chart. Elsevier, Amsterdam.

Sanchez P. A. (1976) *Properties and management of soils in the tropics.* Wiley, Chichester, West Sussex.

SSEW (1983–1984) *Soil map of England and Wales,* in 6 sheets at 1:250 000 plus accompanying regional bulletins (various authors): Soil Survey of England and Wales Bulletins Nos. 10–15. Soil Survey of England and Wales, Harpenden, Hertfordshire.

Young A. (1976) *Tropical soils and soil survey.* Cambridge University Press, Cambridge.

9.3   SOIL AND PROFILE DESCRIPTIONS

Batey T. and Davies D. B. (1971) *Soil field handbook,* Agricultural Development and Advisory Service, Advisory Papers No. 9. Ministry of Agriculture, Fisheries and Food, London.

FAO (1977) *Guidelines for Soil Profile Description*, 2nd edition. Food and Agriculture Organisation, Rome.

FAO–UNESCO (1977) *Soil map of the world,* Food and Agriculture Organisation–United Nations Educational, Scientific and Cultural Organisation, Paris.

Hodgson J. M. (ed.) (1974) *Soil survey field handbook.* Soil Survey Technical Monograph No. 5. Soil Survey of England and Wales, Harpenden, Hertfordshire.

Hodgson J. M. (1978) *Soil sampling and soil description.* Clarendon Press, Oxford.

Kellogg C. *et al.* (1951 with supplement 1962) *Soil survey manual,* USDA Handbook No. 18. United States Department of Agriculture, Washington, D.C.

9.4   SOIL CLASSIFICATION

Avery B. W. (1980) *Soil classification for England and Wales (higher categories),* Soil Survey Technical Monograph No. 14. Soil Survey of England and Wales, Harpenden, Hertfordshire.

Butler B. E. (1980) *Soil classification for soil survey.* Clarendon Press, Oxford.

Clayden B. and Hollis J. M. (1984) *Criteria for differentiating soil series,* Soil Survey Technical Monograph No. 17. Soil Survey of England and Wales, Harpenden, Hertfordshire.

Creutzberg D. (1982) *Field extract of soil taxonomy.* International Soil Museum, Wageningen.

Dudal R. *et al.* (1974) *Soil map of the world,* Vol. 1 *Legend.* United Nations Educational, Scientific and Cultural Organisation, Paris.

FAO (1986) FAO/UNESCO soil map of the world 1:5 000 000: revised legend. World Soil Resources Report 58. FAO, Rome.

Ragg J. M. and Clayden B. (1973) *The classification of some British soils according to the comprehensive system of the United States.* Soil Survey Technical Monograph No. 3. Soil Survey of England and Wales, Harpenden, Hertfordshire.

USDA (1975) *Soil taxonomy,* USDA Agriculture Handbook No. 436. United States Department of Agriculture, Washington, D.C. With amendments (1982), Handbook No. 430-VI, issue No. 1.

Webster R. (1977) *Quantitative and numerical methods in soil classification and survey.* Clarendon Press, Oxford.

9.5   SOIL MAPPING AND INTERPRETATIONS

Bartelli L. J. *et al.* (1966) *Soils and land use planning.* Soil Science Society of America, Madison, Wisconsin.

Beckett P. H. T. and Webster R. (1971) Soil variability — a review. *Soils and Fertilisers* **34** 1–15.

Beek K. J. (1978) *Land evaluation for agricultural development,* Publication No. 23. INRI, Wageningen.

Bibby J. S. (ed.) (1982) *Land capability classification for agriculture.* Soil Survey of Scotland, Aberdeen.

Brink A. B. A., Partridge T. C. and Williams A. A. B. (1982) *Soil surveying for engineering.* Oxford University Press, Oxford.

CDF (1965) *Soil capability classification for agriculture.* Canada Land Inventory Report No. 2. Canada Department of Forestry, Ottawa.

Carroll D. M., Evans R. and Bendelow V. C. (1977) *Air photointerpretation for soil mapping,* Soil Survey Technical Monograph No. 8. Soil Survey of England and Wales, Harpenden, Hertfordshire.

Davidson D. A. (1980) *Soils and land use planning.* Longman, London.

Dent D. and Young A. (1981) *Soil survey and land evaluation.* Allen and Unwin, London.

FAO (1967) *Aerial photo interpretation in soil survey,* Soils Bulletin No. 6. Food and Agriculture Organisation, Rome.

FAO (1974) *Irrigation suitability classification,* Soils Bulletin No. 22. Food and Agriculture Organisation, Rome.

FAO (1976) *Framework for land evaluation,* Soils Bulletin No. 32. Food and Agriculture Organisation, Rome.

FAO (1979) *Soil survey investigations for irrigation,* Soils Bulletin No. 42. Food and Agriculture Organisation, Rome.

FAO (1979) *Land evaluation guidelines for rainfed agriculture,* World Soil Resources Report No. 52. Food and Agriculture Organisation, Rome.

FAO–UNESCO (1974) *Irrigation, drainage and salinity* — an international source book. Food and Agriculture Organisation–United Nations Educational, Scientific and Cultural Organisation; Hutchinson, London.

Jarvis M. G. and Mackney D. (1973) *Soil survey applications,* Soil Survey Technical Monograph No. 8. Soil Survey of England and Wales, Harpenden, Hertfordshire.

Jones R. J. A. and Thomasson A. J. (1985) *An agroclimatic databank for England and Wales,* Soil Survey Technical Monograph No. 16. Soil Survey of England and Wales, Harpenden, Hertfordshire.

Klingebiel A. A. and Montgomery P. H. (1961) *Land capability classification,* Agriculture Handbook No. 210. United States Department of Agriculture. Washington, D.C.

Loveday J., Beatty H. J. and Norris J. M. (1972) *Comparison of current methods for evaluating irrigation soils,* CSIRO Division of Soils Technical Bulletin No. 14. Commonwealth Scientific and Industrial Research Organisation, Canberra.

Mackney D. (ed.) (1974) *Soil type and land capability,* Soil Survey Technical Monograph No. 4. Soil Survey of England and Wales, Harpenden, Hertfordshire.

McRae S. G. and Burnham C. P. (1981) *Land evaluation.* Clarendon Press, Oxford.

Olson G. W. (1981) *Soils and the environment.* Chapman and Hall, New York.

Olson G. W. (1984) *Field guide to soils and the environment.* Chapman and Hall, New York.

Smyth A. J. (1970) *The preparation of soil survey reports,* Soils Bulletin No. 9. Food and Agriculture Organisation, Rome.

Soil survey staff (1966) *Aerial-photo interpretation in classifying and mapping soils,* USDA Agriculture Handbook No. 294. United States Department of Agriculture, Washington, D.C.

Storie R. E. (1978) *The Storie index soil rating revised,* Special Publication No. 3203. Division of Agricultural Science, University of California.

Thomasson A. J. (ed.) (1975) *Soils and field drainage,* Soil Survey Technical Monograph No. 7. Soil Survey of England and Wales, Harpenden, Hertfordshire.

USDA (1978) *Soil potential ratings,* National Soil Handbook Notice No. 31. United States Department of Agriculture, Washington, D.C.

Valentine K. W. G. (1986) *Soil resource surveys for forestry.* Clarendon Press, Oxford.

Western S. (1978) *Soil survey contracts and quality control.* Oxford University Press, Oxford.

White L. P. (1977) *Aerial photography and remote sensing for soil survey.* Clarendon Press, Oxford.

Wright J. W. (1982) *Land surveying for soil surveys.* Clarendon Press, Oxford.

9.6   METHODS

Avery B. W. and Bascomb C. L. (1974) *Soil survey laboratory methods,* Soil Survey Technical Monograph No. 6. Soil Survey of England and Wales, Harpenden, Hertfordshire.

Black C. A. (ed.) (1965) *Methods of Soil Analysis,* two volumes. American Society of Agronomy, Madison, Wisconsin. (See also Page *et al.* (1982); Klute (1986).)

Dewis J. and Freitas F. C. R. (1970) *Physical and chemical methods of soil and water analysis,* Soils Bulletin No. 10. Food and Agriculture Organisation, Rome.

FAO (1976) *Prognosis of salinity and alkalinity,* Soils Bulletin No. 31. Food and Agriculture Organisation, Rome.

FAO (1980) *Soil and plant testing and analysis,* Soils Bulletin No. 38/1. Food and Agriculture Organisation, Rome.

Hall D. G. M., Reeve M. J., Thomasson A. J. and Wright V. F. (1977) *Water retention, porosity and density of field soil,* Soil Survey Technical Monograph No. 9. Soil Survey of England and Wales, Harpenden, Hertfordshire.

Hesse P. R. (1971) *A textbook of soil chemical analyses.* John Murray, London.

Klute A. (ed.) (1982, 1986) *Methods of soil analysis, physical and mineralogical methods* 2nd edition. American Society of Agronomy, Madison, Wisconsin. (2nd edition of Black (1965).)

McCoy D. E. and Donohue S. J. (1979) Evaluation of commercial soil test kits for field use. *Communications in Soil Science and Plant Analysis* **10** 631–652.

Page A. L. *et al.* (ed.) (1982) *Methods of soil analysis, chemical and microbiological properties,* 2nd edition. American Society of Agronomy, Madison, Wisconsin. (2nd edition of Black (1965).)

Phillipson J. (1971) *Methods of study in quantitative soil ecology.* Blackwell, Oxford.

Richards L. A. (ed.) (1954) *Diagnosis and improvement of saline and alkali soils,* USDA Handbook No. 60. United States Department of Agriculture, Washington, D.C.

van Reeuwijk L. P. (ed.) (1986) *Procedure for soil analysis.* International Soil Reference and Information Centre, Wageningen, The Netherlands.

9.7 OTHER REFERENCES CITED IN THE TEXT

Arlidge E. Z. and Wong, Y. C. Y. (1975) *Notes on the land resources and agricultural suitability map of Mauritius,* Occasional Paper No. 29. Mauritius Sugar Industry Research Institute.

Brady N. C. (1974) *The nature and properties of soils,* 8th edition. Macmillan, New York.

Burnham C. P. and McRae S. G. (1978) *Kent: The Garden of England.* Paul Norbury, Tenterden, Kent.

Burton R. G. O. and Seale R. S. (1981) *Soils in Cambridgeshire I:* Sheet TL18E/28W (Stilton), Soil Survey Record No. 65. Soil Survey of England and Wales, Harpenden, Hertfordshire.

Cerutti J. R. (1985) *Soil survey of Warren and Forest Counties, Pennsylvania.* Soil Conservation Service, USDA, Washington, D.C.

Churchward H. M. and Flint S. F. (1956) *Jernargo extension of the Berriquiln irrigation district, New South Wales,* Soils and Land Use Series No. 18. CSIRO Australia.

Findlay E. C. *et al.* (1984) *Soils and their use in South West England,* Bulletin No. 14. Soil Survey of England and Wales, Harpenden, Hertfordshire.

Greenland D. J. and Lal R. (1977) *Soil conservation and management in the humid tropics.* J. Wiley, Chichester, West Sussex.

Hammond R. F. (1973) *Soil Survey of Derrybrennan Farm,* Soil Survey Bulletin No. 28. An Foras Taluntais, Dublin.

Higgins G. M. and Kassam A. H. (1981) The FAO agro-ecological zone approach to determination of land potential. *Pedologie,* Ghent **31** 147–168.

Hill I. D. (1969) *An assessment of the possibilities of oil palm cultivation in Western Division, The Gambia,* Land Resource Study No. 6. Land Resources Division, Ministry of Overseas Development, Tolworth, Surrey.

Hodge C. A. H. and Seale R. S. (1966) *The soils of the district around Cambridge.* Soil Survey of England and Wales, Harpenden, Hertfordshire.

International Society of Soil Science (1982) 12th International Congress of Soil Science, Delhi, 1982, Guide Book, Tour No. 6.

Jarvis M. G. and Mackney D. (1973) *Soil survey applications,* Soil Survey Technical Monograph No. 13. Soil Survey of England and Wales, Harpenden, Hertfordshire.

Jarvis M. G. *et al.* (1984) *Soils and their use in South East England,* Bulletin No. 15. Soil Survey of England and Wales, Harpenden, Hertfordshire.

Laing D. (1976) *The soils of the country round Perth, Arbroath and Dundee.* Memoir Soil Survey of Scotland. HMSO, Edinburgh.

McGraw J. D. (1964) *Soils of Alexandra district,* Soil Bureau Bulletin No. 24. New Zealand Department of Scientific and Industrial Research, Auckland.

Matthews B. (1971) *Soils in Yorkshire I:* Sheet SE 65 (York East), Soil Survey Record No. 6. Soil Survey of England and Wales, Harpenden, Hertfordshire.

Ministry of Agriculture, Fisheries and Food (1984) *Soil texture,* Leaflet 895. MAFF, Alnwick, Northumberland.

Rigdon T. A. (1975) *Soil survey of Appling and Jeff Davis Counties, Georgia.* Soil Conservation Service, USDA, Washington, D.C.

Rudeforth C. C. *et al.* (1984) *Soils and their use in Wales,* Bulletin No. 11. Soil Survey of England and Wales, Harpenden, Hertfordshire.

Shankarnarayan K. A. *et al.* (1983) Application of the FAO framework for land evaluation to an arid area of Western Rajasthan, India. *Soil Survey and Land Evaluation* **3** 59–68

Smith, R. E. *et al.* (1967) *Soils of the Lac de Bonnet area,* Soils Report No. 15. Manitoba Soil Survey.

Sturdy R. G. (1971) *Soils in Essex I:* Sheet TQ59 (Harold Hill), Soil Survey Record No. 7. Soil Survey of England and Wales, Harpenden, Hertfordshire.

Thomasson A. J. (1979) *Assessment of soil droughtiness.* Soil Survey Technical Monograph No. 13 43–50. Soil Survey of England and Wales, Harpenden, Hertfordshire.

van Heesen H. C. Presentation of the seasonal fluctuation of the water table on soil maps. *Geoderma* **4** 257–278.

Veldkamp W. J. (1979) *Land evaluation of valleys in a tropical rain area — a case study.* State Agricultural University, Wageningen, The Netherlands.

Many scientific journals specialising in soils are published, most dealing with all aspects of soil science including pedology, and a few specialising in this area. Particularly noteworthy are the following: *Journal* (formerly *Proceedings*) *of the Soil Science Society of America, Soil Science, Journal of Soil Science, Canadian Journal of Soil Science, Pedologie, Pochvovodenie* (translated as *Soviet Soil Science*) and *Geoderma.* Every 4 years the International Society of Soil Science holds a congress whose proceedings are published in several volumes. Tours associated with the congress have very useful guides containing much local information and descriptions of soils. The regular bulletins of the International Society of Soil Science give comprehensive reviews of all new soil science publications. National and international soil survey organisations also publish a wealth of pedological material in the form of maps, reports and scientific papers.

All this information, of course, needs an efficient abstracting system, and for many years the monthly publication *Soils and Fertilisers*, produced by the Commonwealth Bureau of Soils, has provided such a service.

Acknowledgements

The author and publishers are grateful to the following authors, publishers and institutions for permission to reproduce or draw on published material for the figures and tables listed below:

Table 1.3 — Dr D. Dent and Booker Agriculture International Ltd; Table 1.4 — Macmillan Publishing Co. Inc.; Fig. 1.5 — Dr E. A. FitzPatrick and Longman Group UK Ltd; Tables 1.9 & 6.8 — Ministry of Agriculture, Fisheries and Food; Table 3.2 and Fig. 3.1 — An Foras Taluntais, Eire; Tables 3.4, 4.7, 7.11 & 7.12 — The Food and Agriculture Organisation of the United Nations and also UNESCO for Tables 3.4 & 4.7; Table 4.9 — Booker Agriculture International Ltd; Tables 5.3 & 7.14 and Fig. 5.8 — Drs S. G. McRae and C. P. Burnham; Tables 6.2 & 7.17 and Figs 5.3 & 5.4 — Macaulay Land Use Research Institute, Aberdeen; Tables 6.25 & 6.26 — Pedologie, Ghent; Table 7.2 — New Zealand Soil Survey; Table 7.3 — Dr M. Churchward; Table 7.4 — Overseas Development Natural Resources Institute; Table 7.13 and Figs 7.1, 7.2 & 7.5 — Elsevier Scientific Publishing Co.; Table 7.15 — Manitoba Soil Survey.

Table 6.5 is reprinted by permission of John Wiley & Sons Ltd. Figs 5.1, 5.2 & 5.8 were drawn by Andrea McClintock of Rural Planning Services plc.

Special thanks are due to the Soil Conservation Service of the United States Department of Agriculture who are the source of Tables 1.7, 3.5, 4.11, 4.13, 6.24, 7.5, 7.6, 7.16 & 8.3 and Figs 2.1, 2.2, 2.8, 2.9, 2.10, 2.11, 2.12, 2.13, 2.14 and 6.2, and in particular to the Soil Survey and Land Research Centre of the Cranfield Institute of Technology for permission to draw so heavily on material from the Soil Survey of England and Wales, both throughout the text and specifically for Tables 4.4, 4.6, 5.2, 5.4, 6.1, 6.3, 6.8, 6.9, 6.11, 6.12, 6.13, 6.14, 6.16, 6.17, 6.18, 6.20, 6.22, 7.1 & 7.8 and Figs 2.7, 3.2, 4.1, 6.1, 6.3, 6.4, 7.3 & 7.4.

Index

A horizons, 85, 109
accumulated temperature, 156–157, 209
acid–sulphate, *see* sulphuric
acidity, *see* soil pH
acric, 116
acrisols, 14, 26–27, 109, 112, 116–117, 124
actinomycetes, *see* soil flora
aeration, *see* soil atmosphere, waterlogging,
    gleying
aggregates, 15–16, 50–51
agric, 120
Agricultural Land Classification, 205–206
agro-ecological zones, 177–179
agroclimatic databank, 155–159, 162
air capacity, 16
air photographs, 136–139, 153
air-dry, 18, 216
albic, 110, 116, 120
alfisols, 122–124
alluvial, 83, 91, 94–100, 102–103, 129
aluminium oxides, *see* sesquioxides
andosols, 14, 26–27, 107–108, 114, 116–117, 124
anaerobic, *see* soil atmosphere, waterlogging,
    gleying
anthropic, 120
AP, *see* available water
apedal, 51
arenosols, 14, 26–27, 107–108, 114, 116–117, 124
argillic, 34–35, 86–87, 91, 95–100, 110–111, 120,
    124
aridisols, 122, 124
associations, 132, 136–137
augers, 140–143
available nutrients, 29–32, 236–238
available phosphate, determination, 236–238
available water, 18–20
available water capacity, 18–20, 162–165,
    195–196, 218
AWC, *see* available water capacity
azonal soils, 125–126

B horizons, 86–87, 110
bacteria, *see* soil flora
base maps, 138–140

base saturation, 26–28, 111
bleached sand grains, 86
blocks/blocky, 50, 54, 56
boulders, 48, 210
boundaries, horizon, *see* horizons, boundaries
boundaries, soil, *see* soil maps, boundaries
broken, 72
brown earths, 83, 95–97, 103, 129
brown sands, 83, 95–97, 103, 129
brown soils, 83, 95–97, 102–103, 124
brown-, 91
bulk density, 16, 163
bulk density, determination, 218–220
bulletin, *see* report

C horizons, 88, 110
calcareous soils, *see* carbonates
calcaric/calcaro/calcic, 91, 110, 116, 120
calcimorphic, 127
calcium, 32
calcium carbonate, *see* carbonates
calcium sulphate, *see* gypsum
cambic, 91, 110, 116, 120
cambisols, 109, 112, 116–117, 124
capillary water, 17–20
capped, 56
carbon dioxide, 23
carbonates, 15, 27–28, 37, 56–57, 62, 65, 91, 110,
    116
carbonates, determination, 56–57, 224–225
catena, 137, 193–194
cation exchange (capacity), 14, 25–27, 29
cation exhange capacity, determination, 232–236
CEC, *see* cation exchange capacity
cementation, 61–62, 64, 87, 110–111
CG horizons, 88
chemical analyses, 150, 224–239
chernozems, 14, 26–27, 107–108, 112, 116–117,
    124
chroma, *see* soil colour
chromic, 116
classification, *see* soil classification
clay, *see* soil texture
clay illuviation, *see* clay translocation

clay minerals, 13–14, 25–26
clay translocation, 34–35, 64, 86–87, 91, 110
climate, 11, 74–75, 155–162, 174–177, 209
clods, 50
coatings, 64
coding, *see* soil classification, codes
colloids, *see* clay minerals and organic matter
colluvial, 91
colour, *see* soil colour
complex, 131–132
concretions, 64, 110
consistency, *see* soil consistency
crop suitability, 186–202
crumbs, 55
crystals, 64
cultivated, *see* A horizons
cutans, 35, 64, 110

depth, 69, 210
derived maps, 182–184
descriptions,
    horizon, *see* horizons, descriptions
    profile, *see* profiles, descriptions
    soil sample, *see* soil sample, descriptions
detailed soil maps, 127–135, 143–147
diagnostic horizons, 82–89, 109–111, 119–120
discontinuities, 89–90, 111
discontinuous, 72
drainage, 20–23, 74–75, 165–173, 182–187
drainage classes, 167–173
drawings of profiles, *see* profiles, drawings
droughtiness, 158–159, 161, 165–167, 195–196,
    210–211
dry, 60
duripan, 120
dystric, 116

E horizons, 85–86, 110
earthworms, *see* soil fauna
EC, *see* electrical conductivity
electrical conductivity, 28, 230–231
eluvial, *see* E horizons
entisols, 121–122, 124
epipedons, 120
equipment,
    profile description, *see* profiles, descriptions
    soil analyses, *see under each particular analysis*
    soil surveying, *see* soil maps, surveying
        equipment
eutri-, 116
evapotranspiration, 158–159, 161–162
examples,
    horizon nomenclature, 90–91
    Land Capability Classification for Agriculture
    machinery work days, 174–176
    profile descriptions, 75–79, 90–91, 149–150
    soil analytical results, 150
    soil classification, 90–91, 118–119, 121
    soil map units, 148–151, 191
    soil sample description, 37, 65
    soil surveying, 140–143
    wetness classes, 171–173

excessively well drained, 168–171
exchange acidity, determination, 232–236
exchangeable bases, determination, 232–236
exchangeable rodium percentage, 28
exposures, 66, 143
extractable iron, determination, 238–239

F horizons, 84
family, 121
FAO framework for land evaluation, 197–202
FAO/UNESCO soil map of the world, *see* soil
    classification, FAO/UNESCO
fauna, *see* soil fauna
FC, *see* field capacity
ferralic, 116
ferralitisation, 33–35
ferralsols, 14, 26–27, 107–108, 112, 116–117, 124
ferri/ferric/ferritic, 77, 91, 116
fertilisers, 13, 29–32
field capacity, 16–20, 161–162, 173–176
field sheets, 127–133, 144
fine earth, 12, 42, 216, 221
finger assessment of soil texture, 45–48
firm, 61
fissures, 58
flood risk, 212
fluvisols, 14, 26–27, 107–108, 113, 116–117, 124
forestry, 202, 204
fragipan, 111, 120
fragments, 50
free survey, 133, 137–138
friable, 61
fungi, *see* soil flora

G or g horizon, *see* gleying
gelic, 111, 116
geological maps, 139
gleyed, *see* gleying
gleyic, 89, 91, 116
gleying, 21, 34, 36, 88–89, 91–92, 110–111,
    167–173
gleysols, 107–108, 113, 116–117, 124
glossic, 116
gradient, *see* topography
granular, 50, 55
gravitational water, 16–19
great group, *see* soil classification, Soil Taxonomy
great soil group, *see* soil classification, zonal
greyzems, 109, 113, 116–117, 124
grid survey, 133, 137–138
ground-water gley soils, 83, 99–100, 102–103, 124
group, *see* Soil Classification for England and
    Wales; soil classification, FAO/UNESCO
growing season, 156–158
gypsic, *see* gypsum
gypsum, 15, 62, 110–111, 116, 120

H horizons, 84, 109
halomorphic, 125
handling properties, *see* soil consistency
haplic, 116
hard, 60

250 INDEX

histic, 120
histosols, 14, 26–27, 107–108, 114, 116–117,
  122–124
horizons,
  boundaries, 69–74
  descriptions, 66–79
  diagnostic, 82–91, 109–111, 119–120
  intermixed, 89
  master, 109–111
  nomenclature, 82–91
  recognition, 69–72, 82–91, 109–111
  sampling, 72, 215–216
  slowly permeable, see permeability
  subdivision, 98, 111
  suffixes, 85–89, 110–111
  transitional, 101
hue, see soil colour
humic/humo/humose, 48, 63, 84–85, 92, 117
humus, see organic matter
hydraulic conductivity, see permeability
hydrometer method, see particle size analysis
hydromorphic properties, 111, 125
hygroscopic water, 17–19

illuvial, see B horizons
imperfectly drained, 167–171
inceptisols, 77, 79, 122–124
index, see available nutrients
indicators (pH), 230
induration, 110–111, 120
infiltration, 21, 218
intergrades, 133
intermixed horizons, 89
intrazonal soils, 125–126
iron (extractable), determination, 238–239
iron oxides, see sesquioxides
irregular, 72
irrigation, 161, 182, 189

kastanozems, 107–108, 113, 116–117, 124
key, FAO/UNESCO soil map of the world,
  108–109, 118–119
key, Land Capability Classification for
  Agriculture, 209–213
key, Soil Classification for England and Wales,
  92, 102–103
key, soil series, 105–106, 128–133
key, soil texture by finger assessment, 45–48

L horizons, 84
land, 154–155
Land Capability Classification for Agriculture,
  206–214
land capability classification, 132, 151, 204–214
land evaluation, see soil maps, interpretation
land judging, see soil maps, interpretation
land use, see vegetation
landscape, see topography
laterite/latosols, 35, 125
leaching, 20–21, 33–34
legend, see soil maps, legend
length of growing season, 156–158

leptic, 117
lime, see soil pH and carbonates
lithomorphic soils, 83, 93–94, 102, 124
lithosols, 107–108, 113, 116–117
loam, see soil texture
location, 74–75
loose, 60
loss-on-ignition, 227
luvic, 117
luvisols, 14, 26–27, 77, 109, 113, 116–117, 124

machinery work days, 174–176, 196
macroporosity, 58
magnesium, 30, 32
major group, see Soil Classification for England
  and Wales
man-made soils, 83, 92, 100, 102
manganese oxides, 15, 62
massive, 51, 56
master horizons, 109–111
MD, see soil moisture deficit
mechanical analysis, 220–224
mechanical resistance, 21
memoir, see report
micro-nutrients, 30–32
micro-organisms, see soil flora
mineral soil, 84
moderately well drained, 167–171
moist, 60
moisture content, see soil moisture content
moisture deficit, see soil moisture deficit
mollic, 109, 117, 120
mollisols, 122–124
mor, 24, 33, 84
mottling, 21, 37, 40–41, 65, 167–170
mull, 24, 33
Munsell, see soil colour

natric, 110, 120
nitrosols, 109, 114, 116–117, 124
nitrogen, 30–32
  determination, 228–229
nodules, 64
non-agricultural uses of soil maps, 197, 202–204

O horizons, 84–85, 109
observation points, see soil maps, observation
  points
ochric, 109, 117, 120
order, see soil classification, Soil Taxonomy and
  zonal
organic matter, 11–12, 14, 24–25, 29, 33, 47–48,
  62–63, 167–170
  determination, 225–227
organic soils, 12, 14, 26–27, 48, 71, 83–85,
  101–103, 107–109, 114, 122–124
orthic, 117
oven dry, 18, 216–218
oxic, 35, 110, 120
oxisols, 122–124

paleo-, 87, 92

pans, 61, 64, 99
parametric systems of land classification, 205–206
parent material, 11, 74–75, 88–89, 110–111
particle size analysis, 220–224
particle size classes, 12, 41–45
peat soils, 12, 14, 26–27, 48, 71, 83–85, 101–103, 107–109, 114, 122–124
pedogenic features, 64
pedon, 80
peds, 15–16, 50–56
pellic, 117
pelo-, 92
pelosols, 83, 94, 102, 124, 129
permanent wilting point, 19–20, 218
permeability, 16, 20–21, 171–175, 218
petro-, 120
pH, *see* soil pH
phaeozems, 107–108, 113, 116–117, 124
phase, *see* soil series, phase
phosphate/phosphorus, 30–32
phosphate (available), determination, 236–238
photographs, 67–69
physical analysis, 150, 217–224
pipette method, *see* particle size analysis,
placic, 117, 120
plaggen, 120
planosols, 14, 26–27, 107–108, 115–117, 124
plant remains, 63, 84, 123
plastic, 61
plates/platy, 50, 52, 56
plinthic/plinthite, 35, 111, 117, 120
plough layer, *see* A horizons
podzolic soils, 83, 92, 97–98, 102, 124–125
podzolisation, 34–35, 85–87, 92
podzols, 14–15, 26–27, 98, 107–108, 114, 116–117, 124
podzoluvisols, 107–108, 112, 116–117, 124
poorly drained, 167–171
porosity, 16, 20, 37, 57–59
porosity, determination, 218–219
potassium, 30, 32
potential evapotranspiration, *see* evapotranspiration
precipitation, *see* rainfall
prisms/prismatic, 50, 53, 56
pro-forma sheets, 65, 72–75
profiles,
    classifying, *see* soil classification
    descriptions, 66–79, 90–91, 145–146, 148–151
    discontinuities, 89–90, 111
    drawings, 70–71
    preparation, 68–69
    selection, 66–67, 147
PSMD, *see* soil moisture deficit
PT, *see* evapotranspiration
PWP, *see* permanent wilting point

R horizons, 88, 110
rainfall, 158–161
rankers, 83, 93–94, 102, 107–108, 115–117
raw gley soils, 83, 93, 102, 124
raw humus, 24, 33, 84

raw soils, *see* terrestrial raw soils, raw gley soils
reaction, *see* soil pH
reconnaissance maps, 132, 134–137
record, *see* report
regosols, 107–108, 114, 116–117, 124
rendzinas, 83, 94–95, 102, 107–108, 112, 116–117, 124
report, 147–151, 191–192
retained water capacity, 16, 165–168, 174–175
rhodic, 117
roots, 21, 23, 37, 58–59, 62–63

safety, 67, 140, 225–226, 228, 235, 237
salic, 120
salinisation, 23, 34, 36
salinity, 15, 23, 28, 33, 36, 110–111
    determination, 241–242
salt-affected soils, *see* salinity
sampling, horizons, *see* horizons, sampling
sampling, soils, *see* soil samples, collection
sand, *see* soil texture
sand fraction, 12, 48
sand-/sandy, 92
saturation, 16–17, 170
saturation extract, 28, 241–242
scale, *see* soil maps, scale
series, *see* soil series
sesquioxides, 14–15, 35, 62, 85, 87, 110–111, 249–250
silt, *see* soil texture
single factor maps, 134, 182–184
single grain, 51
site characteristics, 74–74, 149
slickensides, 64, 111
slope, *see* topography
slowly permeable horizons, *see* permeability
smooth, 72
sodic, *see* salinity
sodium adsorption ratio, 28
soft, 60
soil additions, 36
soil associations, 132, 136–137
soil atmosphere, 23–24
soil augers, 140–143
soil biology, *see* soil flora, soil fauna
soil boundaries, *see* soil maps, boundaries
soil chemical analyses, 150, 235–250
soil chemistry, 25–29
Soil Classification for England and Wales, 81–106
soil classification, 80–126
    codes, 82–83, 93–101, 104–117, 135–136
    FAO/UNESCO, 35, 77–78, 81, 106–119
    soil map of the world, *see* soil classification, FAO/UNESCO
    Soil Taxonomy, 35, 77, 79, 81, 106, 119–124, 160, 176–177
    zonal, 81, 125–126
soil colour, 37–41, 65, 167–170
soil complex, 131–132
soil consistency, 37, 60–61
soil depth, 69, 210
soil erosion, 21, 36, 74–75, 223

soil exposures, 66, 143
soil family, 121
soil fauna, 21, 24–25, 30, 37, 58–59, 63–64
soil fertility, 13, 29–32
soil flora, 12, 21, 24–25, 58–59, 63
soil formation, 11, 32–36
soil group, see soil classification, FAO/UNESCO
soil handling properties, see soil consistency
soil intergrades, 133
soil map of England and Wales, 82–83, 135–136
soil map of Scotland, 135–137
soil map of the world, see soil classification,
    FAO/UNESCO
soil maps,
    boundaries, 127–147
    interpretation, 134, 180–214
    legend, 127
    mapping symbols, 127–133
    mapping units, 127–137, 148–151, 191
    non-agricultural uses, 197, 202–204
    observation points, 127–130, 134, 137–138
    purity, 128–133
    purpose, 137
    report, see report
    scale, 131–138
    surveying equipment, 140–143
    surveying procedures, 127–153
soil mineralogy, 13–15, 44
soil moisture content, determination, 59, 228–229
soil moisture deficit, 158–162, 165–167, 195–196,
    209
soil pH, 25–28, 56–57
    determination, 240–241
soil phase see soil series, phase of
soil physical analyses, 150, 228–235
soil profile, see profile
soil reaction, see soil pH
soil samples,
    collection, 143, 226–227
    description, 37–65
    pre-treatment, 227
soil series, 81–82, 104–106, 121, 127–133, 145–146
    phase of, 81–82, 132–133, 148–151
soil solution, 25, 29
soil structure, 15–16, 37, 50–56, 58, 65, 222
soil surveying, see soil maps
Soil Taxonomy, see soil classification, Soil
    Taxonomy
soil temperature, 156–158, 176–177
soil testing, see available nutrients
soil texture, 12, 37, 41–48, 65, 163–165, 168,
    231–235
soil units, see soil classification, FAO/UNESCO
soil water, 16–23, 162–176
    content, determination, 59, 228–229
    movement, 20–23, 33–34, 159, 161
    state, 16–17, 37, 59–61
solodic, 117
solonchaks, 15, 107–108, 116–117, 124
solonetz, 107–108, 114, 116–117, 124
soluble salts, see salinity
sombric, 120

spodic, 110, 120
spodosols, 122, 124
stagno-, 92
stagnogley soils, 83, 99, 103, 129
stagnogleyic, 89
stagnopodzols, 83, 98, 102
sticky, 61
stone content, determination, 49, 230–231
stones, 12, 37, 42–44, 47–50, 56, 65, 164, 210
streaks, 40–41
structure, see soil structure
subgroup, see Soil classification for England and
    Wales
suborder, see soil classification, Soil Taxonomy
    and zonal
subsoil, see B and E horizons
suffixes, horizon, see horizons, suffixes
sulphur, 30, 32
sulphuric, 14, 26–28, 92, 111, 117, 120
surface water gley soils, 83, 99, 102, 124
surveying, see soil maps

takyric, 117
temperature, 155–158, 177–179
termites, see soil fauna
terrestrial raw soils, 83, 93, 101, 124
textural triangle, 12–13, 42–45
texture, see soil texture
thionic, see sulphuric
topography, 11, 74–75, 210
topsoil, see A, L, F, H and O horizons
trace elements, 30–32
trafficability, 161, 174–176
transitional horizons, 89
transpiration, 158–161
typical, 92

ultisols, 122–124
umbric, 109, 120
undulating, 72
unit, see soil classification, FAO/UNESCO

value, see soil colour
vegetation, 74–75, 140
vertic, 111, 117
vertisols, 107–108, 115–117, 121–122, 124
very detailed maps, 132, 151
very poorly drained, 167–171
vitric, 117

Walkley–Black method, 225–227
water movement, see soil water movement
water state, see soil water state
water table, 16, 183–184
waterlogging, 21, 36, 60, 167–171
wavy, 72
weathering, 15, 33, 87
well-drained, 167–171
wet, 60
wetness classes, 169–174, 211–213
wilting, 19–20
wind, 209

winter playing fields, 202–203
workability, 173–176, 195–196, 212

xanthic, 117
xerosols, 107–108, 115–117, 124

yermosols, 78, 107–108, 115–117, 124
yield predictions, 192

zonal soil classification, *see* soil classification
    zonal
zonal soils, 125–126